DETROIT NEVER LEFT

LATINA/O SOCIOLOGY SERIES
General Editors: Pierrette Hondagneu-Sotelo and Victor M. Rios

Family Secrets: Stories of Incest and Sexual Violence in Mexico
Gloria González-López

Deported: Immigrant Policing, Disposable Labor, and Global Capitalism
Tanya Maria Golash-Boza

From Deportation to Prison: The Politics of Immigration Enforcement in Post–Civil Rights America
Patrisia Macías-Rojas

Latina Teachers: Creating Careers and Guarding Culture
Glenda M. Flores

Citizens but Not Americans: Race and Belonging among Latino Millennials
Nilda Flores-González

Immigrants Under Threat: Risk and Resistance in Deportation Nation
Greg Prieto

Kids at Work: Latinx Families Selling Food on the Streets of Los Angeles
Emir Estrada

Organizing While Undocumented: Immigrant Youth's Political Activism Under the Law
Kevin Escudero

Front of the House, Back of the House: Race and Inequality in the Lives of Restaurant Workers
Eli Revelle Yano Wilson

Building a Better Chicago: Race and Community Resistance to Urban Redevelopment
Teresa Irene Gonzales

South Central Dreams: Finding Home and Building Community in South L.A.
Pierrette Hondagneu-Sotelo and Manuel Pastor

Latinas in the Criminal Justice System: Victims, Targets, and Offenders
Edited by Vera Lopez and Lisa Pasko

Uninsured in Chicago: How the Social Safety Net Leaves Latinos Behind
Robert Vargas

Medical Legal Violence: Health Care and Immigration Enforcement Against Latinx Noncitizens
Meredith Van Natta

Contested Americans: Mixed-Status Families in Anti-Immigrant Times
Cassaundra Rodriguez

Private Violence: Latin American Women and the Struggle for Asylum
Carol Cleaveland and Michele Waslin

Latino Fathers: Challenging Myths, Negotiating Ideals
Fatima Suarez

Detroit Never Left: Black Space, White Borders, Latino Crossings
Nicole E. Trujillo-Pagán

Detroit Never Left

Black Space,
White Borders,
Latino Crossings

Nicole E. Trujillo-Pagán

New York University Press
New York

NEW YORK UNIVERSITY PRESS
New York
www.nyupress.org

© 2026 by New York University
All rights reserved

Please contact the Library of Congress for Cataloging-in-Publication data.

ISBN: 9781479826803 (hardback)
ISBN: 9781479826810 (paperback)
ISBN: 9781479826841 (library ebook)
ISBN: 9781479826827 (consumer ebook)

This book is printed on acid-free paper, and its binding materials are chosen for strength and durability. We strive to use environmentally responsible suppliers and materials to the greatest extent possible in publishing our books.

The manufacturer's authorized representative in the EU for product safety is Mare Nostrum Group B.V., Mauritskade 21D, 1091 GC Amsterdam, The Netherlands. Email: gpsr@mare-nostrum.co.uk.

Manufactured in the United States of America

10 9 8 7 6 5 4 3 2 1

Also available as an ebook

CONTENTS

List of Figures and Tables — vii

Introduction: If Detroit Could Talk — 1

1. This Bridge Called My 'Hood: Latina/o/x Experience and Southwest Detroit — 41
2. Producing Neighborhoods: From Redlining to Diversity — 59
3. "Where You From?" Property Claims as Abstractions — 91
4. Big Data, Big Money: Gerrymandering, Bankruptcy, and Demolition — 123
5. Affirmative Action or Reverse Racism? The African Town Proposal — 141
6. Public-Private Partnerships: Regime Change and "Some New Form of Management" — 151

Conclusion: Getting Past the Overlay to the Underplay — 189

Acknowledgments — 201

Appendix I: Bordering Practices — 205

Appendix II: Methods — 207

Appendix III: An Example of How a Street Sign Is an Abstraction — 215

Notes — 219

Bibliography — 241

Index — 273

About the Author — 287

LIST OF FIGURES AND TABLES

FIGURES

Figure I.1. "Free the Water" Graffiti (2016)	31
Figure 1.1. "Keep St. Anne's Street Open" Sign (2024)	42
Figure 1.2. Google Map of Southwest Detroit	57
Figure 2.1. Majority Black Detroit Matters (2020)	61
Figure 2.2. Knight Foundation's Six "Neighborhoods" (2003)	69
Figure 2.3. Next Detroit Neighborhoods Initiative (2006)	71
Figure 2.4. Neighborhood Stabilization Plan Map (2008)	73
Figure 2.5. Creative Use of Empty Lots in Front of Detroit Public Theatre (2024)	75
Figure 2.6. Detroit Future City Framework Zones (2012)	76
Figure 2.7. Blight Removal Task Force Report, "Defining Blight" (2014)	79
Figure 2.8. Blight Removal Task Force Report, Tipping Point Geographies (2014)	81
Figure 3.1. Census Tracts in Southwest Detroit	102
Figure 4.1. Direction of Money Transfers in Metropolitan Detroit (1971)	138
Figure A.1. No Warning, 518 Wabash (2009)	215
Figure A.2. "Warning: Car Break-In Area" (2019)	216

TABLES

Table I.1. Population change in Detroit city and Wayne County (2000–2020)	36
Table 2.1. Public-private investment targeted neighborhoods	70
Table 3.1. Southwest Detroit population by census tract (2010, 2020)	103
Table 3.2. Household income and poverty in Southwest Detroit (2010, 2012, 2022)	106

Table 3.3. Homeownership and vacancy rates in Southwest Detroit (2010, 2022) — 107

Table 3.4. Average poverty status in past 12 months, select suburbs (2019) — 112

Table 6.1. Timeline of JPMC's investment in Detroit — 174

Table A.1. Examples of prominent bordering practices — 205

Introduction

If Detroit Could Talk

People suddenly had nice things to say about Detroit. It had only been two years since the city exited the largest municipal bankruptcy in US history when a JPMorgan & Chase director called the city "the new Brooklyn".¹ She spoke at a 2016 national conference where other philanthropic and corporate elites took turns crediting the influx of outside organizations and resources for the city's "economic revival." They seemed to have manufactured a miracle. Two years later, a professor at one of the most highly ranked business schools in the world agreed the city's "explosive rebirth . . . [was] one of the biggest urban stories in the United States."² Prominent awards over the next ten years confirmed the quick turnaround: UNESCO designated Detroit an example of a "City of Design," *Lonely Planet* suggested it was the second "best city in the world" to visit, and *TIME* magazine concluded it was one of the "world's greatest places."³ Readers of *USA Today* concurred with national leaders, academics, and journalists when they chose three Detroit locations first among the nation's 10Best riverwalks, public squares, and art museums.⁴

Detroit's purported turnaround was a story that differed dramatically from the one that the media parroted in the brief three years between the 2010 US Census and the 2013 bankruptcy. Outlets as diverse as *The New York Times*, *The Economist*, *The Wall Street Journal*, *The New Yorker*, and *Forbes* used their front pages to propose their explanations for Detroit's troubles, but they transformed a complex city of places into a thing.⁵ *The New York Times* declared Detroit was a "city that some have declared dead again and again."⁶ National news outlets catered to diverse, international audiences, but were remarkably consistent in their insistence that the problem was too much (square miles), too little (population size), too late (decades).⁷ Their coverage repeatedly associated the nation's largest Black city (in proportion to its overall population) with population loss in ways that tied people to space; headlines like "Detroit Shrinks Itself" reinforced the conflation.[8] Journalists used generalized terms, if they acknowledged residents at all.[9] Even the business school professor signaled the audience that mattered were outsiders when he said Detroit was a city "that many people were ready to let just fail . . . let just disappear. The last person out, please shut off the lights."[10]

The city's miraculous revival seemed to depend on outside observers, but if Detroit could talk, she would scream about this whitewashing of her story. She would fume about how people who did not live with her talked over, for, and about her. They erased her residents' shared struggle to have a home, hold property, and determine their collective destiny. She would insist she was not a thing, but instead a collective experience cultivated over generations. If Detroit could talk, she would dare you to explain why the 1970s campaign to "Say Nice Things About Detroit" only happened when white people were running the city government, taking over its anchor institutions, and turning public resources over to private interests.[11] She would object to news coverage of a bankruptcy that all but ignored that she was among the hardest hit by predatory lending practices that led to the 2008 Great Recession. She would explain that what happened in the decade leading up to and following the bankruptcy were repeated indignities over federal indifference, state preemption, and emaciated versions of democracy.

If Detroit could talk, she would point out that over a third of the city's population was still in poverty in 2022, that the median income of her residents was less than half that of their national counterparts, and that her foreclosure crisis did not end in 2008.[12] She would show you other national recognitions she received, like the one in 2023 for the worst K-12 student performance in the nation. She received this distinction repeatedly for over a decade while her residents' tax dollars were siphoned from her schools and libraries to fuel downtown development.[13] If Detroit could talk, she would ask why developers were not seen as welfare dependent since they relied on public funds. She would give you countless examples of property transfers to confront journalists and investors who used her to exemplify revitalization and reflect on a possible future for other metropolitan areas. She would point out that their story about the latest change in her fortunes coincided with a broader, national drama about race, urban areas, and who made

America "great again." Their version of events that distracted collective attention from how powerful groups redirected shared public resources into their own pockets.

If Detroit could talk, she would ask you to reflect on what Ta-Nehisi Coates said about her. In 2011, the journalist and MacArthur Fellowship (the "genius grant") recipient wrote that he couldn't wait to get back to Detroit because it was a writer's dream. He did not think he had "ever seen more animus between a city and a suburb than in the Detroit area. It was actually really bracing, and I'm tempted to say beyond even what you see down South."[14] He presented himself like other journalists, just beyond their story's frame as a passive observer. Their stories nonetheless made Detroit and her residents real for national and international audiences. The kinds of dreams that Coates referred to were part of a broader trend in journalists' stories that projected abstractions about population shifts, demographic change, and vacant space onto our collective imagination. Outsiders' dreamy reflections transferred an animus that largely ignored Detroit residents' lived experiences and hid their struggles against racism and for space.

Outsiders' dreams abruptly ended when they reached the ears of Detroit residents. "Detroiters" challenged the narrative that "Detroit is Back" with T-shirts that read "Detroit Never Left." Stickers appeared around the metro area, repeating the slogan. A song, a mural, and online videos and debate followed, attesting to a collective dispute between new city boosters and residents who felt disregarded for keeping the city going through its toughest times. Residents shared a conviction that mainstream media maligned Detroit because it was the country's largest Black city. The animus proved size mattered, especially when it involved issues of space, size, Blackness, and racial inequity.[15]

This book argues that the tensions surrounding the years leading up to and following the foreclosure crisis and the city's bankruptcy involve broader claims about social and spatial mobility that underpin the American Dream. The ideal implied anyone, regardless of origin, could work hard and succeed in the United States of America. The dream seemed realized through industrial production: Immigrants arriving in the early 20th century to the city hoped they would be part of a collective vision of national prosperity.[16] They built cars in the Motor City that put many Americans on wheels. The city's promise stretched across national boundaries: President Franklin D. Roosevelt referred to Detroit as America's "arsenal of democracy" because it became a hub of World War II armament production. Detroiters had given the country both a large middle class and dominance over international affairs. The city was one of the earliest examples of a global city.[17]

The dominant narrative about iconic status of "the D" shifted abruptly after the 1967 rebellion (alternately referred to as a riot), which was one of the bloodiest in US history.[18] A variety of commentators blamed the civil disturbance for white flight and postindustrial decline.[19] Their interpretation transformed an icon of the American Dream into one of concentrated poverty. This second storyline obscured how the American Dream was associated with whiteness. After all, Detroit continued to deliver the dream to African Americans who moved into the middle class and positions of governance and leadership in the city. African Americans were more likely to own than rent their homes in the city in the years preceding the 2008 national foreclosure crisis: Detroit had some of the highest levels of Black homeownership in the country.[20]

For many Americans, Motown symbolized Black power, home (or local) rule, and self-determination. The city's story preceded the version focused on industrialization and a predominantly white wave of immigration that reinvented the Motor City. Codenamed "Midnight," Detroit was one of the last stops on the Underground Railroad. The 1833 Blackburn protests (a riot according to the governor) also registered African Americans' active resistance to the Fugitive Slave Act. White people reacted to Black action with dispossession: they assaulted African Americans and burnt many of their buildings. Mayor Marshall Chapin increased the surveillance of Black Detroiters and ordered them to post a $500 bond or leave the city.

Detroit became a "Black Mecca" again during the Great Migration (1916-1930) of African Americans from the South to Northern Cities. Detroit was the fourth largest city in the number of migrants it received, but it was first in terms of the migrants' relative impact on the city's population size.[21] The new residents were important political actors who organized the nation's largest branch of the National Association for the Advancement of Colored People (NAACP). They developed Black Bottom and Paradise Valley and created one of the largest Black middle classes in the United States. They made Detroit the city with the greatest number of Black-owned businesses in the country.[22] White people again reacted to Black action with dispossession. Black Bottom and Paradise Valley were demolished by the late 1950s and early 1960s in favor of urban renewal projects that included highway expansion. The area's residents were abruptly displaced, and many moved into public housing projects.[23]

Detroit fostered critical civil rights gains that included the 1971 election of Coleman Young, the city's first African American mayor. It registered countless historical figures who were drawn to (and drew strength from) the Black city. They transformed American culture and politics, including, C. L. R. James, Stokely Carmichael, Kenneth Cockrel Sr., Kenneth Cockrel Jr., John Conyers, Berry Gordy, Rosa Parks, Marvin Gaye, Michael Jackson, the Jackson 5, Aretha Franklin, Rick James, and Stevie Wonder. Smokey Robinson, Anita Baker, and Diana Ross were born in "Hitsville USA." Malcolm X was nicknamed "Detroit Red," delivered his most important speeches in the city, and married a Detroiter. Reverend Martin Luther King Jr. practiced and recorded his famous "I Have a Dream" speech in the city two months before he delivered it during the March on Washington. Even today, Black and brown Detroiters comment on how they are only reminded that their color is a problem once they leave the city.

The Detroit metropolitan area maps social and spatial mobility through the highways, exchanges, detours, and borders of the nation's color line. The city persistently represents the American Dream, albeit a globalized one. It's a border city whose trade crossings generate significant import and export value for both the United States and Canada. The metro area's immigrant populations are supported by developed community infrastructures. The international dimensions of the American Dream and its ties to the color line are reflected in the city's Latina/o/x population, which is concentrated in the southwestern part of the city.[24] The area known as Southwest Detroit, herein "Southwest" or SWD, includes both recent immigrants from Latin America and Detroiters who trace their Mexican ancestry back over five generations, albeit with disruptions that included the forcible removal of US citizens of Mexican ancestry. Many Southwest residents produced space through their travel across roads and interstate crossings out of Detroit, across some of the whitest and wealthiest suburban towns in the United States, and into

Mexico. A major international border crossing divides Southwest: the Ambassador Bridge is one of the few privately held ports of entry into the United States. Despite the significant wealth that transfers through the area, its poverty rate remains three times the national average.[25] Many residents nonetheless foster a sense of "Southwest Pride," a form of what scholars call place identity, by branding their resilience onto T-shirts, caps, and hoodies.[26] Other areas of the city similarly market the city's grit with songs and clothing brands, including "Detroit versus Everybody." The racial divide between the city's urban and suburban areas and the exchanges that cross national borders are not things, but practices that produce the relation between race and space in America.

If Detroit could talk, she would explain something she learned over generations, lifetimes of labor, and boom and bust economic cycles: Journalists talk about her as if they know something about her that she does not know about herself. Their news articles contributed toward our collective ability to make sense of Detroit in much the same way that they help us make sense of the noise of our own everyday lives. They authored a reality promoted by powerful groups, including photographers, urban planners, economists, lawyers, investors, and policymakers. The professional groups traded on words, images, and "empty abstractions" that were based on their own life experience. Their abstractions were reductionist because they failed to compare and reconsider residents' patterned experiences. In this book, examples of empty abstractions include "blight" and "tipping point," but we see these oft-repeated buzzwords echoed and endlessly recycled everyday by politicians, business executives, media, and a variety of other professionals and intellectual workers. Abstractions are words and images, reduced models that extract from reality. They can be used to promote the conditions that currently exist in society or, alternatively, to reveal the relations that underpin their production. We can also critique abstractions to imagine alternatives to the relations that currently exist.

Abstractions are a method for a general understanding of the relations that produce race and space. Detroit is an ideal case to study because the city's residents have been remarkably consistent in distinguishing abstractions from their own experience. Detroiters insist national media has consistently mischaracterized the city. Their persistent protestations explain why the phrase "Say Nice Things About Detroit" resonates over half a century after it was popularized as a marketing slogan. This book's approach differs from the one used by many scholars in one important way: Other scholars tend to rely on a variety of administrative boundaries and static conceptions of space in ways that reflect what is more commonly known as the container theory of space and the geography of opportunity.[27] People share this way of conceptualizing space and recognize it when they wonder, for instance, about what happens when a tree falls in a forest with no one around to hear it. This book demonstrates the value of focusing instead on human actions. It assumes human perception occurs before conceptualization.[28]

Detroit as Abstraction

Detroit Never Left explains how space is produced by people. My analysis found that the relation between human experience and conceptualization was mapped through words. At issue was not just that there were different versions of a story, or even that what people said reflected what they thought. Instead, words were critical to how powerful groups advanced their interests. For example, the stories that were published about Detroit indicated that what mattered was less about what an individual journalist might have thought than what was eventually published. Publication was an action that depended on editors. Their actions were constrained by media whose ownership was concentrated among a few conglomerates.[29] The actions that the conglomerates took surrounding publication were examples of the relation between most people and powerful groups: this relation shaped the ways we understand each other and our collective experience.

One important example of how abstractions worked in the period leading up to Detroit's bankruptcy involved the words "nature" and "population," which recurred in news articles published by *The Wall Street Journal*, *The New York Times*, *USA Today*, and *Forbes*. One representative 2010 *New York Times* article described city "blocks that are being reclaimed by nature, complete with pheasants nesting in vacant spaces where people once lived."[30] The twinned abstractions of nature and vacancy, or the absence of people, were partial truths. Residents' lived experiences confirmed that there were many unoccupied residential structures in the city. This was a partial truth because the article (and others like it) rarely mentioned that predatory mortgage lending forced many people to lose their homes: Journalists ignored the relation between people (especially bankers and real estate investors) and space. Their articles instead vaguely charged "the twin blows of the foreclosure crisis and jobs lost to the recession" for "population loss."[31] The story focused blame on the city government for "ignoring its [Detroit's] hemorrhaging population."[32] The *New York Times* article exemplified a point of view shared among outsiders, or people who lived outside Detroit: Many books and articles repeated the abstract association between nature and the population of a majority Black city.[33]

Journalists' references to nature and population demonstrate how words are empty abstractions. They are weapons that invert the relation between people and space. Articles tied journalists' and editors' assumptions about the reduced population size to vacancy of residential structures. They made the city synonymous with its human and nonhuman residents (nature), and portrayed both as things that coexisted and were unmanaged in Detroit. The stories appealed to a longstanding legal relation that protected property's productive use but largely ignored the struggles people faced to stay in their homes and avoid foreclosure. Their abstractions hid the relation between people and space and inverted the reality: powerful groups engaged in predatory investments that dispossessed predominantly Black and Brown people and forced them out of their homes.

Journalists' stories about Detroit's bankruptcy demonstrated how abstractions promoted a specific set of relations between people and space. The Detroit case implicated predominantly white outsiders and the city's predominantly Black residents. Journalists cited experts to position themselves as authorities on what happened in Detroit, which inverted another theme in their stories: Local government and city residents did not "acknowledge" and would not "face," Detroit's reality.[34] Journalists positioned nonresident outsiders, including Michigan's governor, the state review board, and the city's state-appointed emergency manager, as active and creative. They turned city residents into problems in one of three ways: They identified municipal pensioners as impediments who sought to block bankruptcy proceedings, current residents as "largely poor and minority" who "live like this," and past residents as to blame for the city's main problem, population loss.[35] These inversions produced problems that politicians and investors who lived outside the city could "solve."[36] The relation spanned beyond the city's boundaries and even across international territories; journalists observed that people came from all over the world to the "Urban Laboratory and the New American Frontier."[37]

The word "decades" was another theme and an abstraction in national news coverage leading up to Detroit's bankruptcy. Journalists concurred that the city's financial crisis had been "decades" in the making, which demonstrated how abstractions could be deceptive mystifications. The references mystified how time (decades) had caused the city's bankruptcy. News stories either harkened back to the 1920s when Detroit was the largest city in the country, the 1950s when the city's population peaked, or they more generally referenced city government and the public sector. For example, one front-page article in a 2011 issue of *The New York Times* announced a formal state review of Detroit's finances. It claimed that "in the eyes of some leaders, this financial crisis . . . was decades in the making: the city never shrank its operations enough to match a shrinking tax base, and it delayed its woes with borrowing, exaggerated revenue estimates and accounting shifts."[38] In this use, "the city" was equated with its local government.

The stories' focus on city government was mirrored by local newspapers. For example, in a *Detroit Free Press* article with the headline "How Detroit Went Broke," the subtitle was "The Answers May Surprise You"—and "Don't Blame Coleman Young"—implying readers should *not* blame a Black mayor who had been outspoken about racism, Black Power and governance, and white disinvestment in the city.[39] The article nonetheless faulted Young's "fiery rhetoric [that] may have contributed to metro Detroit's racial divide."[40] The authors also blamed city government for over five "decades of mismanagement," which inverted the relation between banks and bankruptcy because it blamed political leaders rather than predatory lending practices.[41] The authors nonetheless acknowledged a critical 2005 financing deal that had been "applauded" by Wall Street.[42] In other words, the speculative lending practices that banks had pursued with the city's residents were mirrored by those extended to the city government. These practices were concentrated over a decade, which the article revealed when it summarized its data in a table with a subheading that recognized "bankruptcy [was] avoidable—until decadelong [sic] borrowing binge."[43] The authors' reference to decades was a deceptive mystification because it was unclear how time caused the city's bankruptcy. Journalists used the abstraction to resolve the presumed contradiction of a city government dominated by Black people.[44] The contradictions included ostensibly colorblind markets tied to Wall Street and a state government dominated by white people who claimed to treat all people equitably.

The abstraction of decades obscured a long-standing relation that Mayor Young had observed twenty years earlier when he observed that "white investors were not too interested in investing into a city where blacks made up both most of the population and city hall. Instead, they opted for the mostly white surrounding suburbs."[45] The abstraction of decades also inverted the focus onto local government and obfuscated the state's role in appointing an emergency manager who filed for Detroit's bankruptcy. The state government's actions included changing a law in 1999 (almost two decades before the bankruptcy) that shortened the time for foreclosing on properties with unpaid taxes.[46] The action meant that the state became another institution that wrested property from city residents' control. The deceptive mystification of decades enabled violent dispossessions and extractions from residents.

The abstractions of nature, population, and decades are examples of how partial truths and deceptive mystifications produce race and space. Abstractions are different from words that appear synonymous but refer more narrowly to discourse rather than concrete actions, including "doublespeak," "gaslighting," and "fake news." Abstractions are important to study for several reasons. First, they can elucidate the relation between people and space. Second, the examples above demonstrate how abstractions are productive and violent extractions from reality. Third, abstractions mirror violent struggles over power groups' attempts to colonize Detroit and residents' experiences. In other words, key abstractions shaping urban development survive intellectual challenges because the relations that produce them continue to exist. Other scholars echo how abstractions turn relations into things, appear to resolve contradictions, settle claims, and make private property seem self-evident and natural.[47]

What Scholars Say About Race, Space, and Abstraction

The 2019 COVID-19 pandemic may have forever changed our commonsense understandings of people and space. Our lives were upended as we developed new routines and increased our physical distance from one another. Many of us struggled to do more than simply occupy our homes; some recreated our spaces with the help of furniture makers and appliance suppliers, while others struggled with how builders or contractors produced our homes. Some people fought with mortgage companies, while others tried to avoid eviction by landlords. Our experiences indicated that space was not a thing; it was a product of struggles in relation to other people.

Many of us assume space is racially neutral, but where and how one lives in the world is conditioned by a variety of social differences. Residential segregation is only one example, albeit a significant one, of how racism shapes our lives, our communities, and, ultimately, our world. We experience life through spaces that are shaped by ideas about racial differences. We should not take space for granted. It is not something that "just is" because we do not all understand, organize, and experience "the world from a stable (white, patriarchal, Eurocentric, heterosexual, classed) vantage point."[48] Our relative access to different spaces maps our daily struggles to produce space. For example, thousands of videos and memes online attest to the phenomena where white people judge a Black person "out of place."[49] Hashtags like #BBQBecky, #PermitPatty, #GolfcartGail, and #CentralParkKaren documented white women's settled expectations to control public space. The recent public attention to these events on social media was part of a much longer history. We glimpsed the latest examples of this history when we watched violent videos online shared under the #BlackLivesMatter hashtag, including the murder of George Floyd. This history—in which Black people struggle for space to live life—stretches back centuries.[50] It underscores how white supremacy depends on controlling physical and conceptual space.

Our experiences demonstrate that we produce race and space in relation to other people, but this reality contradicts the ways we think about space. For example, W. E. B. Du Bois had already observed over a century ago that spaces were not simple facts. He identified a relation between

Philadelphia's Seventh Ward and the "removable causes" of racial segregation that were located "far beyond" the area's political boundaries.[51] His research indicated administrative boundaries were abstractions that concealed and mystified how powerful groups produced what they called a "slum."[52] Henri Lefebvre also argued space was "neither a mere 'frame,' after the fashion of the frame of a painting, nor a form or container of a virtually neutral kind, designed simply to receive whatever is poured into it."[53] He considered that space had been subordinated to the abstract principle of private property. Du Bois and Lefebvre's work elucidates how people produce race and space, especially in the form of property.

There is a significant body of literature that indicates race and property are fictions, but they rarely overlap. For example, Karl Polanyi argues that land was a "fictitious commodity" because humans had not produced it for sale.[54] The making of land into something that could be bought and sold (commodification) was part of a grander fiction of a self-regulating market. More recent scholarship confirms that real estate markets depend on fictions about vacant land, hidden housing demand, and public interest.[55] Speculative real estate projects are particularly illustrative of the work these fictions do because people are displaced and dispossessed of their homes *before* property values rise, *before* regulatory approvals are secured, and *before* demand increases.[56]

A different scholarship examines race as an illusion. For example, a 2003 documentary, *Race: The Power of an Illusion*, remains frequently viewed in public and academic libraries. The film stands the test of time because it challenges a persistent belief that there is a biological reality to race. Scholars consistently find racial difference was a fiction used to justify colonization and enslavement. Some use frame theory to explain the illusion. For example, Joe Feagin explains that people rely on a "white racial frame" to understand, act on, and make race real in their everyday lives. He points out this frame is a dominant worldview for "an overwhelming majority of white Americans—as well as many other people seeking to conform to white norms and perspectives."[57] Scholars like Vanessa Rosa demonstrate that urban planners framed diversity, surveillance, and consultation as responses to residential segregation, but in practice, they used the constructions to produce precarity and vulnerability for residents.[58]

A complementary body of scholarship emphasizes the "sincere fiction" that underpins ideas about the relationship between racial superiority and inferiority.[59] Eduardo Bonilla-Silva identified an ostensibly colorblind ideology in which white people rationalized that racial inequalities were the result of "market dynamics, naturally occurring phenomena, and blacks' imputed cultural limitations."[60] Scholars like Christopher Mele found powerful groups relied on this ideology to deceive people and promote their version of urban development.[61]

Scholars demonstrate that powerful groups turn race and property from illusions into reality, but they have been less consistent in turning these productive fictions inside out to reveal the relations that produce these abstractions. Detroit activists are experts in this exercise. They built what is frequently called a "movement city"[62] and rely on intergenerational discussions to distinguish their reality from the ways powerful groups talk about race and space.[63] Activists interpret the ways politicians, lenders, developers, and the media laud recent development as an "overlay for the underplay." Activists use the expression to demonstrate that what a powerful group says (the "overlay") conceals, mystifies, and inverts its objective (the "underplay"). An example of this patterned relation involves the ways politicians justify business incentives that benefit developers and investors at the expense of legacy residents: the people who lived in Detroit before its bankruptcy. For example, policy makers argue that the captures of tax increments promote development, but they also redirect residents' property taxes toward downtown development at the expense of the city's public schools and libraries.[64]

In this book, I draw on several examples to examine key abstractions that produce the relation between race and space. Powerful groups present abstract ideas as things, like puppets that perform as partial truths and deceptive mystifications. The abstractions include words like "broken windows," "tipping points," "blight," and "sprawl" that imply urban development follows natural laws and obscure how powerful groups make decisions about, among other things, where to direct public and private investment. We can use words like mirrored searchlights, turn them on their authors, focus on action and lived experiences, and reveal the relations that codify, institutionalize, and concretize the interests of powerful groups. This method allows us to "see in and through" whiteness and ownership and expose the doubleness of abstraction.[65]

My analysis is guided by scholarship on abstraction and dialectical materialism, subjects that were central to Lefebvre's thinking on space.[66] He pointed out that bodies perceived space through their physical senses before they could conceive of it in their mind. Senses mirrored a social relation: People tried to scale their immediate actions and experiences to abstract concepts as they produced and consumed space.[67] This dialectical approach implied our analyses should prioritize human action and experience, a perspective that was shared by many scholars from the Global South who criticized Western rationality for its insistence on an opposition between subject and object.[68] They argued it was a dualism that operated like a "straitjacket," led Western culture to overemphasize speech and "the written word," and concealed social practice.[69] Words and images are abstractions; they are part of a dialectic that struggles to conquer actual, lived experience, but they can also be inverted and used to reveal relations between social groups and struggles to produce race and space.[70]

The concepts of abstraction and dialectical reasoning have a long history that can be traced to the ancient Greeks. This long history culminated in scholarship that distinguished conceptual from concrete abstraction. Scholars like Karl Marx, Henri Lefebvre, Alfred Sohn-Rethel, Alberto Toscano, Brenna Bhandar, Jason Moore, and Sara-Maria Sorentino explain that powerful groups make abstractions real through their dominance over social relations of production, consumption, and exchange.[71] The distinction between the empty, formal abstractions authored by powerful groups and concrete abstraction made real through our lived experience has operative force in the material world. Consider the example of money: The paper it is printed on, its shape and size, and the symbols printed on it do not make it real. Money becomes real through human actions that create value, particularly by its ability to rely on government and markets to be exchanged and to act as money.

The concept of "population" is another particularly illustrative example of the relation implied by abstraction. It underpinned how journalists produced Detroit in the years leading up to and following the city's bankruptcy. Their repeated references to population loss reduced Detroit's problems to an abstraction: a group that was absent from the city. This was a partial truth focused on the loss of a predominantly white, and secondarily, a Black middle class population that had voluntarily left the city. Despite the focus on population loss, the 2010 Census indicated Detroit still had over seven hundred thousand residents and that over 70 percent of the city's properties were occupied. References to Detroit's population loss was an abstraction that failed to consider how the category was structured; they ignored race and hid the relation between white people who had been incentivized by home lending practices and federal policy to move out of the city and the different forms of interpersonal and institutional racism that prevented poorer Black people from doing the same.

The example of population demonstrates how we can rise from empty to concrete abstractions. This method means analyzing the components of a category, including space, race, and social class, and consider elements that make up those categories. This form of analysis moves toward "ever more simple concepts, from the imagined concrete towards ever thinner abstractions," to conceive of a population "not as the chaotic conception of a whole, but as a rich totality of many determinations and relations."[72] Of fundamental significance, Karl Marx calls this "the method of rising from the abstract to the concrete [and notes that it] is only the way in which thought appropriates the concrete."[73] Approaching data in this way means understanding that not only do abstractions present relations as things, and that science requires reduction, but also that scientists should review what they had initially set aside in their analysis. This review should focus on what is left out of an abstraction, especially when it contradicts what we *think* we know about government, political power, commodities, and economic markets.[74] David Harvey similarly uses "the power of abstraction" to analyze and understand the concrete world, identify the contradictions of capitalist accumulation, and demonstrate that *how* we abstract matters.[75]

Maps are another illustrative example of abstractions because they underpinned efforts to, as one Detroit entrepreneur, mapper, and project leader explained: "monetize" Detroit.[76] Mapping projects were critical to how investors and multiple levels of governments commodified Detroit. Their maps ignored important details about how space was experienced, mystified the ways we produce space, and naturalized the biological and cultural grouping of humans and space.[77] Maps demonstrated how abstractions do things: they produced space in relation to what mattered to the people who commissioned them. The signs and lines on maps were also deceptive; they reified space by bordering it and asserted a truth that insisted on settling ongoing boundary disputes and struggles over space.[78] Maps, their lines, and their signs, revealed how abstractions were codified, institutionalized, and concretized through words and images. They demonstrated that abstractions are not simply ideas but also tools developed by powerful groups to dominate relationships. Maps made conquest and enclosure possible; governments used them to aggressively control land, extract resources, and consolidate their power. Cartographic symbols work like money in capitalist societies because they create "general equivalents" and commodify space.[79]

Images complement words: Both are abstractions that are made real at different levels of social and material existence. For example, urban planners used maps to target areas of Detroit for redevelopment. Journalists complemented these maps with their frequent references to the city's size (in square miles) and comparisons to other city sizes. Planners and politicians also used these maps and numbers to avoid debates with city residents about withdrawing public services from areas of the city. Sara Safransky documented how planners shifted public discussion from distressed markets to high-vacancy areas. One of them explained, "Everyone is looking at language. It's highly scrutinized."[80] Planners also changed the words they used from "distressed" to "vacant" areas. They made the idea of shrinking the city seem obvious and natural. They used maps, words, and numbers to obscure their role in producing spaces and promoting the conditions that threatened residents to move (or be removed) from their homes and communities.

People do not share equal or compatible abilities to author or popularize abstractions. Powerful groups depend on abstraction to create differences between people, produce space, and generate profit. My references to "powerful groups" draw on scholarship that identifies leaders and professions associated with abstraction. For example, Karl Marx noted that economists and philosophers developed abstractions that emphasized the conceptual world.[81] Lefebvre adds that epistemologists, urban planners, geographers, and other "specialists in some scientific discipline or other which has a concern with space" similarly advanced abstractions that distorted the ways we understand space.[82] John R. Logan and Harvey L. Molotch pointed to a growth machine made up of real estate entrepreneurs who made their money from land and development.[83] Katherine McKittrick criticized geography for naturalizing race and space by "repetitively spatializing where nondominant groups 'naturally' belong."[84] Scott pointed to people who consolidated their power by commissioning maps to settle boundary struggles. Legal scholars suggested law "has a power of transformation without equals: it is a machine for abstraction which, through the medium of language, translates the real and produces it otherwise."[85]

Other scholars identify other professionals among powerful groups. For example, Keeanga-Yamahtta Taylor explains how public-private partnerships tethered federal housing development and financing to real estate brokers, mortgage bankers, and homebuilders and made the federal government "complicit with private sector practices that promoted residential segregation and racial discrimination."[86] Elizabeth Korver-Glenn states that real estate professionals, "including housing developers, real estate agents, mortgage bankers, and appraisers . . . , actively create racially unequal housing markets and urban landscapes."[87] Johana Londoño details examples of how "urban planners, architects, designers, municipal government officials, settlement workers, policy makers, business owners, developers and urban ethnographers" broker representations of Latinx urban culture across the United States.[88] These insights are useful in mapping the relations between powerful groups and professionals, but they mirror the insights of scholars who study productive fictions: They often focus on unequal outcomes and miss the interest-driven relation between professionals and power. Consider the comparable example of scholars who identify "inequality" as a problem without seeing it as one of several possible outcomes in a relation where some profit at the expense of others. By limiting our scope of analysis to inequality, scholars miss ongoing relational struggles that tie accumulation to dispossession. For example, Taylor documented how the Federal Housing Administration (FHA) guaranteed mortgages that were designed to promote foreclosure.

Abstraction and the Property Relation

Many scholars and professional groups produce knowledge and contribute to social and political projects that underpin what Robin D. G. Kelley calls a "neoliberal variant of racial capitalism."[89] These projects were initiated by classical economists and politicians who wanted to create an economy that was autonomous from society.[90] They did not and could not succeed, but the projects nonetheless promoted white supremacy, US territorial conquest, and slavery.[91] Racial projects were bolstered by political force and they dispossessed and displaced nonwhite people. The project of promoting capitalism did not end colonization or abolish slavery. Harvey points out that capitalism "necessarily and always creates its own 'other'" and depends on violent, predatory practices to promote "accumulation by dispossession."[92] These practices are explored in this book and include a credit system that promoted extraction by commodifying land and forcefully expelling residents from their homes and communities. Harvey believes the state, by which he means law and governance, facilitates, supports, and promotes these practices by privatizing, appropriating, or transferring public assets to private companies. In his conception, the state plays a supplementary role in the relation of accumulation by dispossession.

Du Bois, Lefebvre, Taylor, Kelley, and Harvey are part of an intellectual legacy that implicitly challenged a conventional legal argument that property is a "bundle of rights" held by different and discrete individuals. They would instead argue that property expressed a mutually dependent relation between opposed interests.[93] They focus on the relation between owners and nonowners and those who accumulate through those who are dispossessed. Relational analyses can extend our understanding of other relations, including those of obligation and dependency, dominance and subordination, and protection and the punishment. Abstractions reveal that the state's role in producing these relations between social groups is, and has always been, more than supplemental. In other words, the state is creative in promoting accumulation by dispossession.[94] Jamie Peck and Heather Whiteside suggest that Detroit is simply one case of a broader phenomenon of financialized urbanism that targets municipalities for "financialized restructuring and technofiscal governance."[95] Their insight suggests cities are no longer growth machines, but instead debt machines that take on a postdemocratic form because political power is further removed from residents.

We can explain race and space more effectively when we consider how the state actively produces (and not simply promotes) the relation between race and space. For example, property laws that originated in slavery created "racially contingent forms of property and property rights."[96] These laws were used by a variety of groups, including courts that invented whiteness as a relation to property deployable throughout society. Law "defined and affirmed critical aspects of identity (who is white); of privilege (what benefits accrue to that status); and, of property (what legal entitlements arise from that status)."[97] US courts continue to protect the property interest in whiteness by treating the status quo as a neutral baseline. Their rulings settle and protect whites' expectations of power and control that were manifest in the cases of "BBQ Becky," "Permit Patty," "Golfcart Gail," and "Central Park Karen." An earlier example of the state as creative actor in accumulation by dispossession traces to earlier forms of colonization and property law; the state formalized and registered land titles. The titles created not only land as a commodity, but also humans as natives and savages.[98]

The examples of state action demonstrate how abstractions can be used like a searchlight: They can be inverted and turned against themselves to elucidate the relations that produce race and space. Consider, for example, that the 1896 Supreme Court decided in *Plessy v. Ferguson* and judicial opinion rationalized "separate but equal" to legalize segregation. To focus on the court's reasoning would narrow our attention to business owners who enforced legal segregation, which would obscure the critical role courts had in a relation in which they continued to actively produce and give legitimacy to de jure segregation by upholding laws passed by state and local governments. The case demonstrates how abstractions can be simultaneously mobilized through words like "separate but equal" and yet reflect the relations underpinning the actions of powerful groups. This is one example of the doubleness of abstraction.

The state has a monopoly over the definition of what is legal and over the legitimate use of physical force (violence) to enforce order.[99] This makes abstraction more than an idea tucked away in a person's mind or circulated through frames on newspaper pages. Abstractions are also more than a reflection of shared understanding between powerful groups. They instead make struggles concrete through symbolic, structural, and direct forms of violence. Abstractions and signs are violent, just as "tools cut, slice, assail and brutalize natural materials."[100] Their violence is simultaneously destructive and creative; it insulates powerful groups from critique and undermines people's ability to redress extractive relations.[101] Abstractions can survive challenges as long as the conditions that produce them continue to exist.

The violence of abstraction was mapped through the ways investors worked to repackage, "monetize," and sell Detroit. Repackaging involved dispossessing Black home- and landowners and displacing Black governance. The city was also monetized through mapping and survey projects leading up to and following the bankruptcy. Newly hired consultants and professionals came to the city and took over the city's government and its major institutions, including the Henry Ford Hospital, the Detroit Institute of Arts, and Wayne State University.[102] White investors, including Dan Gilbert, the Fords, and the Illitches, took ownership over a large proportion of the city's downtown and midtown real estate.[103] The involuntary transfers of ownership that happened through bank and tax foreclosures complemented state-imposed emergency management and accompanied an erosion of democracy in the city.

Ownership in the years leading up to and following the foreclosure crisis and the bankruptcy was a social relation mediated through legal and administrative violence. This pitted legacy and recent residents in disputes about who had a legitimate claim to call themselves a "Detroiter." Southwest Detroit residents debated what it meant to be "from" the area, which reflected the difficulties they experienced in the city and their struggles for belonging and identity. These struggles were tied to, but simultaneously greater than, home ownership, legal residency, and citizenship.[104] Legacy residents struggled with a variety of investors, policy makers, and even new residents who believed urban legends about having been forced out of the city after the 1967 rebellion. The tensions raised the question of what abstractions about democracy meant. For example, representation meant that African American and Latina/o/x residents struggled to retain a measure of control over local affairs. Public resources became an asset that nonresidents pursued through legislation that favored their interests even if they had not elected local representatives or paid taxes to the city.

City, state, and federal governments depended on abstractions to promote their partnerships with private corporations. They worked together to attract investments and fund development. Many of these programs and partnerships were neither transparent nor responsive to residents' concerns about exclusion. For example, many legacy residents were dispossessed and displaced by the quasi-public Detroit Land Bank Authority (DLBA). Lenders inverted the relation underpinning loan terms and blamed "irresponsible" borrowers (homeowners, city government, and municipal pensioners) for debt. State politicians similarly shifted blame onto the city for the political decisions that led to the city's bankruptcy. Banks and the state government relied on abstractions like "risk" and "trust" and enabled a variety of outside investors and interests to strip the city of its assets and control over its resources, including the Detroit Institute of Arts, Belle Isle, and the Water and Sewer Department.[105] The experience of bankruptcy demonstrated how both corporations and the federal and state governments made democratic rights contingent for the predominantly Black city.

The relations that produced Detroit and racial difference didn't end when the city exited bankruptcy under its first white mayor in forty years. The experience of dispossession and displacement continued under the state-mandated Financial Review Commission that would oversee the city for at least another thirteen years, until 2027. Detroit's experience of bankruptcy shaped comparable experiences of rights contingent on racialized difference: The federal government relied on abstractions to prevent Puerto Rico from declaring bankruptcy and to restructure and manage the island's debt.[106]

Abstractions as Bordering and Crossing Practices

People share a familiarity with borders that constrain our physical and socioeconomic mobility.[107] I draw on these experiences and refer to social and spatial separations as "bordering practices." Borders are not "things" but a set of practices grounded in patterned human action. (An outline of examples is included as appendix 1.) Thinking about abstractions as bordering practices underscores their materiality and avoids relying on other familiar and related abstractions, including boundaries, frames, and ideologies. Bordering practices also helps us focus on how space is produced through social relations. For example, we produce space when we assign places to where activities should occur in the form of buildings and through gates, walls, and highways, among other things.[108] These enclosures give an appearance of separation; similarly, we produce race when we assign people to spaces. Policing and redlining are examples of bordering practices. In the case of metropolitan Detroit, they also include international tunnel and bridge crossings between the United States and Canada. Bordering practices are also reflected in the two cities within Detroit's territorial boundaries: Highland Park and Hamtramck, incorporated to prevent annexation by Detroit. Even journalists recognize that "locals often refer to the act of exiting or entering Detroit as crossing the border."[109]

Many commentators see racial and spatial borders mirrored in what they call Black and white spaces: geographic locations occupied by a relatively greater proportion of people who are racialized and who identify themselves as Black or white. The conflation of color and space was reflected in Patrick Moynihan's 1967 claim that "the urban Negro is, in a fundamental sense, the 'urban problem.'"[110] He focused on space and race and implied African Americans in cities had been excluded from the prosperity enjoyed by white Americans in suburban areas. Scholars have built a tradition that associates Black space with surveillance, discipline, and exclusion from mainstream institutions. They argue, for example, that Black space is experienced along a "carceral continuum" that puts urban communities in relation to prisons and penal management.[111] They extend a similar conception of numerical majorities and rely on container theories of space in their scholarship on "white space" and Latino urbanism.[112]

The scholarship on "Black" and "white" space obscures a relation that extends beyond segregation, exclusion, police, surveillance, and discipline. My data draws from Latino/a/x experience and indicates the border is not a thing, but a set of practices that do more than invent difference and naturalize race through space: They "connect and divide" and selectively filter people and different forms of circulation.[113] This makes inclusion and exclusion two ends of a continuum rather than opposed to one another. I also argue that crossing practices respond to bordering practices; successful crossings were dominated by corporations and white professionals. The patterns suggested white people dominate the production of abstractions that are expressed in physical and symbolic borders. This is why I refer to "white borders" in this book's title.

Detroiters struggled to undermine the coherence of borders in ways that were reminiscent of an unauthorized US-Mexico border crossing. The Latina/o/x youth that I spoke with engaged in a variety of crossing practices that mapped their lives comparatively and in relation to white and Black residents in the metropolitan area. For example, two Latinas who I interviewed demonstrated a crossing practice when they explained they were not "white" despite their light skin color. They lived in Southwest Detroit and narrated their difference through experiences of traveling into areas for work and school that were predominantly occupied by white people. These were not settled claims of white space. They fashioned their racial identity in opposition to white privilege and in solidarity with "Brown Pride." Their claims reflected a struggle for social as much as spatial mobility.

Crossing practices help elucidate peoples' struggles to produce race and space.[114] They include challenges people face not only in becoming homeowners but in holding on to property. Crossings transcend conventional borders and demonstrate that struggles over race and space are not solely reactive and do not simply resist the way things are. For example, people adapt to segregation in creative ways.[115] Clyde Woods identified a "Blues epistemology" rooted in a tradition of Black working class struggles that envisions a distinct, future-oriented social and ethical vision based on, among other goals, economic redistribution to oppressed and working-class communities and a full recognition of human rights.[116] Saidiya Hartman suggested the *undoing* of "the plot of her undoing" begins with the earth but is unsaid.[117] Katherine McKittrick writes of the nonworld, a relation to experience that produces lessons "that cannot be contained in the main text."[118] The relation between race and space exceeds abstraction.

Bordering and crossing practices help me explain how space and race were produced as a relation rather than as things. This finding stemmed from my extended effort to understand how Latina/o/x youth believed they had opportunities in a city without jobs. I used interviews and learned racial difference and inequality extended beyond an individual's color or identity. Youth understood themselves in relation to a hypersegregated city and its adjoining suburbs. This made their experience of race one that was collective and produced through a history of bordering and crossing practices that were tied to Southwest

Detroit; their lives were lived in relation to abstractions that produced race and space.

Scholars like Brandi Thompson Summers similarly identified this inverted relation. She found displacement and creative placemaking could occur in the same space: Mainstream markets produced a relation that extended the meanings of Black space and "the 'chocolate' moniker" in Washington, DC, beyond the number or proportion of Black residents in the city.[119] Rather than Black space, business owners appropriated Blackness "as an aesthetic," concealed the violence of dispossession, and obscured "the processes and practices of excessive policing, predatory lending, evictions, and increased tax burdens that accompany gentrification."[120]

The implications of Thompson Summers's relational analysis are that the politics and violence that underpin dispossession are concealed by another inverted relation: the "illusion of inclusion."[121] She analyzed a sign to explain how white business owners marketed the post-chocolate city in ways that devalued and displaced Black people.[122] I included a comparable relational analysis of a sign in appendix 3, but as throughout this book, I focus on abstraction and action rather than aesthetics and culture to explain displacement and dispossession.

Abstraction and culture are complementary and informed the meaning of race in the years leading up to and following the city's bankruptcy. For example, a MacArthur Fellowship ("genius grant") recipient wrote several articles and books about Detroit. He was a Chilean-born photographer, Camilo José Vergara, who wrote that the book he published after the city's bankruptcy was for the people of the future. He believed they were participating in building a city of several identities that were "*negotiated online* by the automobile industry, gentrifiers, billionaires, foundations, advertising people, volunteers, urban farmers, artists, and bicycle-riding hipsters as they struggle to understand, imagine, and remake all 139 square miles of Detroit."[123] He suggested the city's new identity would be negotiated beyond its physical borders, by outsiders, and no longer spatialized along the Black-white color line. He imagined an abstract future in which the majority Black city's residents were part of a former identity. Vergara worked to produce a post-chocolate city that was up for grabs.

"The Woods for the Trees"

The reader might accuse me of missing the forest for the trees[124] because I ignore the voluminous literature documenting the conditions leading up to Detroit's bankruptcy: significant population loss after World War II, an eroded tax base, high unemployment, and a high rate of vacant lots and buildings.[125] These explanations have been catalogued in a long list of books about the city. The same can be said for the improvement in the overall quality of life for most Detroiters since the bankruptcy on almost every measure: Poverty and unemployment were reduced, and median income was up.[126] My objective is not to challenge the reality of these phenomena but instead to demonstrate that focusing on indicators obscures deeper relations that underpin the production of race and space. The challenge reminds me of Du Bois's comments about sociologists "gleefully counting" outcomes without understanding the human relations that produce them.[127] In this book I suggest that studying these relations can reveal new insights and explain much of what we take for granted about how we produce race and space.

My goal is not a definitive account but a relational one. Many Detroiters continue to feel the city is so often studied but little understood. In the United States alone, there were at least twenty-five titles published on the city over the ten-year period between 2011 and 2021.[128] The titles were mostly fatalistic and referred to afterlives, autopsies, declines, former greatness, hardships, and wastelands. At least seven book titles used the word "ruins," which represented the city as a passive stage set for spectators to consume.[129] *The Detroit News* confirmed "Detroit bashing was a national [and tiresome] pastime."[130] The problem traced back at least to a 1970s campaign when Emily Gail started the brand, "Say Nice Things About Detroit." The slogan endures as one of many that people use to stake their claim and identify their relation to the city.[131]

From Disjunctures as Events to the *Longue Durée*

This book is an effort to make sense of several events that I experienced as disjunctures. The project seemed to begin when I came from New York City in 2006 to teach at a university in Detroit. I moved to an area of the city that residents proudly call "Southwest" (SWD) where

I found a familiar reception: a Latina/o/x population, Mexican food, friends, and a second-floor balcony where I watched car and truck lights crossing the international bridge over the Detroit River at night. As I settled into a new job and a new home, a student came to the department's front office and introduced himself as a neighbor from across the street. He asked if I was "aware of the raccoons climbing around the roof and living above my apartment?"

Perhaps I should have been embarrassed to live with wild animals in the house, but his message didn't immediately concern me; unexpected events had been a part of my daily life growing up in 1970s New York at a time when the city faced possible bankruptcy. I assumed my experience was familiar enough to most people across the country. They saw the same public service announcements cross their television screens at 10 p.m. that asked if viewers knew where their children were. I believed the announcements indicated everyone cared about youth out on the street at night, but the Central Park Five case identified another disjuncture. What seemed like a normal part of a childhood for me (playing outside, in city parks, with friends, sometimes as it grew dark) was instead an abstract, dangerous urban space that seemed out of control to many Americans. The police not only criminalized the youth in the case but also produced the park as a place where some youth were surveilled. The park exemplified an inverted relation: a public space became safe for white people at the expense of youth of color.

I found a parallel disjuncture recurred every time I came back to the United States after spending several weeks in Mexico City; the culture shock wasn't about individual Karens, because what seemed an important and generalized part of life in the United States was an anxious need to divide spaces into discrete categories, to police them and treat some people as if they were pests, and, in the process, to control nature and animals.

Another disjuncture that showed me the difference between how I thought things were and how things were for residents unfolded over my first few years living and working in Detroit. The city magnified the strains of what eventually grew into a national foreclosure crisis in 2008 and the Great Recession. I taught my students that they experienced "neighborhood disadvantage" as the automotive industry crisis unfolded. It seemed like a straightforward enough lesson: We could all see their schools and homes were closing in on them, but my students didn't see Southwest Detroit (SWD) as a place of concentrated poverty and disadvantage. They understood the story that the numbers told, they read the newspaper headlines, and they even had direct experiences with violent crime, but they were also enrolled in the city's public university, anticipated they would go on to lucrative careers, and had not imagined leaving a city without jobs after graduation. They echoed their families and communities repeated insistence: *Si Se Puede!* Most had been raised to believe there was something unique about Latinos because we "work hard and succeed." We were children of immigrants and shared a belief that "where there's a will, there's a way." They assumed jobs would always be available. For example, a common saying in Spanish translated the idea that *if* someone is looking for work, they must be praying *not* to find it.[132] Neither my Latina/o/x students or interviewees saw themselves in my theories about unemployment, stalled social mobility, or urban decline.

Other disjunctures happened outside the classroom that mirrored the same messages about insiders and outsiders. I attended fundraisers and other community-related meetings where politicians and nonprofit agency leaders repeatedly claimed that SWD was one of the only areas in the city that was growing economically and demographically. They produced the area as a coherent whole, a thing that was simultaneously blighted and yet the best place to invest in the city. The Ambassador Bridge was one of the few privately owned border crossings in the United States, which seemed to justify investors' interest in the area even before the city went into bankruptcy proceedings. A national nonprofit promoted SWD in 2008 as a "good quality product at a reasonable price." The area's nonprofit organizations were particularly significant to SWD residents because of the number of people they reached and the scope of their services. Their efforts to make SWD a bargain coincided with other city residents and nonprofit groups who noted the relatively greater funding SWD nonprofits enjoyed compared to their counterparts in other parts of the city. Some influential figures felt SWD nonprofits had a distinct advantage, not only because the area was consistently targeted for investment, but also because the area was *not* predominantly Black *and* because its non-Black leadership was trusted by white investors.[133]

The emerging "nonprofit industrial complex" presented another important disjuncture.[134] SWD nonprofits were treated by philanthropic organizations as if they were synonymous with community, but many residents complained some nonprofits could be just like any other business that cared more about profits than people. The former president and CEO of one of the area's largest housing development nonprofits explained, "We ran a business. We saw it as a business. Not a charity. . . . [We were] moving that mindset from charity work, to running a business that happens to have a tax status where the assets don't go up to the owners but are plowed back in."[135] The nonprofit operated as a business in other ways: It acquired several smaller community development organizations and became an important property developer and landowner in SWD.

Census data on poverty and educational attainment did not align with public leaders' claims about how wonderfully SWD was doing. Neither did residents' experiences of being profiled by police departments and border patrol. Disjunctures recurred when Latina/o/x youth remembered their experiences of crossing city borders to find jobs, go to college, or access parks to jog or play soccer. They explained they did not enjoy the same ability to go where they wanted to go as suburbanites did.[136] Their unfreedom was physically marked when they crossed the Motor City's borders and were stopped by a police officer or followed in a store. They kept explaining that their American Dreams of freedom were greater than having a job, leaving the city, or keeping their homes. Their struggles to access different spaces were patterned in ways that indicated how other players dominated space: youth struggled with police, urban planners, mortgage lenders, and other rule setters. Their struggles mapped relations between groups who authored and enforced rules, including city, county, state, and federal governments, as well as financial institutions.[137] They shaped my gradual understanding that abstractions were actions made real "behind the backs of the producers."[138]

My interviews with Latina/o/x youth helped me understand the extractive relationships that shaped their lives in and beyond SWD, the city, and the metropolitan area. The difficulty Detroiters faced crossing from a predominantly Black city into predominantly white suburban areas surrounding it were so patterned that it took on cultural forms, including the 2002 movie *8 Mile*. Large entertainment venues, theaters, and museums were concentrated in the city. They benefited from land transfers and tax incentives that shifted the burden for financing the city onto its residents. At the same time, Detroiters were often underrepresented among the employees of new developments and entertainment venues. The extraction was built into the metropolitan area's infrastructure: Highways were built to direct traffic through and away from the city. Suburbanites came into the city during the week for work and the weekends for entertainment. The youth I spoke with lived in Detroit and complained that despite their concrete experiences of relative immobility, they were blamed for outsiders' fear of crime in the city. They complained about suburban kids who came to graffiti SWD but evaded any penalty by driving back out of the city. They also resented suburban residents and businesses that dumped waste in the city and evaded the cost of proper disposal. Youth residing in SWD felt simultaneously blamed for this blight and dispossessed of time and money spent on periodic clean ups.

The disjunctures of development and mobility were compounded by abstractions like "vacancy." People I spoke with who lived in SWD knew at least one person who occupied buildings informally and without authorization. Sometimes the person was living in a home they had once owned, but experienced mortgage or tax foreclosure. This tied the meaning of urban space to a relation that involved negotiating the terms of occupation. For example, informal occupations became dangerous as water shutoffs spread across the city. One man froze in a flooded elevator shaft at the Roosevelt Warehouse with only his legs sticking out for months before firefighters retrieved his body. People occupied the Michigan Central Station across the street, which made claims that the building was vacant seem disingenuous. I watched people huddling in front of the building, warming themselves and holding their hands over open fires in burn barrels. Meanwhile, tourists came from all over the world and broke past the plywood coverings into the towering, eighteen-story tall structure at the eastern edge of SWD. They took pictures and hawked images of urban decay to international audiences. I wondered why journalists didn't consider the vandals to be criminals in their stories. Tourists visited a city where residents were instead blamed for making it the most dangerous place in America.

What we believe to be true guides how we act: the ways we vote, where we want to live, and how we spend our time. Disjunctures are hidden in abstraction but can lead to insights that help us distinguish what is true. Scholars, city planners, and philanthropists created Detroit as a space they imagined it to be, but often their stories of crisis and decay were the opposite of how people lived in and used areas. For example, journalists portrayed Detroit as an urban frontier because they imagined it as a place without rules that had to be conquered. Tourists from all over the world were no different from suburbanites that came into the city to experience freedom without responsibilities or consequences. They joined journalists, politicians, and police who criminalized city residents and shipped Detroiters off to newly built prisons that fed local economies across the northern part of the state. This was the kind of relation that residents felt benefited others at their expense: The urban frontier put Detroiters on the wrong (passive) side of its "where no man has gone before" border. The relation marked freedom for new migrants at the expense of legacy residents.

Disjunctures undermined people's ability to redress extractive relations. For example, only months before the JPMorgan & Chase director claimed Detroit was the "the new Brooklyn," two SWD artists climbed a water tower and painted a Black Power fist and the words "Free the Water." Their action was one of several crossings, or resident struggles against the mass water shutoffs that intensified during and after the bankruptcy proceedings. The crossings were tied to other struggles to produce space. For example, one of the two SWD artists informally occupied buildings. Residents used other forms of direct action to circumvent shutoffs, including sharing keys that could turn the water meter back on.[139] They often relied on mutual aid and shared a variety of resources between homes, including food and electricity. Other actions included protests and litigation against Detroit Water and Sewer Department (DWSD).

The struggles revealed how delinquency operated as abstraction. On the one hand, it obscured (and could be used to reveal) the relation between not only the city and its suburbs, but also residents and outside commercial interests. Suburban residents and businesses were more indebted to DWSD but, unlike Detroiters, were offered greater leniency and did not experience service interruptions. On the other hand, the abstraction inverted the relation and made it seem like the city's residents owed a debt to DWSD. Delinquency implied immoral action or neglecting a duty, but even the United Nations recognized water was a human

Figure I.1. "Free the Water" Graffiti (2016)

right well before the bankruptcy proceedings began. The DWSD's shut-offs inverted a relation characterized by its free access to water from Lake Huron, Lake St. Clair, and Lake Erie.

Delinquency demonstrates how empty abstractions are violent. The relation that delinquency revealed included several forms of dispossession. An overdue water bill could be added to a resident's tax bill and result in a tax foreclosure on their home. A lack of water could lead to a loss of steam heat and people froze in their homes. Buildings where the water had been shut off were considered blighted, which meant the state could forcibly remove children from their homes and take them into protective custody.[140] One outcome of bankruptcy was collective dispossession as the water system was taken out of the city's control and regionalized under the Great Lakes Water Authority (GLWA).[141]

Over time, the disjunctures helped me understand that what people said about Detroit really mattered. Local businesses posted stickers, wore T-shirts, and commissioned murals that both engaged and challenged the city's reputation. My students who lived in Detroit complained about national headlines that turned the city into something they felt it was not. My suburban students created another disjuncture when they insisted their classmates from Detroit made the city seem better than it "really" was to make themselves feel better. The tensions between residents and outsiders were patterned. For example, Vergara lamented that his proposal for the city was criticized as an embarrassment of the city's residents, but he also thanked the "planners, architects, and historians at various universities" he worked with to develop his famous oeuvre.[142] The disjunctures were marked by residents who often criticized the prestigious university that was about a forty-five-minute driving distance away; they felt it treated the city like a laboratory and them as its specimens. This explained how the university and its "Detroit School" colonized from a distance. Words revealed disjunctures were part of more established and patterned relations that produced race and space in the metro area.

One last example of an abstraction merits attention because it was particularly illustrative of how scholars and universities justify the political agendas of powerful groups. The well-known urbanist, Richard Florida, said he was amazed at how quickly Detroit had begun recovering from the foreclosure crisis. He pointed out recovery was "up from the bootstraps. It was not like there was any big government plan to remake Detroit. In fact, most government plans hurt the city over time."[143] His statement fit neatly with neoliberal forms of urban governance that favor reducing state influence over the economy. The following year, however, Michigan's Republican Governor Rick Snyder initiated perhaps the biggest and most significant government plan to restructure the city's economy and, by default, its relation to metropolitan, state, regional, national, and, because of its ties to trade with Canada, international economies. The federal government had bailed out banks and the auto industry, but Snyder instead appointed an emergency manager who filed for bankruptcy. Part of the bankruptcy exit plan cut public pension benefits for retirees who had worked for the city for decades. The "big government plan" had helped powerful corporations rather than many Detroit residents. Snyder's action highlighted the power of a legislature dominated by white politicians who represented a state dominated by white voters. The tension was recognized by a long-time legislative staff member, who said, "There is still an anti-Detroit bias, there has been for a very long time, among Republicans."[144]

The anti-Detroit bias is part of a broader relation to anti-Blackness, which is neither fixed nor permanent, but "must be constantly remade."[145] The latest example was in October 2024 when President Donald Trump warned the country would be "like Detroit" if Kamala Harris was elected president.[146] The anti-Black bias also shaped the experiences of Latina/o/x Detroiters. Lewis Gordon's reflection on the meaning of mixed race throughout the Americas considered distinctions between racism in Latin America, United States, Canada, and the United Kingdom to be "for the most part, a dodge . . . ultimately, the primary distinctions focus on being either white or at least not being black."[147] This conception resonated with Latina/o/x interviewees who tried to make sense of themselves and their experiences of social and spatial mobility in a hypersegregated metropolitan area.

I began interviewing youth living in SWD as they tried to make sense of another disjuncture: uneven development in the city. They were aware SWD had been consistently targeted by philanthropic foundations and outside investors. They shared a sense with community leaders that the area had been overlooked by a Black-led city government, but they enjoyed new attention after the city's bankruptcy under a white mayor's administration. Some were excited by new businesses coming to the area, grants, and new murals on business walls. There were new resources being directed to public parks, activities, and development. But they were conflicted about whether the slow gentrification they saw happening in SWD was a good or a bad thing. Social media confirmed that the disjunctures were not isolated events but instead glimpses of the *longue durée*, a longer history of relations shaped by white supremacy and anti-Blackness.[148]

These experiences shaped my sense that *being* Latina/o/x in Southwest Detroit was a relation that could not simply be thought about as an individual or group identity.[149] The more I reflected on the various kinds of data I had collected before and after the interviews, the more I understood that being Latina/o/x was an experience not unlike driving with a sideview mirror: You look forward to attaining the benefits that white supremacy seemed to offer some people in the richest areas of the metropolitan region, like Bloomfield Hills and Birmingham.[150] At the same time, you keep looking in the sideview mirror to ensure you do not experience the same kinds of exclusion and discrimination that seemed central to the Black experience in the nation's largest Black city. That explained the Afro-Latina/o/x interviewee that said they identified as "brown," when I asked them. Or the dark-skinned Latina/o/x man who said they identified as "brown . . . and white too." The relation between white supremacy and anti-Blackness underpinned the doubleness of abstraction and what it meant to be Latina/o/x in Detroit.

Methods

Detroit Never Left uses Detroit as a case study for its analysis of race and space. The period leading up to and following its bankruptcy involved a variety of actors in thinking about and trying to solve the city's financial woes. They shared a belief that data was critical to understanding and intervening in the city's development. For example, Dan Gilbert was critical to the development of data collection and analysis about the city. He worked with the Detroit Blight Removal Task Force to survey and define a problem that grew as the foreclosure crisis intensified: Other investors similarly believed they could "monetize" the city's parcels and profit from property sales. The city's residents claimed these efforts targeted public assets and supported investors' "land grab" at their expense.

Data is an important way of understanding how scholars have misunderstood the relation between race and space. Conceiving of space as a container explains why researchers take abstraction for reality: They consider census tracts as discreet variables and analyze them in corresponding ways. This misconception implicates other abstractions, including the interaction index that measures the proximity of residence between racial groups rather than meaningful interaction between them. Critical geographers propose focusing instead on relational analyses of lived experience and struggles to produce space. *Detroit Never Left* builds on these insights. The twinned need to understand space not only as a relation but also one that is tied to racial inequity makes Detroit an ideal case study.

Detroit Never Left relies on a variety of data to elucidate the relation between race and space. I draw on over sixty in-depth interviews with

Latina/o/x youth between the ages of twenty and twenty-four who were living in the Detroit metropolitan area, most of whom lived in Southwest Detroit. I conducted three interviews with each individual to understand their social networks, mobility, and understanding of how to "get ahead" in our society. I asked questions about factors that helped or limited an individual's socioeconomic mobility. The interviews provided a context for understanding where they lived, worked, and tried to experience social mobility. Their narratives illustrated their struggles with, among others, police, immigration officials, mortgage lenders, and landlords. Their stories suggested they faced a variety of borders in their everyday lives. I found abstractions like what it meant to "be from" SWD, "paying your dues," "Southwest" identity, and the distinctions between the block, the neighborhood, and the community were fundamental to how they made sense of themselves and how they thought about what they wanted in their future. Their stories could not explain broader trends, including Latina/o/x youths' struggles to stay in SWD or live in the adjoining suburban areas where the Latina/o/x population had concentrated, largely after having left the city. This led me to interview other residents, business owners, activists, nonprofit organization leaders, and city employees. I also spoke with lawyers, nonprofit organization leaders, and a variety of urban planners and scholars who conducted research on Detroit to understand my interviews.

I relied on census data to consider how the Latina/o/x population was part of a broader trend of Detroiters leaving the city. For example, table 1.1 compares the population sizes in Detroit with broader Wayne County. The Latina/o/x population moved out to the suburbs during the foreclosure crisis and as they sought to realize the American Dream. This data indicates that their numbers increased in the city and the adjoining suburban areas where they settled in Lincoln Park, Allen Park, and Melvindale, all located in Wayne County.[151] This data reflected a broader trend of people leaving the city. Two women I interviewed lost their homes in the suburbs, which elucidated why not all crossings into white suburbia were successful. Their experience of dispossession suggested their time living in the suburbs had put them no closer to reaching the American Dream.

I drew on other forms of data to compare lived experiences with abstractions about the city. One important source was mainstream media. I conducted content analyses using keywords related to key events and

Table I.1. Population change in Detroit city and Wayne County (2000–2020)

	2000			2010			2020		Change (2000–2020) as % of 2000 population	
	City	Wayne County	2007-2010 U.S. Foreclosure Crisis	City	Wayne County	2013-2014 Detroit Bankruptcy	City	Wayne County	City	Wayne County
White alone	117,658	1,064,497		55,604	902,180		60,770	857,132	-48%	-19%
Black or African American alone	774,175	866,622		586,573	732,801		493,212	952,462	-36%	10%
Hispanic or Latino	47,257	77,501		48,679	95,260		51,269	117,649	8%	52%
Total	951,270	2,061,162		713,777	1,820,584		639,111	1,793,561	-33%	-13%

Source: US Census Bureau 2000; US Census Bureau 2010; US Census Bureau 2020.

empty abstractions discussed in this book, including blight, demolition, vacancy, tipping points, neighborhoods, and bankruptcy. I performed similar analyses with the city's mainstream newspapers, *The Detroit Free Press* and *The Detroit News*, and the city's African American newspapers, *The Michigan Chronicle* and *The Michigan Citizen*.

I referred to press releases, annual reports, audits, and investigative reports that involved different organizations in Detroit's development before and after its bankruptcy, including the annual reports of JPMorgan & Chase and the Kresge and the Knight Foundations, and the Local Initiatives Support Corporation. I referred to official government documents to understand the factors that shaped the city's fortunes. For example, I analyzed US Government Accounting Office reports to understand how city and state government officials redirected Hardest Hit federal funds meant for homeowners struggling with impending foreclosure that were instead redirected to promote an aggressive demolition program in the city. I referred to US Department of Justice documents to analyze "the largest settlement with a single entity in American history."[152] I traced JPMorgan & Chase's subsequent collaboration with the city government through a variety of documents, including their press releases, a *60 Minutes* episode, a three-part case study of "inclusive capitalism" at the Harvard Business School, and business and finance industry articles.[153]

Much of my data was based on nonparticipant observation. I attended and watched recordings of city council meetings, university presentations, and movies that considered how the city fared in the years leading up to and following its bankruptcy. I analyzed documents and attended meetings associated with major development projects, including those associated with the expansion of what is now the Stellantis Assembly

Plant. I also attended public events in SWD, including Mexican Day Festivals, Cinco de Mayo parades, and community meetings related to policing, bridge expansion, and participatory budgeting. These experiences helped me understand how relations were patterned between residents and powerful groups. For example, the Ford Motor Company purchased Michigan Central Station in 2018 and hosted a well-attended celebration. The company's Chief Executive Officer announced they were going to develop the building and area "with" rather than "for" the city's residents, which implicitly recognized the ways investors contributed to long-standing, racial stereotypes about white saviors and Detroiters' laziness.[154] It also demonstrated how distinctions between business growth (accumulation), philanthropy, and charity were changing. I also attended city council meetings, zoning meetings, land bank meetings, and other public events in Detroit]to understand how bordering practices worked.

Chapter Outline

Chapters 1 and 2 focus on the abstraction of space. Chapter 1 uses the case of Latina/o/x youth living in Southwest Detroit to explain how they struggle to produce space. The case grounds my analysis of the disjuncture between lived experience and abstraction. Only some of our experiences become codified through media, statistics, and maps. Space is instead produced through struggles between embodiment and abstraction. Some people lead relatively borderless lives. Other people struggle to cross borders. These experiences are shaped not only by their own identities, but by bordering practices that shape their daily lives. Whether it be driving beyond the city's borders into adjoining suburban areas, claiming neighborhood boundaries that compete with standard maps, recognizing informal credentials that do not depend on official documentation or mainstream certification, or policing their own neighbors, SWD residents' experiences encouraged new spatial patterns and altered the taken-for-granted nature of social relations.

Chapter 2 develops my analysis of the disjuncture between lived experience and abstraction. It analyzes how powerful groups produce neighborhoods as an abstraction and a bordering practice that both promote and inhibit socio-spatial mobility. The federal government and realtors produced redlined maps in the past, but newer forms of urban renewal continued to follow many of the same patterned practices through place- and impact-based investing that meant targeting and branding neighborhoods. These practices produced not only racial and economic inequality, but also inequities in mobility.

Chapters 3 and 4 focus on the abstraction of property. Chapter 3 draws on Latina/o/x youth's experiences living in SWD to explain how they struggle to hold on to property. They associated belonging in ways that were not exclusively tied to formal ownership, which was an empty abstraction. They instead associated "being from Southwest" with shared collective experiences of struggle, sacrifice, and "paying your dues." Their experiences challenged conventional understandings of ownership in ways that mapped struggles for individual and collective freedom. They compared their ability to access and use land with a broader collective history of repatriation, deportation, and dispossession that traced back to the early twentieth century. I regret that I couldn't find the space in the book to share painful stories, including that of a US-born citizen, a girl who joined her deported parents in Mexico only to be so humiliated when she was asked to stand and unable to speak Spanish that she wet her pants. I focused instead on detailing two youths' experiences with foreclosure and forced mobility that demonstrated how the production of space involved struggles across spatial scales and how youths' struggles surrounding SWD were mirrored by similar struggles for self-determination, local control, and home rule that spanned across and beyond the city.[155] These struggles underpin the American Dream but are only colorblind as abstractions.

Chapter 4 relies on three case studies to explain how abstractions operated as relational bordering and crossing practices. For example, after President Barack Obama's victory, Republican-gerrymandered districts ostensibly promoted representative democracy but instead facilitated emergency management. The context shaped Detroit's bankruptcy in ways that underscored the limits of Black governance. The demolition program that ensued under the city's first white mayor in forty years was a concrete example of how abstractions around blight facilitated new crossing practices after the city's bankruptcy.

Chapter 5 is an interlude to focus on reactions to the 2002 African Town proposal that would have promoted Black entrepreneurship in the city. The proposal grew out of a longstanding struggle for economic self-determination that was vivified by the 2001 publication of *PowerNomics* by Claud Anderson. The idea of an African Town in Detroit preceded his book, but Anderson adapted his development plan for Detroit in ways that *The Detroit News* editor compared to *Mein Kampf*. The abstraction of exclusion became an important way for thinking about how white supremacy and anti-Blackness shaped the options available to other immigrant and native minorities at a local level. This relation was affirmed by the federal government.

Chapter 6 develops my analysis of the disjuncture between belonging and property. It describes an important example of how our federal government structure allows states and cities to serve as laboratories for social and economic experiments. Public-private partnerships drew on federal government support to experiment with new collaborations between public and private entities in ways that not only transformed local control and home rule but also eroded democracy and supported the private sector's dominance over the development of public policy.

The conclusion summarizes the book's findings about how race and space are produced in relation to one another and most often to the advantage of actors who set the rules of the game. It recognizes that the book has paid attention to the dominant and dominated poles of spatial production and encourages future research that can map the field's dynamics. For example, recent scholarship has paid increased attention to the physical and symbolic struggles related to urban commoning.[156] *Detroit Never Left* also uses the concluding chapter to suggest the ways its theoretical and analytical contributions apply to the study of other cities and organizations.

1

This Bridge Called My 'Hood

Latina/o/x Experience and Southwest Detroit

Two well-known Chicana scholar-activists put together a book that many women of color scholars consider a classic. In the preface to the fortieth anniversary edition of *This Bridge Called My Back: Writings by Radical Women of Color*, Cherríe Moraga introduced the "phenomenon" *of the book as* a "bridge" of consciousness that "far exceeds . . . [its] pages and geographies."[1] The phenomenon of an international bridge crossing in Southwest Detroit similarly exceeds its naturalization because of its entries and exits. Bridges are deceptive, like maps, because they simultaneously connect, distinguish, and divide. The Ambassador Bridge spans over a river that connects Detroit, Michigan, to Windsor, Ontario, in Canada. It connects several highway interchanges, intermodal connectors, ports, and rail and truck passenger transit terminals that direct vehicles into and away from Detroit. These borders and bridges shape the experiences of Latina/o/x youth who live in Southwest Detroit (SWD) and map their struggles to produce space.

The Ambassador Bridge is less than a mile and a half long, but the stretch is one of many bordering practices that mark who is out of place. It focused struggles between its owner, Manuel ("Matty") Maroun, and local residents. For example, figure 2.1 shows a "Keep Ste. Anne's Street Open" sign prominently posted in the front window of a duplex (right above a "Not for Sale" sign). The sign was also in the window of nearby Tamaleria Nuevo Leon. It referred to a decades-long struggle with the bridge; residents in the area sought to maintain street access to St. Anne's, one of the oldest Catholic churches in the country. Residents complained about ceding public property to Maroun, especially because it meant sections of their neighborhood would be leveled to expand toll booths and customs inspections. The 2019 negotiations leading up to a series of property transfers between the city and private owners revealed

Figure 1.1. "Keep Ste. Anne Street Open" Sign (2024)

a relation in which the privately owned bridge had not been authorized but had nonetheless occupied public property. This inverted a relation in which media and police focused on and acted against poor individuals who illegally occupied property, even if it was owned by the city.

The relation between the individual and the international was echoed in interviews with young people who live in Southwest Detroit. Their experiences contrasted the types of mobility enjoyed by people who lived outside of the city. For example, they were bordered by police who shaped where they could go and how they got there. Youths' experiences conflicted with those of outsiders who saw the area, the city it was a part of, and its residents as an unsafe and undifferentiated mass. The ways Latina/o/x youth defined their neighborhood boundaries similarly competed with the official maps of the area.

This relation is important for several reasons. First, young people struggled to reconcile their experiential knowledge of the area with more abstract, shared understandings of the neighborhood. They sought to define and produce their community. Second, the abstraction of Southwest Detroit brought Latina/o/x youths' definitions into conflict with those developed by nonresidents. Third, as city officials made space more abstract through websites and publications, young people resisted the ways their neighborhood was seen by outsiders. Overall, this meant that there was an important difference between how young people thought about their neighborhood and the ways it had been characterized by outsiders. Despite this difference, outsiders effectively defined the area and its problems for broader audiences including the very groups whose purpose was to support the development of Southwest Detroit.

Getting Stuck in Detroit

Southwest Detroit is part of the Motor City that prioritized building expressways over developing its public transportation system. Detroiters depend heavily on cars, which often means families struggled to access a reliable vehicle. At least a third of the city's residents don't own a car. They took their chances getting to work on time using what some journalists considered "America's worst transit system."[2] Even public transportation could not ensure equal access across the metropolitan area. Suburban voters consistently resisted regional transit since the 1960s. Some residents used public scooters and bicycle sharing stations that recently cropped up, but the new options failed to impress families who needed to go shopping or visit a medical clinic. Long winter months covered the city in ice and snow.

Detroiters paid the nation's highest average annual premium for car insurance. The high cost was compounded by poor wages: The US Treasury Department determined auto insurance was unaffordable if it exceeded 2 percent of a zip code's median household income, but average rates in Detroit fell between 12 and 36 percent of pretax income in nearly every zip code.[3] Insurers were a powerful group that relied on abstractions to set premiums: they considered indicators of racial bias, including credit scores and educational attainment that were shaped in relation to a hypersegregated city. This meant drivers who lived in predominantly nonwhite paid more than people who lived in predominantly white zip codes.[4] A majority of the city's drivers were uninsured and ran the risk of being ticketed or having their license suspended.[5]

Some city residents registered their cars outside of the city. The crossing practice cost drivers the vote in the district where they lived.

The problems involving transportation in the Motor City reflected how decisions made by the Michigan Legislature favored outside interests, including those involved in cross-border trade, at the expense of the city and its residents. For example, Michigan set the weight limit for trucks at double the federal limit. This led to potholes so big that they destroyed wheels and even entire vehicles. The problem was so significant that the media regularly featured viral videos documenting the latest, deepest hole. The problem was so marked that it persisted in the months before this book was printed.[6]

Another way Detroiters get stuck is that Michigan is that it is one of few states with no-fault auto insurance and the only one with unlimited personal injury protection, which covers medical costs resulting from car accidents. Michigan does not impose standard medical fee schedules, which means that auto insurers are charged more for medical claims than other insurers. This arrangement leads not only to high auto insurance rates but also to a demand for those personal injury attorneys whose services are advertised on the many colorful billboards that line the highways in the metropolitan area, several of whom are listed in a local newspaper among the "30 People Who Are Only Famous in Detroit."[7]

Policing Mobility as an Urban Bordering Practice

The example of racial profiling, or "driving while Black or Brown," plays off the legal trespass of "driving while intoxicated." The profiler engages in bordering practices that include both traffic laws and their selective enforcement. Law enforcement in the Detroit metropolitan area produces a relation between a majority Black city and its predominantly white adjoining suburbs.

Studies indicate property appraisals undervalue homes owned by Black and Latino homeowners. Appraisals are based on comparative market values, which means suburban areas are also valued in relation to the racial and ethnic background of their residents.[8] In practice this means that home values are higher in predominantly white communities. This relation is not only associated with the presumed stability and race of homeownership in the city or the suburbs. This relation between the city and the suburb is also a product of who can travel through (who is trespassing) and who can occupy presumably "public" spaces. Policing mobility involved appraisers and police alike in a relation that depended on abstractions that segregated people and space. The Latina/o/x population of SWD was clearly marked in this relation.

I met Mireya as a student but interviewed her after she graduated with her degree. She felt people from the suburbs could come to Detroit, but Detroiters lacked the same freedom to go to the suburbs. City residents were more likely to be nonwhite and more likely to be stopped by police, which is a common example of a bordering practice. She says people wonder what she's doing when she travels to suburban areas. She thinks this is why salesclerks and security guards follow her in suburban stores.

Mireya is Dominican and had talked in class and in interviews about her struggles to understand what it meant to be a "woman of color." When I asked how she saw herself, she said she considered herself brown. In this majority Black city, however, many people with lighter skin than Mireya considered themselves Black. This "racial innocence" might explain her hesitation to talk about her personal experiences with racism.[9] I asked whether she felt the disparity in accessing suburban spaces resulted from the segregation of Black and white people in the metropolitan area. Mireya replied that she wanted to avoid making definitive statements about racism. I asked if she had ever experienced discrimination. She said yes, but added that she "gets over it." She doesn't let herself think about how she may experience discrimination, she said, because she doesn't want to get angry.

I met Mireya for the second time on a Sunday. I asked if she would be able to identify discrimination. She asked me to clarify what I meant.

NICOLE: To be discriminated against means "I didn't do anything. I mean, I was just driving down the street like somebody else, right? Why'd you stop me?" You know what I'm saying?
MIREYA: Si. Y eso me ha pasado, ahora que lo pienso, pero no sé si fue, no podría directamente decir que fue por discriminación.[10]

Mireya initially vacillated on whether her experience of being stopped by a police officer was based on discrimination, but she was young and had already experienced the first example that came to my mind: police racially profiling nonwhite people in predominantly white spaces. Mireya continued: She drove her car to an adjoining suburb to run at an open track. She was stopped by a police officer when she crossed from the city into the adjoining suburb at night, and the police officer asked

> "¿Oh, tu sabe porque te estoy parando?"
> Yo le dije "no."
> "Oh, because your headlights are, are off."
> And I'm like "But my headlights don't turn off."
> They literally, *son de esos carros que no se la apaga los* headlights, *pero no encontraba nada por cual excusarse, y después me dijo* "Let me get your license and registration."
> *Yo sentí que estaba buscando otra razón por la cual me podría parar. Aparte de que él estaba incorrecto . . .*
> *Allí yo sentí que era una forma de discriminación.*[11]

Mireya referred to the officer's action as an error (*incorrecto*), so I asked why Mireya felt discriminated against. She believed the police officer had marked her out of place.

> MIREYA: *¿Como, que hacía yo en esta ciudad?*[12]
> NICOLE: But what, what was the basis you feel, of, the police officer having stopped you?
> MIREYA: *¿Aparte de lo que él dijo?*[13]
> NICOLE: *Si.*[14]
> MIREYA: *Para mí fue que* "*¿Que hace esa muchacha aquí, en este tiempo, en esta hora, yendo para un parque . . . para correr?*" *O sea, yo le tuve que explicar,* "*o, yo voy a ir a correr.*"[15]

Mireya initially referred to being a woman (*muchacha*) out at night (*en esta hora*), so I asked whether the police office stopped her because "women aren't out that late?" She confirmed: *No. Yo creo que fue por el color.*[16]
I left Mireya's responses in the language she used rather than translating them to English to illustrate the ways abstractions operate through language by converting experiences into concepts. This conversion means they can be more easily compared, interpreted, and exchanged, but the

kinds of code-switching Mireya used would invariably be lost in translation. Mireya was clear about why she was stopped: it wasn't the time of day, her gender, her headlights, but where she was and her color that mattered to the police officer. Whatever the suburban officer's intentions were, the fact was the most immediate example of discrimination was immediately recognized by Mireya. Her experience was real; the empty abstractions that the officer depended on were not.

Mireya's experience demonstrated how police enforcement conflated people and space. He policed an administrative boundary that distinguished city and suburb and a racialized boundary between urban and suburban residents. Mireya related the experienced in terms that confirmed her sense that his judgment of her color had marked her out of place. The practice produced racial inequity as an outcome; it did not depend on the officer's intention but instead, Mireya's sense that she could not travel freely across borders.

The exchange between Mireya and the police offer is familiar to many nonwhite motorists. Officers controlled space by determining who seemed suspicious and out of place. In many parts of the country, police choose to enforce policies labeled "show me your papers" laws.[17] Officers mark suspicion visually and restrict the mobility of nonwhite motorists. Mireya's experience of driving into an adjoining suburb illustrates not only how people *experience* space differently but also how some bordering practices have greater control over people's struggles to produce space.

Even when police are not actively producing space through their patterned bordering practices, their position and authority influences how people struggle. For example, Jorge moved from California to Detroit with his mother. He stayed behind when she returned to California and lived with his aunt, uncle, and cousins.

> They're [his aunt and uncle] undocumented. That's why I have to wake up early every day, like around six in the morning. I'll be doing all-nighters. I'll go to sleep at four or five. But sometimes like, *a veces*, 'cuz I don't pay rent, so I try to contribute as much as I can. And my *tia*, like . . . like she's undocumented so she fears getting deported a lot because, the *migra* be very heavy. So she makes me wake up early sometimes like:
> "Can you please take the kids to school?"
> And I'm like, "Yeah."

Jorge drove his nieces and nephews to school and picked them up to protect his undocumented aunt (*tia*) from being deported. This provided both a measure of protection from law enforcement and stability for his mixed-legal-status family. We cannot know whether color would factor into an immigration official's decision to stop and detain his aunt, but Jorge felt certain that their "heavy" presence in the predominantly Latina/o/x area encouraged them to liberally mark residents out of place. In other words, Jorge recognized racism was not about the officers' intentions but rather the outcome of racialized inequity and inability to freely cross borders and produce space.

Policing mobility was a bordering practice that also produced space and a racial relation between a predominantly Black city and a predominantly white state. In the post–civil rights era, cities like Detroit experienced white flight and a resulting loss of revenue from property taxes. In response, they intensified policing to take advantage of financial incentives from the federal government. These funds helped support not only Detroit, but also the northern part of Michigan where twenty-eight of thirty-three prisons were built after 1970. This was one example of how state and local government controlled the *spatial* mobility of predominantly Black Detroit residents and improved the *social* mobility of many predominantly white residents in northern Michigan who gained new jobs building and working within the prisons.

The Abstraction of Crime Versus the Lived Experience of Safety

I met Fausto as a student, but he emailed me after our class ended to participate in my study. I asked about his neighborhood in our first interview. He initially focused on his block, which, he said, "is pretty calm, because the majority of the people who live there are families." He distinguishes the block from the neighborhood, where "there's a lot of drug dealers, I walk around in our neighborhood, a lot of prostitution." As proof, he said police had raided an empty house two blocks away in the morning and "they weren't there. Yeah, like, their activity happens more at night." His response indicated that police were not always effective at controlling how space in the area was used.

When I asked Fausto whether everyone on his block knew which buildings house drug traffic or prostitution, he replied, "It's not something that's hidden to people." Having lived in a different part of SWD, but sharing a similar experience, I tried to understand the distinction he had drawn between his block and the neighborhood by asking other questions about distances. His narrative shifted:

> *There's really no specific area where bad things happen or where there's drug use or where there's prostitution. It's all spread out in the neighborhood. I guess you kind of just get lucky, you know? It's kind of like a hit or miss. You might have a neighbor who sells drugs or not, you know?*
>
> *On my block, personally talking from experience, a family bought the house where a drug dealer used to live. There's three houses next to me on my left side. And he was, you know, he looked like a regular person. But he sold drugs, you know? He had weapons, he had, so many things. The only reason I know this is because we had communication with him. Like, overall, he wasn't a bad neighbor, but you knew that he was a drug dealer.*

Fausto reflected on his experience with the drug dealer and concluded: "*That guy was always selling stuff. Like, whether, if it was not drugs or weapons. He was selling animals . . . he was selling clothes . . . puppies, dogs, cats, like he was selling all types of things. He was just a . . . Like he just sold stuff. Anything. Like, wide range, which is like a businessman, but not like an official, like 'I went to school and I'm a businessman' type of person.*" Once Fausto reflected on the distinction he originally made between the neighborhood and his block, he found his experience of personal safety differed from his more abstract impression about "hit or miss" levels of crime in the neighborhood. Once Fausto moved beyond his abstract ideas about crime in the neighborhood, he concluded his neighbor was a businessman without a degree.

The distinction Fausto drew between having a skill and a degree has a broader social value that young people don't control. Their community placed a high value on experience and ability. For example, every interviewee completed a survey to identify "things that help someone get ahead." As Fredrico was completing the survey, he asked what I meant by "being smart," explaining that, in his opinion, there are different types of smarts. Did I mean "book smart or . . . ?" He trailed off, as if I should provide other definitions. Fredrico graduated from an Ivy League school. His background might have led him to value higher education, but he distinguished being smart from book learning. The issue wasn't so much a distinction of skill, but an assertion that experience and ability matter.

Over the course of four interviews, Fausto talked about his busy schedule, traveling within and beyond Southwest Detroit for work, school, and to coach soccer. In our fourth and final interview I asked how he *felt* about his neighborhood.

> NICOLE: If someone has never been to your neighborhood asks you "How do you feel about your neighborhood?" What would you say?
>
> FAUSTO: Um, I mean, I feel proud of my neighborhood. But I definitely wouldn't lie to someone and tell them that it's, what it's not. So like, I know, the areas that need improvement, based on living there for so long.
>
> And, uh, but I obviously, I'm proud, like, I feel proud of where I live. I mean, there's, it's . . . I feel like a lot of the things that people talk about Southwest Detroit are a little bit exaggerated. They're a little bit over the top. I mean, a lot of the things people talk about is obviously crime. But I feel like sometimes they make it out to be something that's really not as bad. So like, there is crime, and there are things that happen. But it's not as exaggerated as some people who don't live there put it.
>
> People that I've talked to that have never been to Detroit, they always kind of make it seem like it's a really, really dangerous place, but obviously it's not like that. There's times where like you can be out on the street, and then there's times that you don't, but overall, I mean, it's not as dangerous as people make it out to be.
>
> NICOLE: What do you feel proud of?
>
> FAUSTO: I don't know, I just feel like Detroit's full of really hard-working people in general, people who help people who have come here with nothing and have been able to make something out of nothing. And that gives me a lot of pride.

Fausto's comments treated crime as an abstraction that was disconnected from his experience and overall sense of pride in both his neighborhood and Detroit. He distinguished between two types of people. One type doesn't live in or have never been to Detroit. They exaggerate the extent of crime in the city. The other type includes hard-working people who "could make something out of nothing" even if they lacked formal recognition as entrepreneurs.

Luisa felt safe in the neighborhood because residents policed the community. She had multiple roles in the community: she worked with a domestic violence intervention program and believed they replaced the police in the neighborhood. She relied on social ties to promote public order and control crime.[18]

> *I feel like the Detroit police has always had that sense of not responding on time and I feel like a lot of incidents that have happened in my community, it's like the police never even showed up. It's like how you handle it within like, the community itself. So, I think for a safe neighborhood would be like nothing has ever happened that caused others to feel unsafe. There was never an incident or situation where something just came up. And if it did, it was handled with other residents that live in that same community.*

The distinction between abstract reports about crime and personal experiences of safety were important to understanding how Luisa produced space. For Fausto, people "that have never lived in Detroit" mischaracterized both the city and his "area." Similarly, Mireya distinguished what she imagined was differential access crossing the city's borders between suburbanites and her own experience as a Detroiter. Crime rates did not seem to bear on how Felix, Fausto, or Fredrico felt about their own safety or how they evaluated neighborhood residents. Similarly, the police raid prioritized abstract claims that were disconnected from residents' needs.

The distinction between the abstraction of space and lived experience demonstrates how some people dominate its production. For example, Project Green Light is a public-private partnership in which businesses pay to have a real-time camera surveillance installed that transmits video directly to the Detroit police department. A flashing green light is also installed outside participating businesses. Luisa felt Project Green Light expanded socio-spatial control.

> *How is that going to benefit in the long run? This is very short term, a type of goal where different community businesses have this light. So if*

> anything happens, so you know, that these places have that green light, right? And I think that it brings awareness of someone's always looking at you or like, that business itself always has, like, someone's always like observing them. Versus like, how do you just create a safe space in general? It shouldn't just be individual places. It should be a community as a whole.

Mireya, Jorge, Fausto, and Luisa shared a frustration that they had been mischaracterized and that public resources were unfairly turned against them. The relationship between the abstraction of space and lived experience is important for many reasons that go beyond local control. Project Green Light soon came under criticism for several reasons, including the possibility that police response prioritized crimes against property and produced spaces that were under constant surveillance. The software also cross-referenced images against license, mug shot, and social media data, but was built on white models, which meant a higher rate of false positives when matching darker skin tones. In other words, racism was both input and output of the technology. Project Green Light indicates not only that abstract space can be produced and controlled at multiple scales, but also that these abstractions require political and economic support. Other cities like San Francisco, California, and Cambridge and Somerville, Massachusetts, banned the facial recognition software, but the Detroit City Council extended its contract (with Genetec) for the software in 2020.[19]

Technology appeared objective but coded racial inequity and surveillance.[20] Project Green Light ties into a much longer legacy of categorization and surveillance that informed colonial modernity, including the invention of race as a form of classification, racial science, racial statistics, and racial progress. These codes are codified mappings that produce inequality in spatial production that is scaled to increasing levels of abstraction. For example, even though surveillance is centralized, the hundreds of Green Light camera videos cannot all be continually monitored. Scaling from lived experience to increasing levels of abstraction implies different bordering practices.

What Is Southwest Detroit?

Luisa's narrative was notable. She related her story as a set of interactions between individuals who could access different spatial resources.

In other words, "some people ... from the Southwest" had enough influence to order police patrols. She came from a large family, like many other residents in her abstract "community." Her family was deeply grounded in the neighborhood because they owned a local business that attracted both police and criminals. The borders were monitored as much by residents as they were by government officials. The setting made everyone vigilant.

Ultimately, the patrols did not solve the problem of crime. Instead, as Luisa explained, residents worked "as a neighborhood" and "a community" and reacted to "someone new in our neighborhood" whose outsider status was marked geographically because they were from another state. Luisa explained how neighbors produced a "safe" space. She conflated her feeling of safety with a broader assertion that the neighborhood was safe.

I think California, or some other state. And so my mom was telling me about it. She's like, "Yeah, they come into the store. And they cause all this commotion and, you know, they were at the park the other day, we have a little park by our store. And they were just causing this big scene with my other neighbors [who] have been our neighbors for years. It's just like, you know, they like pulled out like some a weapon on them, and stuff."

And I was like, "Whoa, like, how are we going to allow someone new in our neighborhood, letting them act this way? Like, no, this is a safe neighborhood."

So I called some people that I know from the Southwest. And I was like, "Yo, like this is going on in my neighborhood, I don't feel safe. I've never felt this way, like in my block or anything like that."

They're like, "Okay, we'll send a patrol, like, someone to patrol the neighborhood." So they sent, like two nights of some of patrolling.

And I told my ma: "Somebody needs to tell him something that like that doesn't go down here."

She's like, "You're not going to be the person to tell them that."

And I was like, "Okay, I won't."

But our other neighbor was like, "I'm gonna tell him something, because they're not about to cause ... We have kids living in our block, we have people, like your dad that like, goes to the store. And he's alone, like, all morning, like, we're not gonna have any of that."

> *So they talked to him. And they told him, "You know, this doesn't go down in our neighborhood. I don't know why you have drama with our other neighbor. But you know, cut it out."*
>
> *So yeah, now they're pretty cool. And, I mean, they saw the cops patrolling our area. So I think they are more chill now. But I told my mom, "We're not going to have that around here."*
>
> *That's not safe. I know people that, you know, can help us out. And as a community, we kind of, you know, solve that issue. And I think that that's really important. That's something that's always been a thing on [named] street, like, we hold people accountable, and like, what we work as a neighborhood.*

Luisa was concerned for her father's property (the store) and the safety of public and common space, the "little park." She distinguished between the block, the neighborhood, and the community. I asked about the different terms she used in our third interview.

> LUISA: Community would be like Southwest. Like people, the larger scale.
>
> . . .
>
> NICOLE: *And then you say, neighborhood, so what does neighborhood mean?*
>
> LUISA: *So, and then from Southwest? I think it's broken down into like Springwells Village, Mexicantown . . . um . . . There's like different, So I think my, um . . . my neighborhood would be Mexicantown.*
>
> . . .
>
> NICOLE: *You pointed at "That's always been a thing about [deleted] street," that's different from Mexicantown.*
>
> LUISA: Well I think just the whole idea of . . . like you create . . . so it's like just one street, right? But you create like, a neighborhood within that street . . . you create like your own family within that street or, because you've, it's just been . . . people that have been there for a long time, or expanding from house to house to house. It's like, there's something special about that.

Luisa's understandings of community, neighborhood, and even a "neighborhood within that street" indicated that people produced space in relation to one another and across time. She did not refer to crime or consider the new residents to be criminals. Fausto and Flor similarly refused to see neighbors who engaged in illegal behavior as criminals.

The scale of space was critical because it mapped youths' sense of safety. The women I interviewed and my students from Southwest Detroit were concerned about being able to walk safely because Southwest Detroit is a node of truck and train traffic. They insisted that human trafficking was a problem in the area. For Ariel, it could have impeded their ability to get to work and their socio-spatial mobility.

> The reason I stopped walking to work is because . . . there's this man that I started seeing a lot of the time and a lot of people are telling me about him too, that is very suspicious. And the way he . . . The vibe he gave off was not safe. And he was always kind of walking around the way I would walk to work. Like between my house and there [work]. So I told my mom about that. She was like, "Okay, you're not going to walk anymore."

Ariel works a couple of blocks from their home but is nonetheless most often driven or uses their mother's car. Their concern about walking safely was shared by many residents: Missing bodies were a problem in a city with so many vacant properties. In his annual report for 2019, for example, the city's ombudsman called for cadaver dogs to find missing people in vacant buildings before they were demolished.

Luisa produced space in relation to major boulevards, avenues, streets, and neighborhoods to bound SWD. Other residents felt Southwest Detroit extended south past I-75 to the Rouge River on what is literally the southwestern city boundary. Still others debated whether Delray was part of Southwest Detroit or its own community.

Latina/o/xs residing north of Michigan Avenue felt they were part of "Southwest," but excluded those who resided in other areas. This made mapping a spatial and sociocultural bordering practice.

FREDERICO: I live, uh, Lonyo and . . . McGraw? Michigan. I think Michigan is a bigger Street. So yeah. Lonyo and Michigan.
NICOLE: Do you consider that Southwest?
FREDERICO: I do. Apparently, it's not. [*laughs*]

NICOLE: I don't know how we define what is, what is not, but I think people decide, right?

FREDERICO: Yeah, I do. I consider that Southwest, mmm, on the far outskirts of Southwest. But I technically live in Claytown.

The Department of Neighborhoods produced Clayton as a new neighborhood after the city's bankruptcy. Frederico's use of the name indicated the ways his understanding of where he lived was changing in relation to the planners who were producing the area. Frederico went on to describe the school in front of his house that had "*a very motley mix of teachers as well as students. So it is I'm not gonna say it's predominantly Hispanic, but it's more Hispanic, but it's also heavy. . . . there's a heavy Arabic population. There's also a heavy Black population, and slowly but surely, there's, I think there's a growing presence or just like light citizens as well.*" Other interviewees went on to identify different areas as "cultural hubs" distinguished by the racial and ethnic groups that lived there. Geography became a proxy for racial and ethnic difference, which demonstrated how bordering practices included physical markers, such as street and neighborhood names.

Federico and other interviewees struggled to produce Southwest Detroit, but they could not dominate representations like the ones produced by the city or Google (figure 1.2.). The latter's aerial perspective seemed above the fray of everyday struggles to control the production of space. Google Maps is widely used, which suggests its labels are universally shared. The maps seemed to settle long-standing debates and branded space. Frederico demonstrated how many residents understood this branding as a physical experience that turned the area into an object, a commodity that could be made palatable and sold to outsiders, but that competed with their claims to space.

Labels were part of a struggle to produce Southwest Detroit: The stakes were greater than the residential gentrification of the area. The distinctions and conflations made by outsiders interested in economic development, including Google and foundations, competed with the labels used by residents. For example, Google labeled the area *west* of I-75 as Mexicantown, but considered Southwest Detroit another name for the area. In contrast, the MexicantownCDC referred narrowly to the Welcome Center and Mercado buildings and outdoor plaza located *east*

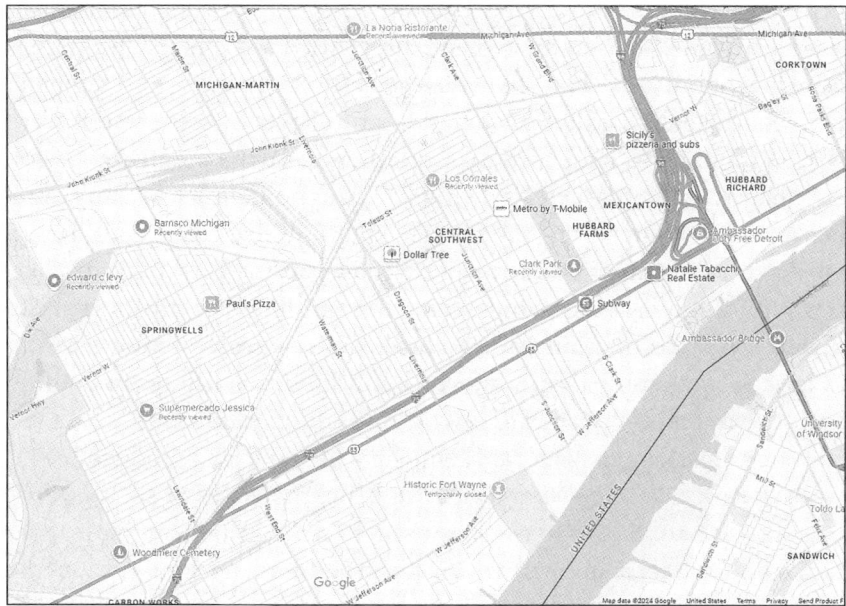

Figure 1.2. Google Map of Southwest Detroit

of I-75. The maps and their labels mapped competitive struggles between corporations, community leaders, and Manuel ("Matty") Maroun and his companies. He expanded the footprint of the Ambassador Bridge after he bought it in 1979.

Google's control over the production of an abstract Southwest Detroit influences how some residents understood the area. For example, Felix distinguished Mexicantown as the area east of I-75 where he grew up living with his grandmother.

> FELIX: That walk is different here [Southwest Detroit compared to Mexicantown] because there's no direct route. You're going up and around blocks instead of cutting through them. But yeah, I feel safe. I've never . . . I mean, when I was younger, I did get jumped. But, like, those are all just like . . . experiences, I don't know.
> NICOLE: Do you think that that still goes on?
> FELIX: Yeah. [*chuckles*] I'm not saying it gives people character but . . . I think there's . . . you learn something from it. Yeah, you . . . you have to learn from it.

Felix distinguished Southwest Detroit, where he was unable to follow a "direct route." He contrasted the direct way that streets and homes were laid out in Mexicantown, which he associated with being "jumped." Homes in what Google considered "Central Southwest" Detroit were also more likely to be fenced in. According to Felix's mental maps, the area he considered Mexicantown had a greater number of empty lots because they were part of the bridge expansion. He could cut through blocks in Mexicantown and create alternate routes to reach his destination. In other contexts, people "cut through the grass" to shorten the distance to a destination and produce "desire lines."[21] These crossing practices compete with more formal and intentional ways of guiding socio-spatial mobility, such as wayfinding and wayshowing.[22]

Felix's crossing practices also compete with Google to produce Southwest Detroit. He referred explicitly to his experiences of socio-spatial mobility: where he *currently* lives (which he described as "better off" compared to Mexicantown) versus his grandmother's house, where he lived for some time. He distinguishes both areas from his life in an affluent college town nearby. Felix felt safe in his neighborhood and considered being "jumped" (mugged) as another learning experience. In other words, like Frederico, experience provided an alternate education.

Felix, Frederico, Ariel, Luisa, Fausto, and Mireya were characters in a South-*West Side Story* who struggled to define and defend their street, neighborhood, and community even when the enemies included their local government. These struggles undermined their access to resources they desperately needed, including police protection, the collaboration and support of a neighbor or family member, and even the planners whose maps simultaneously accomodated bridge expansion and undermined residents' personal safety.

2

Producing Neighborhoods

From Redlining to Diversity

If you brand it, they will come.[1]

"Neighborhood" is a word that is over five hundred years old, but we take it for granted. It is also an abstraction that signals borders of inclusion and exclusion. A neighborhood does not only refer to people who live near one another, but also distinguishes spaces in fraught references to an implied racial homogeneity.[2] In the early twentieth century, scholars considered neighborhoods mapped stages of ethnic difference and eventual assimilation into a white, middle-class, suburban America. After World War II, their analyses complemented the work of developers who branded their housing developments as "neighborhoods" to attract whites to suburban areas. By the late 1960s, journalists and scholars treated urban neighborhoods as synonymous with nonwhite slums, *barrios*, and ghettos. Movies like *West Side Story* reflected minoritized groups' struggles to define and defend neighborhood borders. There was a resurgence of scholarly interest in urban poverty, inner-city neighborhoods, and a so-called urban underclass in the 1980s. These different waves of foundation-funded research attempted to soften demands for meaningful integration. They blurred the boundaries between city and resident-led definitions of neighborhoods. They also set a precedent for urban development that included developers, planners, and new residents in a fierce competition to claim and name new neighborhoods. In Detroit's case, these new groups were making something out of nothing. In contrast, legacy residents saw their sense of a broader collective identity put into play. The new borders of an "official" neighborhood name were erected with signs, maps, and city-commissioned murals.

This chapter identifies how explicit references to neighborhoods changed before and after Detroit's bankruptcy. The city defined 53 neighborhoods in its 2009 master plan. After the bankruptcy, the city added another 156 neighborhoods to its reference maps. The shift in the city government's approach to neighborhoods and the city's footprint was forecast by the mayoral debate leading up to the bankruptcy. The racialized election pitted a white Michael "Mike" Duggan against a Black Benny Napoleon. Both had platforms that centered on neighborhoods. Napoleon focused on safety and proposed placing one police officer per square mile across the city.[4] In contrast, Duggan emphasized marketing the city and changing its appearance in a variety of ways that included criminalizing graffiti, fighting blight, and encouraging demolition.[5]

Duggan's administration hired new employees who had recently been considered outsiders by the city's residents. Duggan's push to change the ways people thought about Detroit was as much spatial as it was conceptual. He sought to promote "20-minute neighborhoods" where residents could quickly walk to shops and schools.[6] The plan seemed particularly ironic in the Motor City where residents historically depended on cars to overcome the effects of geographic isolation and racial segregation. Duggan also wanted to rebrand the majority Black city and use its neighborhoods to produce "diversity."[7] The newly-minted Department of Neighborhoods (DON) delineated and produced 209 diverse neighborhoods that it depicted through maps. A variety of philanthropic and nonprofit organizations distributed these maps to build a new identity for Detroit. Detroiters resisted these efforts in a variety of ways, including lawn signs, T-shirts, and billboards that coincided with national Black Lives Matter protests during the summer of 2020. They insisted "Majority Black Detroit Matters" (see figure 2.1).

This chapter examines a dominant abstraction: the neighborhood. It first identifies how early social science scholars projected their ideas about racial and spatial differences onto neighborhoods.[8] The chapter also introduces an important theme in this book: how public-private interests and partnerships produced space as neighborhoods and as interchangeable, exchangeable commodities for investment. These efforts illustrated how foundations, developers, and investors gained the upper hand in shaping urban development projects. These efforts were not colorblind, but profoundly informed by how predominantly white powerful groups promoted white supremacy in a majority Black city. The chapter concludes by focusing on Southwest Detroit because it was consistently

Figure 2.1. Majority Black Detroit Matters (2020)

targeted for development. It received significant funding and attention but nonetheless lost population over the twenty-year period between 2000 and 2020. The case leaves us with important warnings about data-driven policies that use selective data to target neighborhoods: They do not always meet their intended outcomes, but further entrench urban inequality.

How Scholars Produced Neighborhoods

Urban renewal was one of a series of experiments that not only produced space but also assigned differential value to it. This valuation implicated a variety of local, state, federal, and international dynamics that simultaneously produced racial and ethnic inequities. In other words, the same practices that mapped, planned, and produced space also created racial inequity. Scholars set a precedent for these practices at the beginning of the twentieth century when they used the neighborhood as a unit of analysis. They applied the scientific method to map neighborhoods and produce space as a problem. Scholars made race a central, albeit misunderstood, factor in our thinking about neighborhoods.

W. E. B. Du Bois produced the first sociological analysis of neighborhoods when he analyzed the Seventh Ward in Philadelphia. He was particularly interested in explaining how the physical and social environment shaped the conditions of African Americans' lives. As an African American man, he recognized that many people conflated neighborhoods with the population that occupied them, but he countered that the slum was a symptom of "removable" causes that "takes one far beyond the slum districts."[9] In other words, he understood that policies and practices stemming from racism produced the slum.

Writing two decades later, Robert Park and Ernest Burgess considered neighborhoods were spaces characterized by the culture of their residents, including immigrants, African Americans, homeless people, and other marginalized groups. They were white men who conflated nonwhite groups. They also juxtaposed racially segregated neighborhoods and sociocultural difference that they believed informed an "inner organic completeness."[10] They relied on biological metaphors, deceptive mystifications, and argued social changes were gradual adaptations that mirrored patterns found in nature.

Both approaches considered migration critical to neighborhood development and change, but Du Bois's relational analysis of race and space was overlooked by mainstream urban scholars. Park and Burgess's understandings of race and space instead dominated a long legacy in urban studies that presumed naturalized conceptions of neighborhoods. For example, in trying to understand the effects of neighborhoods on people's life chances, Robert Sampson identified his central concepts as ones involving ecological proximity, ecological knots, and tangles. Other scholars followed Sampson's later recognition that neighborhoods were not natural and that maps created artificial borders.[11] Writing over one hundred years earlier, Du Bois also suggested ecological understandings of urban space overlooked racism.[12] They complemented biological ones because they centered on the Black residents of Philadelphia's Seventh Ward.[13] In other words, understandings of space that were rooted in ecology, biology, or nature took racism for granted. They tacitly consented to and therefore enabled white supremacy.

Park and Burgess's legacy included a focus on crime in neighborhoods. Oscar Lewis inherited a conception of neighborhoods that influenced his writings in the 1960s on the culture of poverty. He argued that the cultural norms of a delimited set of nonwhite groups resulted in social disorder and poverty.[14] These groups included African Americans, Mexican Americans, and Puerto Ricans—groups that represented the majority of Detroit's resident population. Scholars writing in the 1980s returned to the idea of people who were trapped in neighborhoods of concentrated poverty when they defined the "underclass."[15]

Scholars remained focused on the relationship between neighborhoods and residents as they sought to transform urban areas in Detroit. Rather than a set of differentiated neighborhoods, scholars and national media produced Detroit as an undifferentiated mass of spatial and racial otherness.[16] They imagined the city through universalizing images of Blackness, poverty, and empty space. Social science scholarship reimagined development after bankruptcy. Politicians, investors, and urban planners alike sought to create neighborhoods to attract new residents to the city, stimulate economic development, and produce a new Detroit.

The powerful groups that imagined a new Detroit were influenced by the 1982 "broken windows" theory. The idea was popularized by two scholars' commentary on neighborhood safety first published in the popular magazine, *The Atlantic*. James Q. Wilson and George L. Kelling focused their observations of police "foot patrol" and quickly observed it had not reduced crime.[17] What the public performance produced was residents' feeling of security and belief that crime was reduced. The performance also encouraged residents' opinion in favor of police officers. In their conception, foot patrols were a win-win because officers also "had higher morale, greater job satisfaction, and a more favorable attitude toward citizens."[18] Wilson and Kelling's references to "natural forces" and "natural communities" asserted that police should reinforce community controls and maintain order because physical disorder produced crime.[19] They insisted that broken windows were akin to untended property and led to crime and a breakdown of community controls in general. Their claim that "most citizens" liked to talk with a police officer ignored Black and Latina/o/x community's long-standing experiences with racial profiling. The presumption of a straightforward collaboration between citizens and police seemed an almost cartoonish reflection of white supremacy.[20]

By the time Detroit exited bankruptcy, the broken windows theory was thirty years old, but its references to community controls and untended property compelled media, politicians, and city planners to recycle its abstractions as a war on blight. The theory made three claims that were relevant to development plans and priorities. First, the theory emphasized that police should prioritize maintaining order over fighting crime. This revived the purportedly preemptive patrol function that police had during the 1960s and that led to the waves of urban rebellion that followed. The theory also underscored that police should protect property. This phenomenon was exemplified by Project Green Light. Politicians and community organizations sought to reclaim the city by challenging a narrative that associated the city with the 1967 rebellion and the nation's highest crime rate.[21] They focused on crime to make the city seem safe again.

The broken windows theory also threatened "a stable neighborhood of families who care for their homes" and that could become "an inhospitable and frightening jungle" of smashed windows, tall weeds, and abandoned property.[22] The contrasting images echoed the racialized and spatialized contrasts that powerful groups and suburban residents had woven into the Detroit metropolitan area. Homogenous suburban neighborhoods were symbols of law and order. In contrast, references to jungles and nonhuman wilderness in a sprawling and segregated city aligned with the image of a rewilded city just before Detroit's bankruptcy.[23] The implied racial superiority and inferiority were also manifest in ongoing discussions about affordable housing and demolition.

Finally, the broken windows theory recycled the earlier idea of a "tipping point" when it established an antagonistic relation in which "the public order is deteriorating but not unreclaimable."[24] The reference recalled the racial tipping point, which implied white people were provoked to leave a neighborhood as Black people moved in.[25] The idea that there was a racial tipping point assumed an area's transition from white to Black residents was inevitable. It also shifted the focus of a social problem (residential segregation) onto people's actions (moving) rather than onto racism in the housing and mortgage lending industry.

The tipping point was repurposed by a variety of influential groups who targeted areas of Detroit for recovery. For example, the Urban Institute titled its report on Detroit "Tipping Point."[26] It did not define what the tipping point was. Instead, the report used the term as another naturalist abstraction. The report's authors suggested the tipping point was one where "the market would take over" and replace investments made by mission lenders in targeted neighborhoods. The report's failure to define what the tipping point was indicated that the authors reverted to natural explanations when they could not explain how a phenomenon worked. The Urban Institute's report was part of JPMorgan Chase's effort to treat Detroit as (what Peter Scher considered) a laboratory for urban renewal.[27]

The idea of a tipping point has been challenged by scholars. It was an abstraction that borrowed from physics and implied science-based interventions produced their intended effects.[28] The authors of the broken windows theory similarly passed off their own cultural preferences as social science when the theory was originally published in 1982. For example, when Wilson and Kelling asserted that "most citizens like to talk to a police officer," they did not provide any empirical data to support their claim.[29]

The authors similarly vacillated on the causal relationship between foot patrols and crime. They asserted that even illusory effects on resident sentiment were significant but dismissed the real potential for expanding racial discrimination and the reality of police brutality. Despite the inability to correlate sentiment with incidence, the broken windows theory's authors nonetheless drew on their status and influence as social scientists and found a large audience for their prejudices in *The Atlantic* magazine.

The broken windows theory has been repeatedly used to justify repressive policies. Its concerns resulted in quality-of-life laws and police patrols that engaged in "stop and frisk" harassment and aggressive, zero-tolerance, "proactive policing" policies and practices.[30] Some scholars felt these practices expressed "middle-class, white, often-suburban interests," encouraged racial profiling, increased police brutality, and were part of a globalized "social cleansing strategy" of groups that were not considered economically productive.[31] Others noted the kinds of policing that focused on "neighborhood fabric, neighborhood crime, and how residents felt about their own safety and their neighborhood's future . . . have rarely been investigated either by researchers or policymakers."[32] In other words, the public-private partnerships that sought to revitalize Detroit depended on naturalist theories that racialized urban spaces. They conflated their abstract ideas about vacancy and abandonment with community disorder. Their plans sought to shrink the city into neat, manageable neighborhoods.

How Public-Private Partnerships Produced the Neighborhood

Urban renewal projects differed across the country but often included demolition, or "slum clearance," forcible displacement, and redevelopment. When the federal government stopped funding these projects in the early 1970s, the goal of rehabilitating existing neighborhoods became more significant. For example, in 1975, planning consultants suggested that St. Louis adopt a master plan of "neighborhood triage: 'conservation' for areas in good health, 'redevelopment' for areas just starting to decline, and gradual 'depletion' for areas already in severe distress."[33] In 1985, Mayor Coleman Young similarly promoted a neighborhood improvement program focused on four areas of Detroit.

Community development corporations (CDCs) developed across the country in the late 1960s and 1970s. Dorothy Mae Richardson pioneered the model. She was part of a block club in North Central Pittsburgh that brought a local bank and government officials together to give high-risk home improvement loans and advice to her neighbors in 1968. The local Neighborhood Housing Services (NHS) of Pittsburg subsequently became a national model that Congress institutionalized in 1978 when it passed the Neighborhood Reinvestment Corporation Act.

Local community activists mirrored Richardson's efforts across the country. They pushed for legislation to change banking practices that underpinned redlining, including the 1975 Home Mortgage Disclosure Act and the 1977 Community Reinvestment Act.[34] The Federal Housing Administration also passed policies and entered relationships with private industry (real estate brokers, mortgage bankers, and homebuilders) to produce low-income housing. These efforts turned urban areas into "an attractive place of unparalleled opportunity, a new frontier of economic investment and extraction."[35]

A new form of community renewal emerged in the 1980s that was distinguished by its lack of concrete plans for redevelopment.[36] President Ronald Reagan and other conservative politicians insisted government intervention caused urban decay. Federal cuts to social service programs created an opportunity for foundations to turn community development into an industry. The public-private partnerships that resulted replaced government-led efforts. Foundations and private businesses offered high-risk loans to support affordable housing development. For example, the Ford Foundation joined six private companies to form the Local Initiatives Support Corporation (LISC) in 1980. It gained twenty-five major corporate funders in its first year, with another twenty-five "waiting on the back burner."[37] Four years later, "LISC had obtained more than $70 million from 250 corporations and foundations and three federal agencies and set up 31 branch offices, which raised funds from local sources."[38]

In 1982, real estate developer James Rouse founded the Enterprise Foundation to promote affordable housing. By 1991, the Enterprise Foundation joined LISC to form the National Community Development Initiative (NCDI). It brought seven foundations, businesses, and the federal government together to build affordable housing. The president of the Rockefeller Foundation explained that the collaboration's larger objective was to reintroduce "social standards in communities that no longer had them, and whose residents no longer enforced them."[39] Individual funders echoed the broken windows theory's emphasis on community controls and implicit associations with homogenous white suburban areas that were symbols of law and order.

Taken together, these events signaled important features of how the community development industry developed. They indicated that public-private partnerships would be central to affordable housing development. They also signaled that affordable housing for minoritized populations could become important revenue streams for lending institutions and developers. The community development industry mapped new ways of extracting wealth for white investors at the expense of African American and Latina/o/x communities.[40]

How Foundations Produced Detroit's Neighborhoods

The *Detroit Free Press* was the city's local paper with the largest distribution. Its references to neighborhoods during the 1990s were largely general. There were a few areas that were referred to as historic neighborhoods, but the word was most often used as an adjective, as in "neighborhood sports bar" or "neighborhood children." Some stories referred to areas of the city, as in, "the far east side neighborhood." Some areas had more general names that were relatively consistent, such as when the southwest area of the city was interchangeable with references to Southwest Detroit. An alternate way of referencing spaces was by area or major intersection, as in the West Side or East Side (of Woodward Avenue).

By the late 1990s, the *Detroit Free Press* referred to neighborhoods in terms of major cross streets. For example, there were four references to Fort-Schaefer as a neighborhood in the period between 1947 and 2021. Other mentions of Fort-Schaefer used the location to modify a section, an area, or a community. The paper's coverage indicated that specific neighborhoods were not widely known and that readers thought about the city largely through very general references to areas of the city. For example, "the westside" referred to the city west of Woodward Avenue. Even these references lacked consensus. For example, one classified advertisement that referred to Fort-Schaefer considered it was part of Southwest Detroit.

The relative irrelevance of neighborhood names was a vacuum that a variety of groups used to import national neighborhood development trends to Detroit. This effort was led by foundations. A director of a leading philanthropic organization characterized the first decade of the century as one where "there was a lot of movement to do place-based stuff" in the city.

Foundations targeted their investments in Detroit in ways that influenced local, community-based nonprofit organizations. For example, the John S. and James L. Knight Foundation shifted its strategy in 2003 to focus on revitalizing six neighborhoods. It referred to one in general terms with the label "Woodward Corridor/East Grand Boulevard."[41] Ten years later, the Knight Foundation defined Midtown as "a vibrant neighborhood."[42] Meanwhile, the *Detroit Free Press* continued to refer to the same area as Cass Corridor, a name that traced back to at least 1970.[43]

Foundations' focus on place-based investing was reflected in their efforts to map, border, and define neighborhoods. The Knight Foundation's efforts to rebrand the Woodward Corridor as Midtown underscored its inconsistent approach to neighborhood names and boundaries. The Knight Foundation had given another neighborhood a nonprofit organization's name (see fig. 2.2).[44] Only two years later, the Knight Foundation referred to the same area as Northwest Detroit. It similarly added the "North-Central" label to an area it had earlier referred to as "7 Mile/Woodward."[45] The changes nonetheless reflected the organization's

Figure 2.2. Knight Foundation's Six "Neighborhoods" (2003)

developing influence over neighborhood names and boundaries. (For a timeline of investment in Detroit, see table 2.1.)

In 2006, the city adopted a similar approach to targeting areas of the city to diversify the city's economy when Mayor Kwame Kilpatrick announced the Next Detroit Neighborhoods Initiative (NDNI) (fig. 2.3). He spoke about the six areas in ways that underscored that the city had still not adopted widely recognized neighborhood names. For example, he described one area as "Jefferson East, way out Jefferson and Alter. You see it going on up in Chaldean Town, over at John R and Seven Mile, and they are working with us, as well. We're about to pick three new communities—Seven Mile and Livernois is a place we think will be

Table 2.1. Public-private investment targeted neighborhoods

1976	The US Department of Housing and Urban Development created the Community Development Block Grant (CDBG). It allowed greater local control over how federal funds were spent. - Detroit City Council began funding nonprofits through the Neighborhood Opportunity Fund (NOF) program. - Racial conflict undermined the involvement of local communities organizations in NOF decisions.i The organizations were led largely by white people under Mayor Young's administration (1974–1994).
1977	Congress passed the Community Reinvestment Act, which - intended to prevent redlining. - was "one of the seminal pieces of legislation to address systemic inequities in access to credit."ii - uses neighborhoods and communities interchangeably.
1978	Congress passed the Neighborhood Reinvestment Corporation Act and institutionalized the Neighborhood Housing Services of America.
1990	The Ford Foundation worked with the Center for Community Change (CCC) and established the Neighborhood and Family Initiative. It targeted four cities, including Detroit.
1991	The Enterprise Foundation and Local Initiatives Support Corporation (LISC) founded the National Community Development Initiative (NCDI) that focused on bringing capital and technical assistance to Community Development Corporations (CDCs). It targeted neighborhoods across two dozen cities that included Detroit.iii
2003	The John S. and James L. Knight Foundation targeted $24.3 million in funding to six neighborhoods: Southwest Detroit, Woodward Corridor/East Grand Boulevard; 7 Mile/Woodward, East Riverfront, Northeast-East Warren/Alter-Mack and Focus: Hope.
2004	LISC launched the Strategic Investment Areas (SIA) initiative centered on Southwest Detroit, Central Woodward, Northwest Detroit, and the Far East/Lower East Side.iv
2006	The Skillman Foundation announced a ten-year effort that will focus $75 million on six city neighborhoods, including Southwest Detroit, Osborn, Central, Chadsey/Condon, Cody/Rouge, and Brightmoor.
2007	City launches NEXT Detroit Neighborhood Initiative (NDNI), which focused on six neighborhoods: East English Village, Osborn, North End, Brightmoor, 7 Mile-Livernois, and Grand River-Greenfield.
	LISC announces $40 million "Neighborhoods Now" targeting seven neighborhoods, which include Southwest Detroit, Far East/Lower East Side, Northwest Detroit, Central Woodward, Jefferson East, South Fort/Visger Corridor, and Van Dyke-8 Mile.
	The Community Foundation for Southeast Michigan, W. K. Kellogg Foundation and the Ford Foundation create the "Detroit Neighborhood Fund" and awarded over $13 million in grants to the Near East Side.
2008	Federal Government announces the "Neighborhood Stabilization Program" (NSP). In Detroit, the funds - are used to start the Detroit land bank. - included Hardest Hit Funds for demolishing land bank properties in nine target areas that included Southwest Detroit.
2011	NSP ends.
2011	The city, Invest Detroit, and other partners begin "Woodward Corridor Initiative" focused on Greater Downtown.
2014	City announces Strategic Neighborhood Fund (SNF), a public-private partnership to direct $42 million investment toward three neighborhoods: Southwest/Vernor, Livernois-McNichols and Islandview /Villages.

Table 2.1. *(cont.)*

2014	The Detroit Blight Removal Task Force ("Task Force") releases the *Detroit Future City* report that maps "blight" by Census tract.
2018	SNF expands to include another seven neighborhoods with $130 million in contributions.
2020	Hardest Hit funding ends.

i. Shaw and Spence 2004; Bachelor and Jones 1981.
ii. Federal Reserve 2022.
iii. Kohler 2007a.
iv. Thomson (2012, 120) notes that investment varied across SIAa: "Ninety-one percent ($27.7 million) of LISC's total 2008 investment and 93 percent of its 2008 SIA investments went to the Central Woodward and Southwest SIAs."

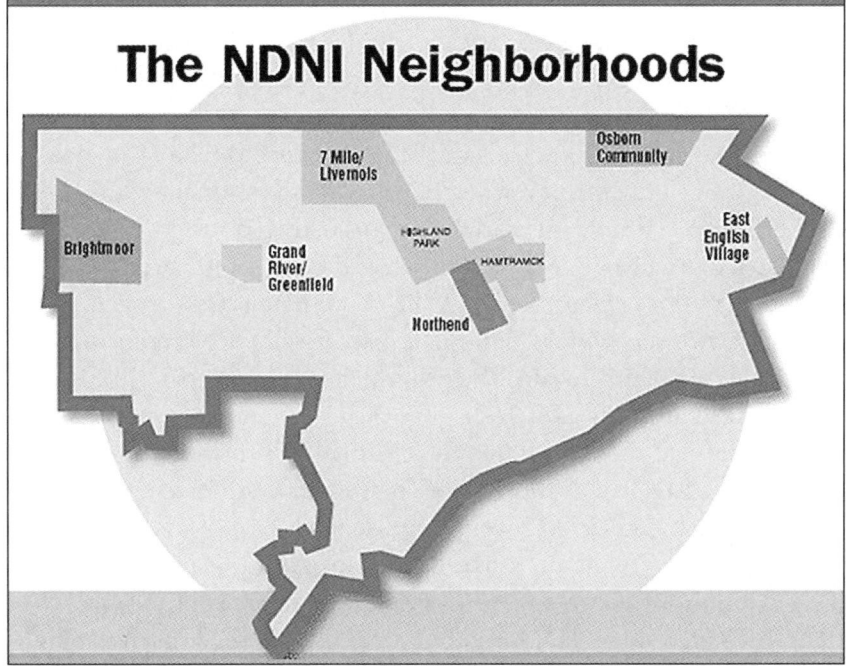

Figure 2.3. Next Detroit Neighborhoods Initiative (2006)

real [sic] hot, that whole Avenue of Fashion."[46] The city's plan differed markedly from the Knight Foundation's approach. Its more equitable approach targeted two areas that were "heavily blighted and in need of major redevelopment; two that had relatively high home ownership and income levels but need help to sustain prosperity, and two in-between areas that are viable but declining."[47] The diversification was markedly different from strategies pursued by other foundations as well.

Following Kilpatrick's announcement, Congress passed the Housing and Economic Recovery Act (HERA) in 2008 to help "states, cities and counties" address the impact of the national foreclosure crisis. The City of Detroit's webpage recognized the impact of widespread foreclosures and quoted HERA's requirement to distribute funds according to "areas of greatest need."[48] In response, the city designed the Neighborhood Stabilization Program (NSP) and targeted nine neighborhoods. The six NDNI neighborhoods were included in NSP, as was Southwest Detroit. The Skillman Foundation and LISC had already targeted four and five (respectively) of the NSP areas. This indicated that foundation spending did not align with the areas that the city targeted. The NSP areas indicated that foundation funding nonetheless influenced the city's decisions prior to Detroit's bankruptcy.

These developments were significant because the city's mayor retained greater influence over neighborhood development plans before the bankruptcy, which reflected the importance of Black governance. As one Black journalist opined, "Kilpatrick and I were both raised to believe that one day, this city's future would lie in our hands, the first generation of black Detroiters with a birth-right responsibility to care for the city, nurture it, see that it regains the prominence it once held."[49] This context changed abruptly after 2008 after the tragic and extractive relation that determined the city's home foreclosures, which were further compounded by Kilpatrick's indictment. It seemed Wall Street, rather than Detroiters or their elected government, shaped the city and its fortunes.

Foundations' focus on place-based investing meant they moved away from more abstract, general references to areas in the city. They instead created maps that bordered areas and defined discrete neighborhoods. Foundations also targeted areas in ways that underscored their belief that the city's footprint should shrink, even though there was no public consensus about whether tax-paying residents desired this outcome or how it should be accomplished. Foundation leaders shared an outsiders' dilemma: They faced 139 square miles of urban space that, to them, seemed a blank canvas. They believed the city had not been comprehensively planned or managed and their first priority was to define the problem through data. The Kresge and the Skillman

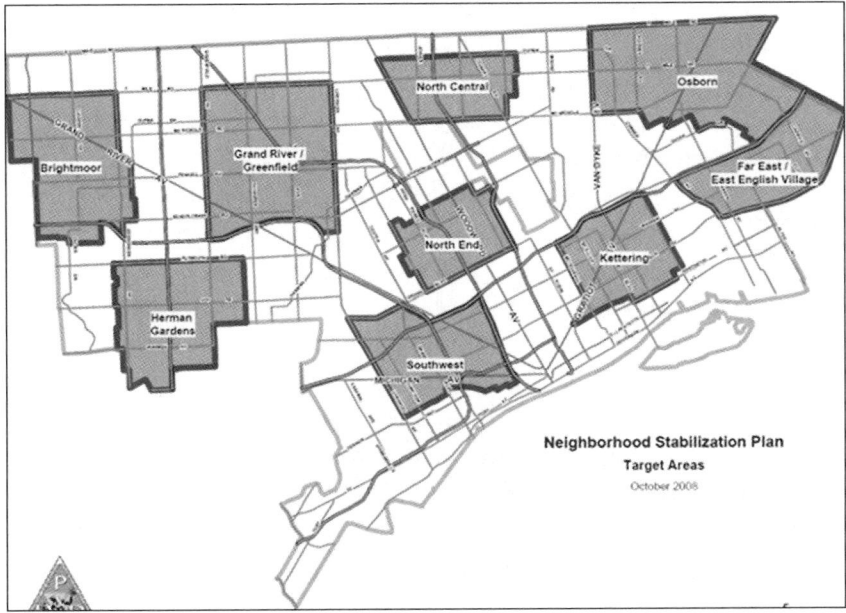

Figure 2.4. Neighborhood Stabilization Plan Map (2008).

Foundations supported the development of Data Driven Detroit in 2008; it was founded by Kurt Metzger. He participated in many data initiatives, including early mapping projects to monetize the city's parcels. We spoke about the mapping project and he confirmed: "We had all these different people looking at neighborhoods, but not the same neighborhoods in many cases."[50]

Detroit's master plan was updated in 2009. It inherited ten areas from the 1990 master plan that it alternately referred to as sectors or neighborhood clusters. It also identified fifty-three neighborhoods. According to the plan, the cluster identification would enable the city to "outline policies focused on providing retail, housing improvements, transportation, and other services" to the city's population.[51] Except for Brightmoor, none of the neighborhood names corresponded with the earlier 2007 NDNI or 2008 NSP maps. The northern boundary of what the previous two maps identified as the Evergreen neighborhood became the southernmost boundary in the new master plan. Rather than competition, the maps demonstrated a lack of strong neighborhood identity, consensus on neighborhood names, and lack of coordination between the city, foundations, and federal funding programs.

The lack of coordination between local government and outside actors shifted in 2012 with the release of the influential Detroit Future City (DFC) report. Its executive summary pointed out that early efforts to engage communities found that "neighborhood appearance" was one of the universal concerns "regardless of neighborhood population, ethnicity, income, or geography."[52] This was significant because, in a more general and national context that extended beyond the report, a neighborhood's appearance was commonly understood to be largely subjective. In any event, the report did not include references to what residents in different areas of the city considered an acceptable, desirable, or attractive neighborhood appearance. The report's discussion instead assumed residents (who were largely Black) and planning experts (who were predominantly white) shared consensus on what constituted a desirable neighborhood appearance. This was consequential because it shaped the abstraction of blight.

The DFC report made many assumptions that disregarded the realities of racial inequity in urban planning. For example, it failed to refer to racism or discrimination anywhere over its 761 pages, even though the patterned practices produced differential real estate values. The report's focus on vacancy and abandonment also ignored that there were many informally occupied properties across the city and that residents used public property creatively.[53] For example, residents used empty lots to host large family barbeques and gatherings, such as pictured in figure 2.5. The ways residents assigned value to space was disregarded. The report instead treated vacant and abandoned parcels as the cause of disinvestment. It also assumed that everyone could live anywhere and that they would have equal and equitable access to more "stable neighborhood options."[54]

The DFC was publicly criticized for two reasons. First, critics argued the report's authors failed to obtain meaningful and representative public feedback. Second, many city residents had been concerned they would lose access to public services with any planned efforts to shrink the city's residential areas. This made the DFC report's proposed framework zones a matter of particular concern because they identified areas of anticipated vacancy (see figure 2.6, especially the text below the legend). The high- and moderate-vacancy areas coincided with those

Figure 2.5. Creative Use of Empty Lots in Front of Detroit Public Theatre (2024)

that had recently been targeted in the NSP, the NDNI, and the Knight neighborhoods. In other words, the report implied the city should reduce services in areas that had recently been objects of foundation attention, investment, and development. The report and its maps imagined green and blue landscapes that projected a dramatic color change for the majority Black city.

The DFC report's discussion of neighborhoods added to the lack of coordination and consensus about what they were, where their boundaries lay, and what their names should be. It dedicated a section to the subject that was located about halfway through the report and suggested Detroit should be a "city of distinct and regionally competitive neighborhoods."[55] It followed with bold-faced lettering that insisted "Detroit must be welcoming to all, including those moving in from neighboring cities [and] those who are originally from other countries," which implied two things: the city was not already welcoming to nonresidents (even though development resources were focused on attracting them) and the shared priority was attracting new residents.[56] The idea that the city was not already welcoming was reminiscent of another inversion: The US Federal Housing Administration's Underwriting Manual repeatedly warned of the "infiltration of inharmonious racial groups" because it would lessen the area's "desirability" and lower its value. The reference assumed the encroachment of nonwhite groups in white neighborhoods.[57]

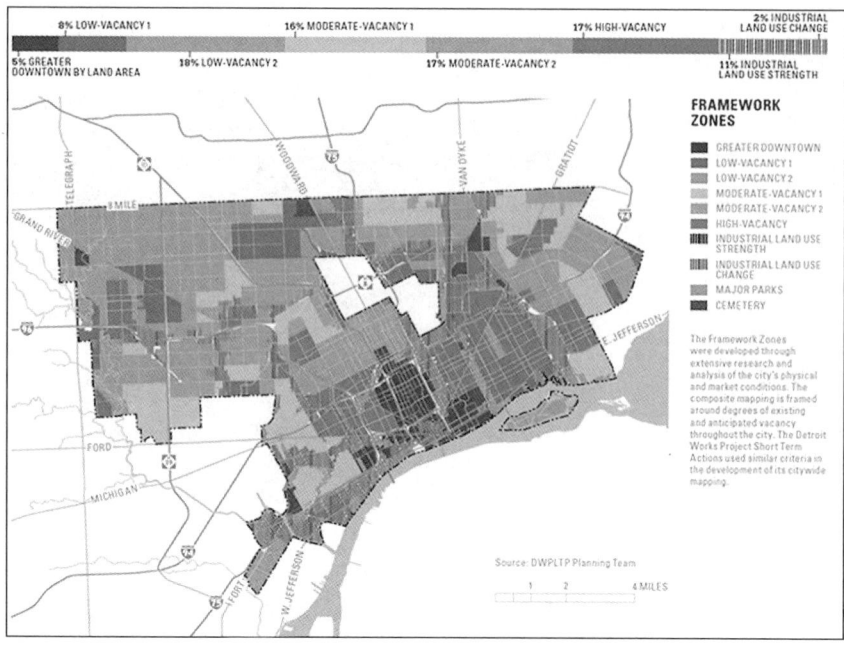

Figure 2.6. Detroit Future City Framework Zones (2012)

The DFC report's discussion of neighborhoods tied into a longstanding problem. Many Detroiters were alarmed that conversations about diversity and attracting new residents often focused on (or implied) white creatives. Media outlets from around the world also participated in depicting Detroit as an urban frontier and a blank canvas, which simultaneously attracted new migrants who considered themselves urban pioneers and disregarded the city's legacy residents.[58]

The report was published only months before the emergency manager filed for bankruptcy. This left the report's relevance in limbo, but the city emerged from bankruptcy in part, because foundations made the Grand Bargain possible. This partly explained why Kresge's investment in DFC and its plan for neighborhoods continued to have political relevance under the Duggan administration.

Criticism of the DFC plan focused on which areas would lose public services and investment and who would have to move. This underscored how the DFC plan produced space even though it did not explicitly refer to race. Detroiters had already experienced similar displacements: urban renewal razed Black communities and leveled business areas, like Paradise Valley. Detroit Future City's plan threatened to do the same. Research published after the report was released found racial disparities in both the areas that would be targeted for investment and those that would be neglected by the DFC plan. Commentators opined on whether people would be forced to move, which reminded the city's residents of earlier waves of demolition and urban renewal that was dubbed "negro removal."

The mayoral election occurred while the city was in bankruptcy proceedings. Political debates focused on the future of neighborhoods. Duggan asserted that development plans had to be "driven by the citizens who live in the neighborhoods on a neighborhood by neighborhood basis."[59] He claimed the mayor should lead a vision for the city's future. He also pointed out that he didn't know of any cities that "outsourced their planning department."[60] The bankruptcy not only restructured the city's debt but also its political authority. The mayor's limited powers mirrored the city's shrinking footprint. For example, the emergency manager intended to remove planning from the city's authority but Duggan convinced him otherwise. Once the city exited bankruptcy, Duggan appointed Tom Lewand to direct economic development and job growth. The latter claimed the DFC report was his "bible."[61]

Nonprofits in the city included quasi-public and community-based organizations that existed largely because of the grants they received from foundations that were active in the city. Despite their reliance on public and private funds, or perhaps because of it, they shared a lack of consensus about neighborhood boundaries. One nonprofit, U Snap Bac, referred to the "east side of Detroit" and used street names to define its "area of redevelopment" on its website. This nonprofit was notable for two reasons. First, U Snap Bac was incorporated in 1987 by a consortium of business associations and neighborhood organizations. It was a public-private partnership tied to the community development industry. Second, the organization's executive director was one of the three chairpersons on the Detroit Blight Removal Task Force.

U Snap Bac's leadership on the task force complimented that of billionaire Dan Gilbert, the real estate investor and founder of Quicken Loans, later Rocket Mortgage, a large mortgage finance company. They framed a federally commissioned analysis that focused on the demolition of property. This was especially significant in a city with significant demand for affordable housing and that had granted Gilbert significant property and incentives for developing them.[62]

The Detroit Blight Removal Task Force

The Detroit Blight Removal Task Force was tasked with reporting on blight, but it centered on neighborhoods. It issued a report in 2014 titled "Every Neighborhood Has a Future . . . and It Doesn't Include Blight." The reference to the future of every neighborhood paralleled both the DFC report and the mayoral campaign. The group's chairs recognized that economic activity in the downtown and midtown areas was not replicated in the city's neighborhoods; they implied the disparity was tied to blight. The chairs also thought the problem of blight undermined the "productive environment" in midtown and downtown.[63] They wrote that blight was a cancer that sucked "the soul out of anyone who gets near it."[64] They implied blight as radioactive, contagious, and synonymous with Detroit. They defined blight as alternately a disease, a place, a symbol, and a calamity.

The report's characterizations of blight created three important problems. First, the report's discussion of blight blamed the city's residents. For example, the introduction implied blight was primarily caused by irresponsible property owners, thieves, and squatters. It briefly referred to speculators and Hardest Hit Fund Program funds without any mention of other significant factors that contributed to property vacancies, including predatory lending, overassessed property taxes, utility shutoffs, and the county auction of tax-foreclosed properties. The taskforce's plan implied the predominantly Black city's residents were responsible for blight, which the report associated with vacancy, danger, and neglect. The abstraction of irresponsibility was one that has been repeatedly used to dispossess Latina/o/x and Black people of land and access to basic resources, including water.[65]

Second, in much the same way that the DFC report's authors assumed definitions of neighborhood appearance were universally shared, the taskforce plan's discussion implied blight would be plainly evident to readers. The problem with this assumption was that the report struggled in at least two sections to define blight (see figure 2.7). Each section

> **DEFINING BLIGHT.** The Task Force's definition and methodology for classifying property as "blight" incorporates the concepts of physical blight, economic blight, the public's interest in protecting the health, safety, and general welfare of people in its communities, and the preservation of property values. Michigan law defines a **blighted property** as one that meets any of the following conditions as determined by the applicable "governing body":
>
> - A public nuisance
> - An attractive nuisance (yes, an oxymoron! See below...)
> - A fire hazard or is otherwise dangerous
> - Has had the utilities, plumbing, heating or sewerage disconnected, destroyed, removed, or rendered ineffective
> - A tax-reverted property
> - Owned or is under the control of a land bank
> - Has been vacant for five consecutive years, and not maintained to code
> - Has code violations posing a severe and immediate health or safety threat
>
> Using the State of Michigan's definition of "blighted property" as a starting point, the Task Force added elements from the Detroit Ordinance governing "dangerous buildings." The Task Force's definition includes properties that are:
>
> - Open to the elements and trespassing, and
> - On Detroit's Buildings, Safety Engineering, and Environmental Department (BSEED) Demolition list.
>
> Accordingly, properties that are exposed to the elements, are not structurally sound, are in need of major repairs, are fire damaged, or have essentially been turned into a neighborhood dumping ground, were classified as "blight" by the Task Force. While the Task Force recognizes that there are other aspects that border on any reasonable definition of blight such as graffiti, un-manicured boulevard grass and litter, the scope of this report addresses blight based on the Task Force definition.
>
> CHAPTER 1: INTRODUCTION   13

Figure 2.7. Blight Removal Task Force Report, "Defining Blight" (2014)

outlined the state's law that undermined a clear definition of a "nuisance." The definition was presented on the right page, and a graphic that attempted to illustrate each bullet point was presented on the left. The two pages were followed by a discussion that elaborated on how the task force added to the state's definition. The narrative provided a narrow description that summarized the kinds of properties that surveyors would consider blighted, but pointed out that properties that might become blighted in the future were also included in their estimation of the problem. The definition of blight vacillated on the criteria that should be used to include and exclude properties. The problem with defining blight was compounded by the speed of data collection (ten weeks), the large number of surveyors (paid and volunteers), and the method used to report data (cellphones used to report data by text message, which became known as "blexting"). The survey lacked reliability. For example, many property owners disagreed that their property was blighted or subject to nuisance violations. Parents disagreed that their homes were blighted if their water was shut off, especially because it meant their child could be removed from their home and their custody.

The Detroit Blight Removal Task Force presented the plan as if it was a scientific survey but ignored problems with the validity and reliability of its data. (This concern will be revisited in a more detailed discussion of public-private partnerships later in this book). Its pages were filled with graphic presentations, maps, and enlarged numbers to magnify the scope of the problem. It referred to databases, mobile phone applications, and live-stream feeds but did not recognize that its definition of blight was an important part of the problem. For example, it estimated that thirty-two thousand properties *could* become blighted because they were owned by the city. The plan did not recognize the longstanding problems that many Detroit residents had in accessing affordable housing. The report instead identified some areas as being at a tipping point to direct demolition (figure 2.8.). The plan's authors identified these tipping points using a variety of indicators, including the density of mortgages, foreclosures, occupied properties, and population under age eighteen. Areas that were at a tipping point ostensibly had the greatest potential impact in terms of the number of affected city residents. Only 22,700 of 78,000 vacant structures were in those areas. In other words, the report suggested removing less than 30 percent of the city's vacant structures would impact the greatest number of the city's residents.

The tipping point is an idea that politicians and planners adapted from physics to represent the significance of their interventions. The task force used the concept to propose immediate intervention in targeted areas of the city. Their report produced maps and spaces where a lack of intervention would "quickly result in significant decline in stability, occupancy, and overall population. Shortly thereafter, disinvestment, increases in vacancy, blighted properties, and crime is likely to follow."[66]

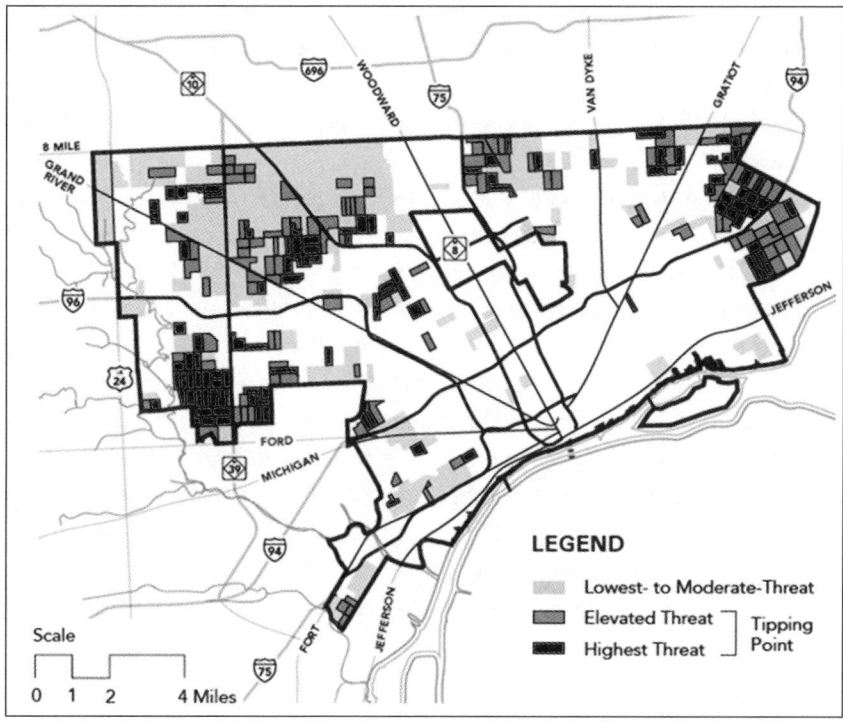

Figure 2.8. Blight Removal Task Force Report, Tipping Point Geographies (2014)

The report characterized spaces as if they were natural and susceptible to decay rather than as creations of a task force whose priorities and actions were directed by prominent actors in the city's real estate and affordable housing markets. Their assessments of markets and real estate value created a relation between intervention and investment. The task force maps also informed subsequent demolition programs that created the conditions for new abstractions and spatial production. Powerful groups depended on these abstractions to normalize their actions and obfuscate their role in the production of (and control over) space.

Department of Neighborhoods

Duggan developed a Department of Neighborhoods (DON) in 2014 so that his office could coordinate work with residents across the city's seven districts. The DON's existence suggested Duggan was interested in promoting economic development across the city's neighborhoods, but the district boundaries were defined in 2013, and two of the seven represented the downtown area. In other words, the city had already planned for downtown's overrepresentation using district boundaries and the DON.

Commentators speculated that public concern about growing inequality under Duggan's administration drove him to create a new chief storyteller in the months leading up to the 2017 election. The position may have been the first of its kind in the United States.[67] The mayor appointed Aaron Foley who explained his job was to counter two limiting narratives about Detroit: a "comeback" story centered in downtown and another about disenfranchised residents. Foley explained he was working against "psychological gentrification," which he defined as the lack of media representations of people who had a home and were "doing quite well . . . or even just maintaining."[68] He wanted to be part of the oft-repeated compulsion among the city's residents to "change the narrative." Foley also competed to redefine the city's identity. Detroit had set an example of Black Power and governance that shaped its identity beyond the city's demographic profile. The storyteller set up a website that told visitors the city was diverse and had "200-plus neighborhoods."[69] His assertion was surprising: The abstraction of diversity is unpopular among historically marginalized groups because it undermines a direct acknowledgement of racism. Scholars argue that references to "diversity" tend to center white people's comfort, commodify otherness for consumption, and reify whiteness.[70] This made Foley's references to diversity a crossing practice that accommodated white supremacy.

The storyteller's website identified 209 neighborhoods. This contrasted with the city's 2009 master plan that had identified 57 neighborhoods. The growth of neighborhood names changed how space and race in the city was imagined. For example, the city's Latina/o/x population was concentrated in part of the sixth district. The area had traditionally been referred to as Southwest Detroit, but the new website divided the area across eleven new neighborhoods. The website produced stories about each newly named neighborhood. It provided links that highlighted different businesses in each of the eleven areas but repeated the same data about private investments and home renovations for the Southwest Detroit area overall.[71] In this way, the website followed the Detroit Blight

Removal Task Force's plan of carefully choosing and selectively curating the way it presented data. The storyteller did not simply produce new stories. He traded on the legitimacy of what seemed like a new local government; one with new resources and many new personnel that, like the city's first white mayor in forty years, had recently moved to the city.

Foley's reference to class did not complement, but instead competed with, the racial difference implied by the two narratives. The contrasting narratives recognized the inequitable development of a downtown area that was dominated by white residents and tourists and its relation to Duggan's neglect of the city's predominantly Black neighborhoods. The racialized difference was not only about who occupied different spaces and the nature of residential segregation but also about the inequitable distribution of material resources and interests they implied. The reference to psychological gentrification also underscored how residents understood the contrast between downtown and its neighborhoods. The term had been used by an African American art dealer and gallery owner in the city to refer more explicitly to issues involving race and space after the city's bankruptcy. George N'Namdi was known for being one of several residents who created schools to promote Afrocentric education. He had used the term in 2014 to refer to "not seeing yourself as often" in new businesses that had opened in the city and the programming of "the powers that be."[72] N'Namdi used the term to refer to visual appearance and implied matters involving race and representation; this interpretation was echoed in the ways other groups in and beyond the city have used it since then.

Foley appropriated the concept of psychological gentrification and put it in service of changing the narrative to one that promoted a broader definition of diversity. This served to distract website visitors from confronting what residents considered to be an intensification of racial disparities. The move was a political one.

Foley acknowledged his work could be put in the service of propaganda.[73] His website promoted projects that generated significant and widespread controversy among a much larger number of city residents. For example, the website published an article that promoted the mayor's controversial Project Greenlight.[74] The controversy was that businesses could pay for a green light that police prioritized in their response to emergencies. The practice hijacked public resources and was not unlike bribery, an otherwise illegal act. Project Greenlight was protested by local groups, including Detroit Will Breathe, the Detroit Community Technology Project, and the Detroit Digital Justice Coalition. It was also part of broader national actions against racial profiling and surveillance by a variety of groups that included the American Civil Liberties Union (ACLU).

Corporations, marketing firms, and city officials produced a narrative about the city's diversity by referencing the number of Detroit's neighborhoods. Their practices seemed comparable to other place making approaches to urban development, but in Detroit, they involved repackaging the city and its long-term residents for outside consumption.[75] This extended to companies that repackaged inequality as a brand. For example, Shinola used Detroit as a prop for its brand and appropriated "the mantle of the 'underdog' from the city's longtime residents."[76]

How Nonprofit Organizations Produced a "Good Quality Product at a Reasonable Price"

Most residents of Southwest Detroit are Latina/o/x. This meant that, depending on the audience, the area was either celebrated as a resilient immigrant neighborhood or dismissed as a blighted, liminal space, the first stop in and the last stop out of the city. Surrounded by a refinery, other industrial facilities, and open stores of petroleum coke, Southwest Detroit was among the most toxic residential areas in the state.[77] It simultaneously symbolized economic growth, legal precarity, and industrial waste. The area's fortunes shifted along with that of the city and the increased traffic across the Ambassador Bridge.

Southwest Detroit was literally and figuratively placed at the border of targeted neighborhoods. It was one of the nine areas identified to receive federal funds as part of the 2008 Housing and Recovery Act's Neighborhood Stabilization Program. It was one of four that LISC identified for strategic investment. In other words, in the same year (2008) that the federal government considered the area one of most impacted by the foreclosure crisis, LISC focused on the "market opportunities" it presented and considered Southwest Detroit "a good quality product at a reasonable price."[78] It marked an attempt to produce a real estate market at bargain prices.

Philanthropic support complemented investors' interest and concentrated resources in the area. For example, the shift in foundation strategy and engagement began in 2003 when the Knight Foundation claimed a commitment to strengthening neighborhoods. It targeted six areas of the city, and its largest grantee was the Mexicantown Community Development Corporation.[79] The trend continued after the bankruptcy; in 2017, JPMorgan Chase gave Southwest Solutions $800,000 of its $1.2 million grant to Detroit.[80]

Southwest Detroit was unlike many areas of the city because it had not struggled with the same kinds of persistent disinvestment. LISC noted its "strategic location for businesses serving both domestic and international markets," among other "competitive advantages."[81] The framing capitalized on distinguishing Southwest Detroit from Detroit more broadly. For example, the president of Southwest Solutions, John Van Camp, boasted that "our rich immigrant history means the people here are especially resilient. Southwest Detroit has always been a hotbed of ideas, arts, culture, and politics, which have and continue to foster the strong sense of community that has held us together through the bad times."[82] His depiction highlighted the area's advantages, which he attributed to people rather than the resources they enjoyed.

The context of how Southwest Detroit was regarded by the city government, philanthropic donors, and investors was important because it mirrored the ways the area continued to receive significant and sustained public investment in the years leading up to and following the city's bankruptcy. This was particularly true in terms of nonprofit funding for community development. For example, one high-level LISC employee felt it was clear which CDC got the city's attention when it came to distributing grants. She explained it was obvious when he was "the only white guy" in the room.[83] She referred to John Van Camp, who became the president of Southwest Solutions in 1973. By the time of his retirement, the organization had expanded from a focus on affordable housing development to healthcare and wraparound services. The organization not only extended service boundaries, but also (and despite its name) crossed spatial and racial borders. It exemplified the ways CDCs were fundamental to the bordering and crossing of neighborhoods.

Nonprofit organizations depend on a variety of funding sources. This encouraged some CDCs to merge. For example, several housing CDCs were absorbed by Southwest Solution, which expanded the boundaries of its service area beyond Southwest Detroit and produced space by colonizing it. As Van Camp explained, "all sectors," including banks, foundations, and government, encouraged "mergers, partnerships and acquisitions."[84] According to *Crain's Detroit Business*, the main business periodical in the city, Southwest Solutions had become "one of the *region's* largest, most complex nonprofits."[85] Van Camp explained Southwest Solutions' development when we talked over the phone:

> People asked me, "What did you do?" And I'll give them a couple words. I said, "Well, I ran a nonprofit." And then I say, "But that just tells you our tax status." I said, "I ran a for-impact organization, that the assets were plowed back in rather than up to the owners." And we ran a business. We saw it as a business. Not a charity. And moving that from . . . and there are some phenomenal charities, okay? But moving that mindset from charity work, to running a business that happens to have a tax status where the assets don't go up to the owners, but are plowed back in. That's another major turning point.[86]

Other nonprofit organizations considered that the work of community development included bordering service areas and developing new neighborhood names and identities. For example, the executive director of Urban Neighborhood Initiatives believed a smaller community size would promote more rigid community norms and reduce drug-related mortality and homicide. As a result, he "reclaimed" the name of an area that had been a township before it was incorporated by Detroit. He received local criticism that the name could promote gentrification. One resident explained this was an example of how nonprofits whitewashed, branded, and marketed a new neighborhood to people who otherwise wouldn't consider the area palatable because "for one reason or another, [they] don't come or don't like it."[87]

In the difficult years between the foreclosure crisis and the bankruptcy, many Southwest Detroit residents became suspicious of community development organizations that seemed to represent outside interests in their neighborhood. This was particularly true in cases like Southwest Solutions, which controlled a variety of housing (market-rate, public, and assisted) in the area. Some residents felt the leadership of the organization magnified their lack of meaningful representation in the city.

Residents were concerned that nonprofits focused on attracting new grants and residents, which could result in the neglect and displacement of existing populations. They were concerned about growing inequalities that resulted from new development. The best-resourced residents (and those with longstanding ties to the neighborhood) were in the best position to take advantage of new sources of funding. They engaged in new business ventures. Other residents and many small businesses faced language and legal borders and struggled to cross them after the city's bankruptcy. Examples of these struggles included the forced relocation of Delray's residents to accommodate plans for a second bridge crossing to Canada (2015–2017), difficulties with the new nuisance codes and business licensing requirements that Duggan had introduced (2014–2019), and debates about rezoning in the neighborhood (2021).

Nonprofit organizations like Southwest Solutions reflected Detroiters' broader criticisms of how speculators benefited from their losses. An important example of this was a shift in ownership from individuals, to the city after a tax foreclosure, to the quasi-public Detroit Land Bank. Affordable housing development in Southwest Detroit often followed this trajectory. As Van Camp explained in one news story about another nonprofit organization, "Serving as the developer of long-term housing can be a good source of income because there was a developer fee for tax-credit projects." Southwest Solutions expanded beyond the conventional model of CDC that limited its service area. For example, operating as Southwest Housing Corporation, it managed more than 238 housing units at fourteen residential properties and 18,000 square feet of commercial retail space in 2005.[88] It took over Detroit Neighborhood Housing Services, Inc., in 2006, which was the largest rehabilitation contractor used by the city. The acquisition also meant that Southwest Solutions paid $1 for "about $600,000 in cash and loans receivable" and a building on Woodward Avenue that was "worth more than $1 million" dollars.[89]

There were other ways that Southwest Solutions reflected residents' broader concerns about border crossing. The organization crossed its service boundaries in Southwest Detroit to develop the Piquette Square for Veterans (PSV). The border crossing enabled Southwest Solutions to expand its services for veterans, which was a population the organization had no experience with prior to developing the property. It claimed PSV was a national model for wraparound services. The move meant Southwest Solutions was a nonprofit organization that was simultaneously a property manager and developer. This enabled Southwest Solutions to cross into the personal lives of its resident clients. For instance, its services for veterans included helping them apply for moving costs, security deposits, and Veteran Affairs benefits. Southwest Solutions also offered its resident clients additional services, including transportation, mental health counseling, substance abuse treatment, and job training. The relationship illustrated power differentials that were magnified by complaints about inadequate housing quality. For example, in one article about bed bugs and inadequate air conditioning at PSV, one resident complained, "It almost has the feeling like we're the inmates, and they're [building managers] the wardens."[90]

Southwest Solutions modeled other crossing practices that concerned city residents. First, they were one of several nonprofit organizations that acquired occupied properties from the land bank. This implicated nonprofit organizations in what many considered a dispossession that was shared between the city and its residents.[91] Second, Southwest Solutions' access to a variety of funding sources also magnified that many residents lacked the kinds of social, cultural, and financial capital the nonprofit enjoyed. The nonprofit had almost doubled its revenue from $1.5 million in 2004 to about $2.5 million in 2006. It was $40 million by 2019.[92] The LISC employee was not the only one to speculate that Southwest Solutions' success depended on the whiteness of its director. Third, unlike individuals, Southwest Solutions was able to adopt multiple names and expand their businesses to profitable development work. It held 501c3 status for its work with community, human, and economic development. It simultaneously offered mortgages and developed properties that it could sell at market rate once the Low-Income Housing Tax Credit compliance period expired.

Southwest Solutions was one example of how references to neighborhood were abstractions. Van Camp bordered Southwest Detroit by referring to its immigrant population, which distinguished the area from the rest of the city. The reference underscored his own location in the racial politics of the city because it ignored the large number of Black immigrants in Detroit. In other words, Van Camp implied there was something unique about the immigrants who lived in Southwest Detroit, which underscored that they were not Black. The implication also bordered who was excluded from the types of services the organization offered, which was consequential because the organization facilitated access to credit and affordable housing. In other words, Southwest Solutions demonstrated how nonprofit organizations could be selective in the groups they served and the services they offered. It magnified the idea that neighborhoods were affinity groups. It also produced Southwest Detroit through loans for entrepreneurs and business development. Southwest Solutions exemplified the ways that nonprofit organizations were implicated in producing race and space through new forms of inequity.

Summary

A variety of groups competed to produce neighborhoods. They included scholars, city residents, local government, foundations, and investors. This competition demonstrated how neighborhoods were abstractions that mapped relations between social groups and the changing racial politics in the years leading up to and following Detroit's bankruptcy. References to neighborhoods were about more than names; they were also bordering practices to direct resources and investments. Struggles over neighborhoods were tied to markets and real estate values.

Scholarship that describes neighborhoods as areas that were primarily or solely produced by their residents traced back to the early twentieth century. This conception obscured the ways spaces were produced "far beyond" a particular area.[93] This was not only true for poorer immigrant, Black, and Latina/o/x communities that social science scholars tend to focus on, but also new white migrants that were incentivized to move into the city's downtown and midtown areas.

The more recent experience of how Detroit planners and politicians used neighborhoods revealed that they participated in producing new relations and values. They did not explicitly consider the legacy of racism in planning for the future. They also produced new racial inequities in their plans to shrink the city's footprint. They competed with residents to remap a new Detroit after the city's bankruptcy, where a downtown area dominated by white residents, tourists, and business owners developed in extractive relation to the rest of the predominantly Black city.

References to neighborhoods mapped not only unequal development, but the inequity of taking resources from poorer areas of the city to bolster richer ones. The inequity was not only a result of long-standing differences between the rich and poor or between white, Black, and Latina/o/x residents. It was also a product of how a variety of groups used data to obscure the political nature of development decisions, despite the significant investment of resources and the struggles that accompanied them.

The bordering practice of targeting some neighborhoods in the city had mixed success. The data-driven interventions claimed they would focus resources to prevent neighborhoods that were at a tipping point from experiencing greater vacancy. The plans looked like their urban renewal predecessors except place-based development did not enjoy federal funding. Southwest Detroit was an ideal case to test these plans. The area continued to lose population across all its census tracts in the period between 2000 and 2020 despite claims that targeted investment and data-driven interventions would stabilize neighborhoods.[94] Data did not take the politics out of urban development plans, it directed investments to favor some areas over others. This plan rationalized planning inequities even as it failed to realize planners' claim that targeting neighborhoods would stem population decline.

3

"Where You From?"

Property Claims as Abstractions

Detroit embodies both the American Dream and the multiple crises it generates. The city grew along with the industrialization of the United States. It developed its predominantly single-family housing and sprawling infrastructure according to Henry Ford's dreams of a city that assimilated immigrants through Americanization classes and livable wages of $5 a day. The manufacturing-centered economy was central to US prosperity following World War II. The 1944 GI Bill promoted low-cost mortgages as a benefit of service for many white GIs who took advantage of mortgages backed by the Federal Housing Authority (FHA) and migrated to the suburbs, creating the country's middle class. Banking practices subsidized white wealth as it redlined and undermined Detroit's development as a majority Black, hypersegregated city. Housing and development policies consistently undermined the ability of Detroiters to keep homes well into the twenty-first century.

The American Dream represents a desire for material prosperity and an aspiration of freedom and equality. It includes ownership of things like a car and a house. The paradox of owning is that the "thing" is rarely what we think it is. Instead, we make claims to ownership based on our rules about who gets what and why. We call these rules a "bundle of rights" that include possession, use, and exchange. These relations vary across time and societies. Land (real property) seems like a thing that can be owned, but in fact, it is a social relation between people that is written into law.

US law produced not only property rights but also whiteness as a form of property. Slave codes passed in 1680 and 1682 initially defined whiteness by default as neither Black nor subject to enslavement. This definition was reflected in John Locke's (1689) famous claim that "every Man has a Property in his own Person," which was a form of possession and a right to exchange not universal to African Americans before the Civil War. The Supreme Court expanded the meaning of white in *Johnson v. McIntosh* (1823) when it decided that the European and Christian arrivals to North America had the right of possession to lands previously occupied by Native Americans. Since then, laws continue to define property and whiteness through the right to exclude. Illustrative examples include Jim Crow laws throughout the South that used the so-called "one-drop rule" to exclude persons with any Black ancestry from a variety of freedoms including property ownership. US court decisions established whiteness as a de facto form of property that was recognized and protected by law.[1]

Latina/o/x and African American populations have collective experiences of being dispossessed of their property. For example, the city's industrial growth at the beginning of the twentieth century brought workers from Mexico and Texas.[2] The railroad intermodal was in Southwest Detroit, which brought many workers who settled in the area. They built families and their children enjoyed birthright citizenship. Despite their legal status, US citizens of Mexican ancestry were forcibly deported to Mexico during the Great Depression.[3] They were rejected as perpetually foreign, neither fully Mexican nor fully American. Their marginalized social status was compounded by Southwest Detroit's location at the border of the city and the United States. The twisted tangle of highways and railroad tracks lead cars and trucks in all directions away from the Ambassador Bridge that crosses to Canada. The area is unique in the city because it retained businesses and a resident population while the rest of the city experienced more significant forms of population loss and infrastructural decay. Some residents held onto property in the neighborhood by migrating back and forth from Texas and Mexico to Detroit for seasonal employment.[4] Others held onto real estate by renting to coethnics that may have had difficulties regularizing their legal status. This became an important avenue for social and spatial mobility because landlords could afford to buy additional property and more expensive homes in adjoining suburbs.

Latina/o/x who live in Southwest Detroit place a high value on owning their home despite the significant challenges associated with living amid heavy commercial traffic. They struggled with effective property tax rates that rank among the highest in the nation.[5] Detroit has a property tax exemption based on income, but the city denied access to many eligible residents.[6] The 1963 Michigan Constitution established property taxes could not exceed 50 percent of a home's value but the city "systematically and illegally inflated the assessed value of most of its residential properties."[7] Tax foreclosures were a fourth, but not necessarily final, among the myriad forms of dispossession facing Detroiters, including utility shutoffs, predatory lending, eviction, and mortgage foreclosure.

The difficulty many Southwest Detroit residents have in holding onto property meant they defensively guarded a sense of belonging as a form of honor they expressed in a variety of ways, including wearing caps and sweatshirts that emblazoned "Southwest Pride." When youth ask "Where you from?" they are likely to hear "Southwest" in response, as if Detroit was a separate entity. Latina/o/x youth living in the southwest area of the city traded on symbols of association as if they were part of a chest full of treasured beads and trinkets. What it meant to "be from Southwest" corresponded with large streets and highways crisscrossing the area whose borders mapped "the block," "the neighborhood," and "the community." For many residents, it also meant attending Western International High School, known for being in the heart of Southwest Detroit and for having a large population of Latina/o/x student and teachers. I interviewed youth who attended Western while Detroit Public Schools (DPS) struggled under emergency management and school closures. They felt living in the city while it experienced significant challenges legitimated their more authentic claim to "really be" from Southwest Detroit. This was one way of defensively bordering the area and distinguishing themselves from their peers who attended schools of choice outside of the city. Their borders mirrored those of Latina/o/x families who could trace back four generations of living in the area and who felt they had "paid their dues." They shared a conviction that they had earned the right to be in Southwest Detroit, even if that right had been inconsistently guaranteed by law.

"Paying your dues" drove many Latina/o/x Detroiter's defensive stance that they should be free to participate in the area's long-standing expressions of public art, worship in churches that traced back to the city's founding, and travel freely along the streets of Southwest Detroit regardless of a family's mixed legal status. It was an expression that challenged the abstractions of legal residence and citizenship. Legacy residents had stayed despite crime, arson, a lack of public services, expensive car insurance, high rent, and high property taxes. They had lived through daily experiences of struggles for property, which they felt bolstered their claim to freedom in the city. In their experience, however, they were not free from foreclosures, precarious housing, or crime. They were not free from a city government that had historically overlooked the neighborhood and from police officers who would arrive hours after they were called, if at all. They were not free from the collective abandonment symbolized by the vacant and decaying five-hundred-thousand-square-foot building that had once been the Michigan Central Station. They were not free from the exhaust of trucks that waited to unload at one of the railroad intermodals and idled illegally on residential streets. They were not free from the industrial waste emissions surrounding the area that continuously polluted the soil, water, and air. They were not free from disenfranchisement under multiple forms and periods of emergency management.

Latina/o/x Detroiters could not enjoy political representation once the city had declared bankruptcy. Unlike adjoining predominantly white suburban areas, they were not free to control land use, set property taxes, or determine zoning policies.[8] Unlike white homeowners, they were not free to take out prime mortgages that their income and credit history made them eligible for.[9] They were not free from unfair banking practices. They could not even walk freely in their own neighborhood, or *barrio*, because of the green lights flashing from businesses on all major streets. The lights indicated cameras that continually surveilled and racially profiled residents that were part of the Green Light Project and the "New Jim Code."[10]

Property as a Bundle of Rights

US law treats property as a "bundle of rights."[11] The founding fathers considered that these rights included "not only external objects and people's relationships to them, but also all of those human rights, liberties, powers, and immunities that are important for human well-being, including freedom of expression, freedom of conscience, freedom from bodily harm, and free and equal opportunities to use personal faculties."[12] In this conceptualization, property embodied the tension between the individual and the collective. The legal tendency to consider property claims in relation to an individual's racial identity preceded national independence; a 1662 Virginia law determined a child was free or enslaved based on its mother's status. The Constitution reinforced this tendency when it counted slaves as "three-fifths of all other persons" for the purposes of taxation and representation. As property was based on race, whiteness became "an object of law and a resource deployable at the social, political, and institutional level to maintain control . . . it became usable property, the subject of the law's regard and protection."[13] Whiteness became protection from the threat of being commodified. The seizure of Native Americans' land underscored that whiteness was required for the enforceable possession of land (*Johnson and Graham's Lessee v. McIntosh*, 1823). Since then, US laws continue to treat the status quo as a neutral baseline, normalizing the relationship between whiteness as freedom and granting white people the right to exclude.

US law prioritizes private property rights and exchange over common access and use. Reflecting general forms of neoliberal governance, Michigan and Detroit governments prioritized private over public interest. For example, in 1980, the city used eminent domain to seize a neighborhood known as "Poletown" for the promise of General Motors (GM) jobs. The lawyer representing the residents called the GM plant expansion plan a "one-way deal" between the company and the city government because it displaced a community of 1,500 homes, 144 local businesses, and 16 churches.[14] Governments' use of eminent domain for development projects has historically disadvantaged poor communities and people of color.[15] Most often, residents' mobilization was of little consequence relative to development goals. For example, Hamtramck cleared areas in the 1950s and 1960s for the Chrysler Freeway. The housing was not replaced, and almost three-quarters of the displaced residents were African American. Some of the residents filed a class action lawsuit in 1968 that would take over forty years to be settled. Even then, the settlement was limited to ordering new housing to be built and offered at below-market rates for the descendants of the original plaintiffs. The use of eminent domain continues to remain embattled with concerns about whose interests are advanced in the name of public interest and the common good.

Urban renewal projects and highway construction disrupted areas where racial and ethnic groups could concentrate their resources and build their communities. For example, with the support of the federal government, Detroit razed Black Bottom and Paradise Valley in the 1960s. The eastern and southern parts of Southwest Detroit were zoned industrial districts, but nonetheless home to a settled Mexican American community. The community remains beleaguered by highway expansions surrounding the international crossing. For instance, many African American and Latina/o/x residents were forcibly relocated from the area south of I-75 to accommodate the new Gordie Howe International Bridge.

The ways governments use the law to dispossess urban residents of property elucidates a more general way that treating private property as a right is not only an empty, but also an antisocial abstraction. Property takes on meaning through social relationships over time; property law is produced by powerful groups who treat property as if it has no social function or responsibility. Property becomes a thing, a commodity, that produces social relationships that prioritize individual ownership. One consequence of how US law treats property as a thing is that housing can remain vacant while people are homeless. US law does not consider property speculation that keeps a home or building vacant to be an illegal activity even though the speculation reduces housing supply, increases demand and cost, and damages communities.[16]

Laws in the United States are abstractions that compromise Latina/o/xs' social mobility. As a result, when people who identify themselves as of Latin American ancestry have moved to the suburbs, they have found a tenuous hold on socio-spatial mobility. For example, one resident I spoke with was Flor, who worried about her Deferred Action for Childhood Arrivals (DACA) status. She became pregnant, expected a different kind of bundle, and moved in with her boyfriend. When they became strapped for cash, they moved into his mother's house in a Detroit suburb about eight miles east of the city's border. Flor had lived her life up to that point in her parents' home in Southwest Detroit. She did not experience her move to the suburbs as a form of social mobility for several reasons, including that she was "scared" someone would break into the house and that the neighbors were gang members. After a couple of weeks, Flor learned her mother-in-law was facing foreclosure. She didn't understand what monies were owed and to who: "We were trying to figure that out and we weren't able to do much so they ended up taking the house away."[17] She spent two years after her baby was born fighting foreclosure on a house she did not own. Her struggle to secure a better life, at least in terms of owning a home, was unsuccessful. She paid in time during her youth for a negative experience of living outside Southwest Detroit.

The impending foreclosure was only one of a series of documentation-related abstractions that dispossessed Flor's family. Her boyfriend's father had been deported because his legal permit expired, and he "got pulled over" by police. The mother's permit was also about to expire, and, Flor explained, "it was a time where Trump was like, not letting anybody just renew anything. He [Flor's father-in-law] didn't renew it." In Flor's narrative, moving to the suburbs was tied up with a series of experiences and legal abstractions, including her status as unauthorized and undocumented, that left her feeling vulnerable and unsafe. She contrasted this with her current home in Southwest Detroit where she said she felt safe even though there was a bar on the corner.

Contrasting her move to the suburbs, Flor associated socio-spatial opportunity with a desire to control both her access to higher education and her housing. I asked what she considered an opportunity in our last interview. Her first response was almost immediate, "education," but then she paused for a long while. I restated my question: "How about this? I wish I could . . ." She thought for a bit and completed the sentence: "own my own house." I asked what that meant for her.

> I think being able to . . . do whatever you like to it, being able to make it your own home not having to worry about if something breaks, or it's not as much of a stress than if it's your own house. And I think even if you're paying it off, but it's not rent, you're not paying someone else for your . . . it's like you're paying, and at the end of the day, it's gonna be your own. And you're not worried about maybe getting kicked out or something happening. Yeah, I think those things. There's no having to worry about something else. Because you know, at the end of the day, it's going to be yours.

Flor's American Dream was not even about social mobility, but security. Her repeated emphasis on worry meant she associated owning her home with a freedom she still didn't have as a renter who had to rely on a landlord to get things done.

Gabi was another Detroiter that I interviewed who similarly suffered significant housing instability after a suburban home she had grown up in was lost in a fire. She was twenty years old when I interviewed her.

> So I was originally born here [Southwest Detroit]. And we lived here until I was about four years old. And then we moved out of the city, I lived with my grandparents.
> *She [Gabi's grandmother] was very, when she grew up here, being raised here, it was always about getting out of the city, you know what I mean? And escaping whatever was going on here and looking for a better life. That was kind of the narrative that my great-grandmother taught them [her kids].*
> *She left the city and we left. I was about four years old. And we stayed out there up until we lost our house, when I turned sixteen. We moved around a little bit. But there was a fire, so we lost our house.*
> I was just staying from place to place. And since I didn't really have somewhere I just got more and more involved with like, the community here [in Southwest Detroit] *and more involved with volunteering and just figuring out ways to spend my time so that way, I didn't have to find a place to stay.*

Gabi experienced significant housing instability during an important transition from her teen to adult years. Her grandmother and great-grandmother marked an intergenerational struggle for socioeconomic mobility. She felt living in the suburbs dispossessed her of something that was very important to her: a sense of self, stability, community, support, and belonging. She traced her family's settlement in Southwest Detroit to her great-grandparents, which suggested she had a fourth generation claim to being "from" Southwest Detroit. Unlike her grandmother and great-grandmother, she lived outside the neighborhood from four through sixteen years of age. Gabi felt living in the suburbs was a form of dispossession that she associated with space and property.

> *I struggle with it. I still consider this* [Southwest Detroit] *my community. And I consider that to myself. And I know that for me . . .*
> *I have a hard time really admitting that to other people, because I just feel I didn't go through the same struggle, and I don't want to*

own that struggle. I don't want to say that I represent that because I don't. I don't represent who grew up here and who had to face the hardships when they were a child, because I didn't, and I don't ever want to claim that.

Gabi's narrative indicated how she understood space in relation to individuals she knew and groups she wanted to be a part of. On the one hand, she felt her grandmother associated moving out of Southwest Detroit with a sense of accomplishment, of having "made it." According to Gabi, this also influenced her grandmother's marital choices and disregard for speaking Spanish in public. On the other hand, Gabi's own sense of not wanting to "own that struggle" of people who lived in SWD during their teenage, high school years reflected her belief about the difficult hardships that kids living in Southwest Detroit had experienced. She believed that experience legitimized their claim, because they had lived (and struggled) continuously in Southwest Detroit. Unlike them, Gabi's struggle involved her sense of self relative to "my community." Her claim was not one of ownership or possession, but of belonging because she had been born in Southwest Detroit (birthright) and her parents, grandparents, and great-grandparents had lived in the area (lived experience). Her personal history shaped her sense that she had a right to live, work, and belong in (to access and use) Southwest Detroit. The desire for authenticity versus the reality of not having shared daily experiences reflected broader trends that related to gentrification and neighborhood change.[18]

Gabi's claim was not limited to physical access and use of Southwest Detroit as a space of direct experience and struggle. Instead, she considered Southwest Detroit to be also a community whose struggles crossed time and space. Gabi had not considered that her experience of dispossession may have been shaped across generations.

So that was the, what, '60s? At the time when they came here?
And they came here from [city in Southern Texas], supposedly by . . .
When she was alive, she denied that she was born in Mexico. She had all of her papers burned, any identifying things. So there's no acknowledging that you're where we actually came from.

> *Supposedly she was born in California and then they moved to Texas at some point, but, there's no confirmation and I don't . . .*
>
> *During the time when my great grandma was alive, she always told my grandparents, and my aunts, and stuff like, that would never speak Spanish out of the house.*
>
> *"Do not acknowledge your heritage." She completely whitewashed them, so that way they could survive. Because when she was growing up, people always taunted her for speaking Spanish and they harassed her for it. And so, she did the best decision that she could at the time, and she thought that by erasing her culture that her kids would grow up and have a better life.*

Gabi's reference to her family's migration history indicates how law ties race to property. Her reference to her great-grandmother burning identity-related "papers" implies a form of property held in political membership.[19] Gabi suggested her great-grandmother was born in California, but experienced racialized otherness because she was taunted and harassed. Her great-grandmother "whitewashed" her children "so that way they could survive." These experiences reveal that "American" is an abstraction defined in relation to whiteness.[20]

Gabi said her family came to Southwest Detroit in the 1960s. One can infer her grandmother was born between 1940 and 1955. In other words, her great-grandmother was likely born in the 1920s and experienced the Great Depression. Gabi did not know about their history because "they don't talk about it." I told Gabi repatriation meant even citizens who were born in the United States were forcibly deported to Mexico. I explained people who eventually returned to Southwest Detroit had participated in an oral history project and expressed a consistent fear of being taken from their homes and, therefore, denied being born in Mexico. Many people of that generation, including in Southwest Detroit, told their kids, "Don't speak Spanish."[21]

Gabi struggled to understand her life experiences, because she hadn't "met anybody who has been taken out of the city and had to deal with it." She had only heard second hand that her uncle had also been sent to live in the suburbs and *"ripped away from everything, because we had family here. And suddenly, at the time where he was going through puberty and he needed support the most, he was completely ripped out and moved to a white neighborhood and went to white schools where nobody understood him."*[22]

Flor and Gabi illustrate very different understandings of private property. For Flor, having her own home represented an opportunity to avoid further housing instability and the associated experience of insecurity. For Gabi, private property marked dispossession from community, which she felt was greater than owning a house. Gabi's narrative underscored how forced migration could bind a group beyond limited conceptions of private property. It also reflected American families' lived experiences of physical and social instability.

(Southwest) Detroit Is Back . . .

Detroit symbolized the American Dream because it was a place where generations of people without a degree could work, own their own home, earn equity, and attain a measure of social mobility. Just before the housing crisis, the majority of African Americans residing in Detroit owned their own homes.[23] Census figures demonstrated that Hispanics shared a similar trajectory in Southwest Detroit where overall homeownership increased while it decreased in the city. Table 3.1 identifies the eight census tracts that the city defined as Southwest Detroit for one of its public-private partnerships, the Strategic Neighborhood Fund (SNF). Those tracts are mapped by the US Census (see figure 3.1).

There were at least three important distinctions between the area that the city and residents defined as Southwest Detroit. First, the city's "recovery" was an abstraction undermined by the concrete reality of continued population decline across the area (see table 3.1). The area was targeted not only by the city's SNF, but also by a variety of foundations that focused on creating jobs, increasing commerce, improving safety, and raising home values. The SNF-targeted southern area and the northern tracts of Southwest Detroit enjoyed unequal resources but lost a similar percentage of population over the twelve-year span. These trends were mirrored by the Hispanic population. The tracts north of John Kronk Street (census tract 9842) gained 360 Hispanic residents in

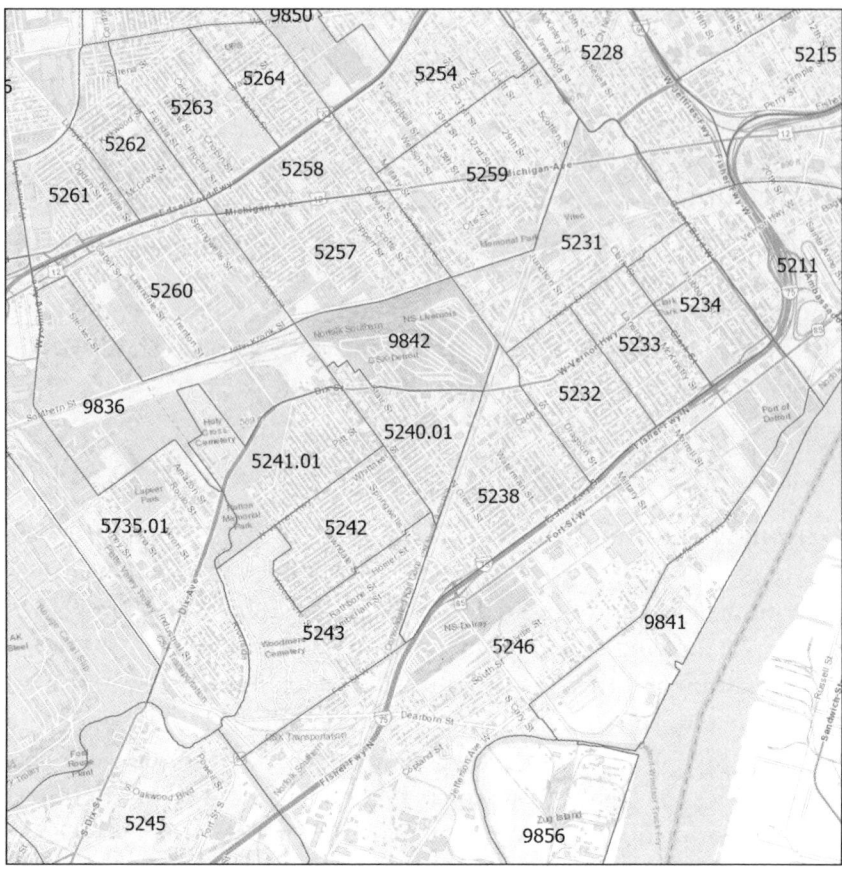

Figure 3.1. Census Tracts in Southwest Detroit

the period between 2010 and 2020, but the SNF-targeted tracts lost 1,570 Hispanic residents. Census tract 5231 lay east of 9842 and seemed to reflect the trajectory of the border area: it lost 212 Hispanic residents. Even northern tracts where the population of Hispanics grew by more than one hundred residents (5263 and 5264), saw greater overall loss in the total population. Dominican and Colombian restaurants opened in tracts 5262 and 5263 and a Honduran food truck parked in 5264, which reflected the growing diversity and relatively recent arrival of new migrants to Southwest Detroit. These trends indicated that the growth of Hispanic representation across Southwest Detroit was the result of general outmigration from area more than it was any significant growth in

Table 3.1. Southwest Detroit population by census tract (2010, 2020)

	Census Tract	Total Population			Percent Hispanic		
		2010	2020	Change	2010	2020	Percent Change
	5231	1,648	1,336	-18.9%	62.6%	61.4%	-20.5%
	5246	-	1,401	-	-	52.1%	-
	5257	5,445	4,403	-19.1%	66.6%	80.7%	-2.0%
	5258	2,091	1,781	-14.8%	65.9%	79.0%	2.1%
	5262	3,176	3,026	-4.7%	53.1%	57.8%	3.7%
	5263	3,635	3,345	-8.0%	69.7%	81.9%	8.1%
	5264	1,600	1,417	-11.4%	58.9%	76.1%	14.3%
	Total	14,347	12,555	-12.5%	63%	70%	7%
SNF-Targeted	5232	3,850	3,247	-15.7%	76.3%	80.7%	-10.7%
	5233	3,326	2,914	-12.4%	76.8%	80.5%	-8.2%
	5234	2,720	2,196	-19.3%	51.9%	45.1%	-29.8%
	5238	4,582	3,759	-18.0%	70.2%	76.9%	-10.1%
	5240	2,985	2,553	-14.5%	75.6%	80.1%	-9.5%
	5241	3,942	3,730	-5.4%	70.0%	74.2%	0.3%
	5242	4,964	4,366	-12.0%	72.0%	79.2%	-3.1%
	5243	2,812	2,626	-6.6%	70.9%	76.6%	0.9%
	Total	22,005	19,230	-12.6%	70%	74%	4%

Source: US Census Bureau 2010a; US Census Bureau 2020.

the numbers of the Hispanic population. The city mayor protested the 2020 Census counts for undercounting Black and Hispanic residents.[24] The city's website identifies the response rate for each tract: the average for Southwest Detroit was less than 50 percent.[25]

Census tract 5211 was only partly included in the SNF-targeted area and, therefore, excluded from this analysis. Tourists, residents, and the Google map referred to the area as "Mexican Town." The area had a Hispanic majority in 2010 but lost over a quarter of its population by 2020. It was the oldest part of what residents associated with Latina/o/x settlement in Southwest Detroit. For example, it hosted a variety of Mexican restaurants along Bagley Street that opened in the 1970s and that were located to the west and east of an eighteen-lane system interchange. The area also included other significant buildings that made up the Mexican American history of the eastern part of Southwest Detroit, including the Basilica of Sainte Anne, the second oldest continuously operating parish in the United States. The area was divided by a spaghetti highway that adjoined the Ambassador Bridge Toll Plaza and the US Customs and Border Protection Inspection Facility. It had experienced significant stress from the Ambassador Bridge owner's multiple (failed) attempts to build a second span, which included buying parcels in the area and demolishing homes. Mr. Krueger was an older white gentleman who lived in the area. I first met him in 2006 when I moved to Southwest Detroit and visited the home he bought from the city, gutted, and renovated. I saw him again at a July 2019 meeting when he asked to offer public comment. He cried as he begged attendees to abandon the Fiat Chrysler Automobile expansion proposal. He explained the bridge company had demolished properties next to his home and had been "a bad neighbor."[26]

A second important distinction between the city and resident defined boundaries was that the SNF-targeted area excluded seven Hispanic-majority census tracts (5231, 5246, 5257, 5258, 5262, 5263 and 5264) from its definition of Southwest Detroit. The SNF focused on tourism and commerce in the southern part of Southwest Detroit but minimized the interventions targeted at improving conditions for Hispanics in the area overall. Hispanic-majority tracts formed a pattern on the map that looked like a backward C: it started on the upper left of the map at 5262 and ended on the lower left in Delray (see figure 3.1). The heart of the C underscored the impact of John Kronk Street on the area: census tract 9842 was dedicated to a massive intermodal "non-place," or a transient space of circulation marked by a low degree of sociality.[27] It served trucks that traded across the international border with Canada. Homes north of John Kronk St. were degraded by highways, a high volume of truck traffic across six lanes, on and off ramps that slowed movement and concentrated noise and air pollution, gas stations, and collision, tire, and auto parts stores. Underpasses under the intermodal allowed traffic to cross to the southern side of Southwest Detroit along West Grand Boulevard, Clark, Junction, and Livernois Avenues, and Central Street. Many residents crossed several times a day to shop, conduct business, and foster personal ties across the Hispanic-majority area. The intermodal acted as one of several experiential borders in Southwest Detroit.

A final important distinction between the city's definition of Southwest Detroit only compounded Detroiters' frequent disregard for Delray and Oakwood Heights, which were areas that fell on the far southwest side of Southwest Detroit, west and south of the I-75 Fisher Highway. The vast swath of land along the Detroit River once housed thousands of families, churches, and a vibrant community.[28] Detroiters who lived in this far along the southwestern border area of the city felt trammeled by plans that Canada and the US Department of Transportation had made to develop another international crossing: the Gordie Howe Bridge. The city and the Marathon Refinery bought many residents out of the area: the city used a community benefits agreement tied to the Gordie Howe project and the refinery justified the expense as part of its environmental remediation efforts. These efforts meant few Hispanic residents (22/83) remained in Oakwood Heights (census tract 5245). Comparative census-tract-level data was not available for Hispanics in western Delray (census tract 5246), even though the 2020 US Census indicated they remained a majority in that area. City Council District six staff reported that Delray residents demanded to be acknowledged as part of the broader area.

The homes that remained in Delray shared among many empty lots, abandoned factories, and empty buildings surveilled by private security companies. The area was poorer and coexisted uncomfortably with truck traffic crossing the Ambassador Bridge and the variety of logistical and industrial companies (see table 3.2). The Marathon Refinery and Zug Island exemplified the surreal quality of life in the area: the island was off-limits to the public, the waters of River Rouge that surrounded it seemed to glow green like antifreeze, and summertime winds compelled residents' worries about uncovered metal ore and complaints about the foul smell in the air. It seemed no wonder that people passing through the area on the interstate preferred to close their windows and pretend people did not live there.

The fortunes of Hispanic residents in the northern and Delray sections of Southwest Detroit were neglected by how foundations and the city targeted their investments. Poverty rates among Hispanics decreased in the SNF-targeted area but barely budged in the northern section. Mean household incomes among Hispanics seemed comparable across Southwest Detroit, but the higher median incomes indicated that poor residents depressed averages within tracts (see table 3.2). This trend was particularly marked in tracts with high poverty levels: almost half of the Hispanic population fell below poverty in tracts 5231, 5246, 5262, 5263, 5264, 5232, 5241, and 5242. The median household income in Southwest

Table 3.2. Household income and poverty rate in Southwest Detroit

Census Tract	Household income (in the past 12 months) by Hispanic or Latino origin (of any race) of householder						Percent below poverty level in the past 12 months, Hispanic or Latino origin		
	Median			Mean			2012	2022	Change (2022 less 2012)
	2010	2022	Change	2010	2022	Change			
5231	29,206	45,833	16,627	9,078	13,434	4,356	23.5%	50.0%	26.5%
5246	31,898	18,986	-12,912	-	12,158	-	-	50.4%	-
5257	40,208	41,667	1,459	11,363	12,996	1,633	25.5%	23.5%	-2.0%
5258	40,208	43,452	3,244	8,771	13,556	4,785	66.0%	35.9%	-30.1%
5262	35,699	40,682	4,983	8,667	9,444	777	36.4%	48.4%	12.0%
5263	28,393	41,139	12,746	10,753	13,817	3,064	44.5%	46.4%	1.9%
5264	24,063	41,394	17,331	7,988	27,288	19,300	48.8%	44.9%	-3.9%
Average	32,811	39,022	6,211	9,437	14,670	5,912	44.2%	42.8%	-1.5%
5232 (SNF-Targeted)	21,172	47,623	26,451	6,361	11,898	5,537	42.4%	46.9%	4.5%
5233 (SNF-Targeted)	30,639	68,542	37,903	10,591	16,129	5,538	40.7%	21.1%	-19.6%
5234 (SNF-Targeted)	27,593	41,172	13,579	7,590	20,277	12,687	21.8%	18.0%	-3.8%
5238 (SNF-Targeted)	39,470	36,726	-2,744	9,209	16,066	6,857	36.6%	26.3%	-10.3%
5240 (SNF-Targeted)	36,438	57,401	20,963	-	19,655	-	-	19.3%	-
5241 (SNF-Targeted)	24,085	40,035	15,950	-	13,659	-	-	47.5%	-
5242 (SNF-Targeted)	34,856	40,810	5,954	12,932	14,763	1,831	29.9%	45.7%	15.8%
5243 (SNF-Targeted)	26,652	49,167	22,515	8,996	14,385	5,389	41.4%	21.9%	-19.5%
Average	30,113	47,685	17,571	9,280	15,854	6,307	35.5%	30.8%	-4.6%

Source: US Census Bureau 2010e; US Census Bureau 2012; US Census Bureau 2022b, 2022c, 2022d.

Detroit was $31,372 in 2010, but by 2022, it increased to $43,642. Average household incomes in Southwest Detroit fell well below the 2022 national average of $75,149.

Hispanic homeownership in Southwest Detroit in 2022 ranged from 17.6 percent to 68.2 percent (see table 3.3). Most Hispanic households were owner occupied: they owned the home they lived in. The majority of Southwest Detroit residents also owned their home, but there was a marked pattern of increased homeownership in the SNF-targeted census tracts. In contrast, there were declines in owner-occupied homes in the northern census tracts of Southwest Detroit, notably in 5258 that was bound on the south by the five-laned Michigan Avenue, on the east by another five-landed Livernois Avenue, and on the north by the I-94 Edsel Ford Freeway. The political decisions and human actions that produced the area created the sense that it had abandoned families who already experienced significant noise and air pollution from cars and trucks. For example, Martin Street bounded the eastern side of a three-block wide green space in the middle of the tract that was turned into a park. It was one of the tracts where the median home value of owner-occupied homes declined between 2010 and 2022. The tracts that experienced the greatest increases and declines in value were in the SNF-targeted area. The median value of a home in 5234 was more than double the city's median, but 5242 saw median home values decline by 36.8 percent.

Homeownership was high in Southwest Detroit and increased in the 12-year period between 2010 and 2022, while it decreased in the city overall. Hispanics were more likely to be homeowners than renters in Southwest Detroit, which was a trend that was not mirrored by the rest of the city where most residents became renters after 2010. Median value also increased across Southwest Detroit, especially in 5234. These trends indicated that homeownership in Southwest Detroit surpassed the city overall, even in non targeted tracts. In other words, homeownership and equity supported Southwest Detroiters' social mobility.

Table 3.3. Homeownership and vacancy rates in Southwest Detroit (2010, 2022)

	Census Tract	Homeownership (owner-occupied units/total occupied units)			Hispanic Homeownership (Hispanic homeowners/ Hispanic households)	Median Value of Owner-Occupied Housing Unit (dollars)			Occupancy Status (Vacant/Total)	
		2010	2022	Change	2022	2010	2022	Change	2010	2022
	5231	62.7%	66.3%	3.5%	66.2%	54,400	94,300	39,900	24.9%	17.5%
	5246	-	35.8%	-	27.6%	-	44,400	-	-	27.6%
	5257	53.4%	53.4%	0.0%	54.3%	59,800	53,500	-6,300	24.3%	11.9%
	5258	62.5%	48.1%	-14.4%	54.1%	50,700	40,000	-10,700	37.9%	21.3%
	5262	64.2%	59.8%	-4.4%	54.4%	60,300	52,100	-8,200	37.4%	15.6%
	5263	48.1%	57.4%	9.4%	64.3%	57,300	57,600	300	31.3%	16.0%
	5264	46.0%	47.5%	1.5%	42.7%	48,700	50,400	1,700	20.1%	21.8%
	Average	58.2%	53.5%	-4.7%	52.0%	56,500	56,983	3,000	31.2%	18.3%
SNF-Targeted	5232	51.9%	67.5%	15.5%	68.2%	76,100	82,500	6,400	30.0%	22.1%
	5233	38.1%	61.1%	23.0%	66.9%	64,200	64,800	600	26.8%	24.9%
	5234	21.9%	39.4%	17.6%	57.6%	77,600	183,100	105,500	21.5%	30.2%
	5238	56.5%	59.9%	3.5%	52.6%	60,900	75,500	14,600	25.5%	13.7%
	5240	40.9%	51.4%	10.4%	56.9%	57,200	79,800	22,600	14.0%	11.8%
	5241	40.1%	48.1%	8.0%	60.0%	74,700	55,900	-18,800	13.4%	19.1%
	5242	50.7%	64.5%	13.9%	60.5%	71,700	45,300	-26,400	27.0%	17.1%
	5243	44.0%	50.4%	6.4%	50.8%	57,200	62,300	5,100	20.1%	16.5%
	Average	43.0%	55.3%	12.3%	59.2%	67,450	81,150	13,700	22.3%	19.4%
	Detroit City	54.5%	48.8%	-10.5%		80,400	82,500	2,100	25.8%	22.8%

Source: US Census Bureau 2010a, 2010c; US Census Bureau 2022a, 2022d.

Vacancy tended to be lower in Southwest Detroit compared to the city overall in 2010. The exceptions were three northernmost tracts: 5258, 5262, and 5263, which were higher than the city's average. By 2022 those tracts fell below the city's average. In contrast, 5232 and 5233, both in the SNF-targeted area, fell above the city's average vacancy rate in 2010. Although 5232 fell below the city's average by 2022, 5233 remained above the city's average. The vacancy rate in a tract that abutted Clark Park mirrored the rapidly gentrifying tract of 5234 that also came to have a vacancy rate higher than the city's average in 2022. Investors may have bought properties in these tracts and kept them vacant in hopes of reselling for a higher price. This was a common complaint about the YMCA building that had been boarded up and vacant since 2001, when it was purchased by Dennis Kefallinos. Residents considered him a real estate speculator and lamented the visible reminder of a resource the community had lost. Vacancy in Delray tract 5246 was also higher than the city's average in 2022. It was one of only two tracts in Southwest Detroit that had higher vacancy rates than the city.

Property and homeownership differ in Southwest Detroit. For example, when compared to other tracts in Southwest Detroit, census tract 5234 had the lowest rate of homeownership in 2010 and a low rate in 2020. Most residents were renters, but it was the tract where the difference between the median and the mean household income was greatest, which signaled a concentration of high-earning households created greater inequality in the area. The area's diversity extended to Vinewood Street whose residents tended to be professionals. The area's diversity extended to Vinewood Street, part of Hubbard Farms, whose residents tended to be professionals and well-organized to advocate for their block. Their street was lined with stately homes that have brick and greystone exteriors. The tract also included similar grand homes along four-lane wide West Grand Boulevard that accommodated a tree-lined median. Clark Park lies within the tract and offered residents a recreational space almost entirely transformed since the bankruptcy by new streetlights, brick columns with iron signs on top announcing the park name, exercise equipment, manicured flowerbeds, and trees buffering I-75 on its southern border. There was a higher rate of turnover in that area because of how quickly its property values increased after the city's bankruptcy and because of the sale of the nearby Michigan Central

Station to the Ford Motor Company. The City advocated for the park as an important destination in Detroit.

Homeownership increased the most in census tract 5233. The area's northern border is marked by Vernor Highway that cuts across Southwest Detroit. Duly's Place Coney Island is a Detroit institution, in part because it is over a hundred years old and made memories for generations of the area's youth. Many young adults continue to visit the twenty-four-hour diner in the early morning hours after going to El Club, a relatively new music venue open until 2 a.m. all week. The two businesses mark the old and new: Duly's runs a Facebook page with frequent posts about the neighborhood's past. In contrast, El Club's owner came to Detroit after its bankruptcy and after his club in Los Angeles had failed. He made headlines several years later for wage theft and racial discrimination.[29] The Mutiny Tiki Bar, Flowers of Vietnam, and Flamingo Vintage were other new businesses that also opened after the city's bankruptcy. They drew a new form of tourism to the area that sought more than Mexican food at the area's long-standing restaurants. Legacy residents did not tend to frequent the new establishments.

Vernor Highway mapped the "two Detroits."[30] It continued west from Duly's with chain businesses like the Dollar Tree, Dollar General, McDonald's, and Burger King on its northern and southern sides. Seven railroad tracks crossed over it before heading northwest and splitting off into dozens more rail lines toward a coaling tower. Vernor Highway followed under two underpasses to a five-way intersection and turned abruptly southwest when it divided from Dix Street. It cut through the center of census tract 5240 and followed west as the southern border for census tract 5241, which lie at the northwest edge of Southwest Detroit. Census tract 5241 had a mix of renters and owners who, in 2022, had the lowest median and mean income in Southwest Detroit. Its residents also had the highest poverty rate in 2022 compared to all other census tracts in Southwest Detroit, even considering the areas in the northern part of Southwest Detroit that saw an increase in its relative Hispanic population. This census tract abutted the large industrial area north of Dix Street whose businesses included salvage yards, scrap metal dealers, and sand, gravel, concrete, and aggregate suppliers. The mounds of gravel and dump and haul trucks looked over Holy Cross Cemetery, which occupies about a third of the census tract. It was filled with beautiful headstones and sculptures marking graves of people born in the late nineteenth and early twentieth centuries. The residents here were poorer and their vinyl-sided homes were more modest. Poverty in 5241 and 5242 increased after 2010. Tiny front yards, older cars, and battered work trucks lined the area's streets. It did not differ appreciably from census tract 5242, which lay just south of Vernor Highway and west of Central Street. Homes in both tracts were worth more in 2010, before the city's bankruptcy. The homes in 5243 that are just south of these areas and that abut Woodmere Cemetery only gained about $5,100 in value over twelve years, which demonstrated how little the area's residents benefited from the city's celebrated renaissance.

When the Bough Breaks: Local Dispossession and the National Foreclosure Crisis

There were many ways Detroiters were dispossessed of real property after 2000, when interviewees like Gabi and Flor were children. There were also several reasons why the housing bubble burst earlier in Detroit. One was that the state-appointed emergency manager controlled and closed public schools. Many residents opted to give up on their struggles for the city and move out to suburban areas.[31] Another reason was that unemployment increased in the years preceding the national, and then global Great Recession. Homeowners in Detroit felt especially desperate to sell as they saw their taxes continue to increase because assessments were not adjusted for decreasing real estate values, which only compounded the troubles associated with the decreasing value of their homes.

Well after its bankruptcy in 2013, the city continued to place the burden of learning about and proving eligibility for the property tax exemption for homeowners in poverty. Estimates were that anywhere from 53 to 84 percent of residential properties had taxes assessed over the state constitutional limits of 50 percent of a property's market value. The disparities increased for middle- and lower-valued properties. In other words, the 20 percent of residential properties having the lowest value (less than $9,000 in sales price) were most likely to be assessed over the constitutional limit.[32]

The city inflated the assessed value of residential properties and the county also foreclosed "at historic rates for non-payment of property taxes."[33] Most (90 percent) tax auction purchases since 2002 were principally to bulk buyers who neglected their properties, destabilized neighborhoods through eviction, and withheld property taxes only to buy the same properties back at another tax foreclosure auction.[34] The shifting ownership often left structures unoccupied and untended for long periods of time, which resulted in their rapid decline. The inflation of tax bills and foreclosure of properties was only the beginning in a series of events that could turn an occupied home into a vacant property that might be considered blighted and then demolished by the city.

Tax foreclosures only added to myriad forms of dispossession, including utility shutoffs and liens that were subsequently put onto tax bills, evictions, and mortgage foreclosures. The lack of government regulation across the country enabled such scale of subprime mortgage lending to African American and Latina/o/x homeowners that the term predatory lending gained increased prominence.[35] Many cities increased their reliance on practices that dispossessed vulnerable populations, but states and the federal government also facilitated practices that treated homeowners like prey. Michigan, the Wayne County Treasurer, and Detroit created land banks that facilitated access to foreclosed properties for speculative buyers. The Emergency Economic Stabilization Act of 2008 seemed to ensure wide-scale economic speculation. Federal funds that should have helped homeowners were redirected to the mayor's demolition program. Detroit was a city of homeowners that became one of renters: approximately 36 percent of its homes went into foreclosure between 2005 and 2014.[36]

At a national level, the Latina/o/x population was particularly devastated by the bank foreclosure crisis. Unlike Sunbelt cities that were impacted by overheated demand, Rustbelt cities like Detroit were particularly hard hit due to unemployment and weak housing demand. If Sunbelt cities were excluded from the analysis, the Detroit-Warren-Livonia Metropolitan Statistical Area (MSA) was first in the nation for real-estate-owned property (REO) density in the period between August 2006–2008.[37] Latina/o/xs made up 11 percent of mortgage originations between 2005 and 2008, but 16 percent of foreclosures in the 2007–2009

Table 3.4. Average poverty status in past 12 months, selected Detroit metropolitan suburbs

Gabi's suburb	Flor's suburb	Southwest Detroit	Detroit City
24%	35%	39%	35%

Source: US Census Bureau 2019.

period.[38] Analyses traced the disproportionate impact of foreclosure on the Latina/o/x population to a number of variables, including marketing of subprime loans to borrowers of color, targeting racially segregated areas, and exploiting social networks of trust.[39] Flor's case indicated how foreclosures also increased with intensified internal immigration enforcement.[40] The federal government passed the "Secure Communities" program in 2008 that required that police share information about arrests with federal authorities. The effects of the foreclosure crisis also stretched over a much longer period for the Latina/o/x population. Over the 2001–2013 period, Hispanic homeowners were more likely to enter foreclosure than Black or white owners.[41]

Flor and Gabi's experiences indicated how the consequences of losing a home meant many Latina/o/x families moved to neighborhoods that were more segregated and had higher poverty rates.[42] Homes in minority neighborhoods experienced smaller growth in equity over time. The housing crisis not only intensified Latino-white disparities in the period between 2007 and 2009, but it also had a disproportionate effect on leaving Hispanic homeowners with negative equity.[43]

Detroiters' access to housing became increasingly dependent on renting, occupying property without authorization, and alternate financing for a home, including risky land contracts in areas where there was a lack of traditional financing.[44] Detroit's district court treated land contract holders the same as landlord-tenant cases, which facilitated eviction. Low-income renters might pay close to market rent for accommodations that might not meet city codes, but they were particularly vulnerable to landlord and land contract abuses that helped them avoid being evicted, homeless, and experiencing the compounded effects of displacement, including missing work, losing a job, and/or securing another home with a record of an eviction.[45]

The Latina/o/x community of Southwest Detroit has long relied on neighbors and family living nearby to finance homes. Land contracts are often informal. Many residents purchased homes and side lots from the city but complained about code violation enforcement that expanded following the city's bankruptcy and the city's efforts to combat what it considered blight.[46] Many vacant lots adjoined one another, creating wide open areas throughout the neighborhood that hosted illegal dumping and that were patrolled by stray dogs. There were protective neighborhood norms that discouraged residents from involving city officials in cases where occupancy codes were violated. Southwest Detroit residents looking to rent or own a home were particularly vulnerable to individuals and companies who monopolized financial and human capital. As one resident explained, "It's difficult if you don't know the rules and regulations."[47]

Another factor that intensified the metro Detroit area's experience of the housing crisis was that land contracts became increasingly common as people lost their homes. For example, residents in Southwest Detroit purchased properties in need of significant repairs and offered informal contracts to tenants who may not have had the credit or legal status to qualify for a mortgage. This attracted residents who might draw on personal experience or relationships with someone in the construction industry to help them fix a roof or install a furnace. Many Southwest Detroit residents felt it was in their interest to engage in these transactions in order to keep their block from having too many vacant properties that might become a fire hazard. For example, Fausto talks about how Southwest Detroit and familial connections helped his uncle's family recover from their foreclosure.

> Through my mom, my uncle was able to get advice, like, "Oh, um, you know, we're in a really bad financial situation right now. How is Detroit? You know, how expensive are the houses? What are the rules of how things work over there compared to over here in [suburban area in a neighboring state] where things are done kind of . . . more the right way? We have to make payments on the house. And now we can't do it anymore. So, we got to foreclose, you know?"

Fausto implied his uncle could not follow the formal rules of making regular monthly payments. He said his mother told his uncle that there were other informal options for owning a home that were available in Southwest Detroit. Many of these options attracted new people to the city.⁴⁸

Property Claims: The Scale of Abstraction and Its Impacts on Local Control

Gabi and Flor were young children in 2000, but they shared experiences that were shaped by collective struggles over property. Over the course of the next twenty years, as they grew into adults, Detroiters continued to struggle to realize the American Dream of owning your own home. For the Latina/o/x population of Detroit, however, this version of the American Dream was locked in struggles over property claims whose meaning was informed by generations of dispossession.

The Mexican-origin population of Southwest Detroit shaped the area's character. Early migrants from Mexico followed other immigrants who were pulled to the city by the demand for industrial labor. Struggles over land drove some migrants to settle during the Mexican Revolution. Many of these settled migrants and their children who were US citizens were nonetheless quickly dispossessed and repatriated to Mexico during the Great Depression.⁴⁹ Families were stripped of constitutional protection and right to due process when they were deported. The removal was complemented by President Herbert Hoover's plan to promote "American Jobs for Real Americans," which deprived US citizens of Mexican ancestry of other forms of cultural belonging. For example, local laws barred people of Mexican descent from government jobs and Ford was among major employers who laid off thousands of Mexican American workers.⁵⁰ Some residents of Southwest Detroit were displaced when the Ambassador Bridge was built (1927–1929), others when the I-75 highway cut through the Mexican American community abutting St. Anne's Basilica, and still others when the bridge expanded in 2009. Residents continued to be forcibly displaced and relocated in 2016 to accommodate a new international bridge crossing the Detroit River, the Gordie Howe International Bridge project.

This history shaped the meaning of owning your home in Southwest Detroit, including the front gate many homeowners installed to visibly mark their property. The gate was a bordering practice that produced space as part of their lived experience. It exercised nonhuman agency in ways that stood opposed to the kinds of abstraction used to dispossess

Flor and Gabi of their family's property.[51] Gabi and Flor's experience of losing their homes indicated how space was produced through competition with businesses and policymakers.

Abstractions furthered some property claims at the expense of others. For example, "sprawl" implied unmanaged spatial expansion and a decline in population density. It produced Detroit as a problem for spatial management and intervention. In contrast, when applied to its adjoining suburb, Oakland County executive Brooks Patterson proudly declared he loved sprawl; that he needed it, promoted it, and his county couldn't get enough of it. He believed sprawl represented jobs and population growth, generated taxes, and funded schools and services, which attracted yet more people and jobs.[52] The contrasting use of sprawl when it referred to Detroit City and Oakland County demonstrated how different actors produced space in relation to different people (racialized as white, Latino, or Black) and their to move into and out of the city.

Patterson's comments illustrated that abstract population shifts did not produce suburban growth. Instead, business and government engaged in bordering and crossing practices and produced the metropolitan area. For example, the development of a large suburban ring surrounding Detroit depended on access to water from the Detroit River. The Detroit Water and Sewer Department (DWSD) supported that growth in two ways. First, it created an infrastructure for water delivery and sewage. The city took on significant debt to finance that expansion: "Between 1956 and 1968 . . . the City of Detroit issued a total of US $147.5 million in bonds to finance expansion and received at least US $50 million in federal aid."[53] Second, DWSD provided water to suburban areas at wholesale prices, but municipal authorities would sell the water to residential and commercial customers at retail prices with "some charging almost 1,000 percent of the wholesale rate."[54] In practice, this meant white suburbanites resented the city's control over DWSD. Their political leaders' rhetoric repeatedly challenged the DWSD's management and water rate increases in the courts from the mid-1970s through the 1980s.

One consequence of suburban growth was that the Environmental Protection Agency (EPA) sued the DWSD in 1977 because of wastewater that overflowed into the Detroit River. Federal Judge John Feikens was put in charge of overseeing DWSD for the next thirty-five years. His authority over DWSD was an example of how space was scaled to ever-increasing levels of abstraction and control because it mirrored and expanded white suburban politicians' frustration at not being able to control DWSD. He opined, "One of the things that we have to give black people the time to learn to do is to learn how to run city governments, to run projects like the water and sewer plant. Unfortunately, they're still in an era of development, many of them, in which they think that all you have to do is talk about this thing."[55] Feikens and suburban leaders used law to control DWSD from a distance. He signed an order in 1999 that shouldered Detroiters with 83 percent of the construction costs for the "'Non-Detroit Only' and 'Non-Common to All'" parts of a combined sewer outflow (CSO) system.[56] Similarly, Feikens's administration and the master plan of 2004 directly undermined Young's earlier attempts to rely on revenue to run DWSD. They reorganized DWSD and made it more dependent on debt capital.

Patterson and Feikens are examples of struggles to border and limit the meaning of home rule and local control in a Black-governed city. They competed at different scales of authority to produce Detroit. Their authority was codified through abstract laws and administrative boundaries that conditioned how people could exercise local control.[57]

Home Rule, Local Control, and Self-Determination

The US Constitution provided a legal framework for Patterson's and Feikens's different types of authority. It also outlined a government structure that valued private property and granted states broad powers to shape their relationship with municipal governments. Michigan is one of about ten "home rule" states in the United States, which means it shifts significant control over legislation to local governments. The concept of home rule parallels private property ownership insofar as one generally equates the latter with the ability to "rule" over one's home. Similarly, albeit at a grander scale, the abstractions of home rule and local control underpinned many Detroiters' struggles for democracy and self-determination.

Michigan's 1908 constitution made it a home rule state. Over 90 percent of Detroiters at the time were white. They framed and adopted their first charter in 1909 and established local home rule for the city. The period between 1909 and 1967 bookended an important demographic shift between Detroit's emergence as a major urban center and residents' sense they no longer controlled their government. The proximate reason for the 1967 rebellion (alternately referred to as a "riot") was a police raid of a blind pig, but similar instances of civil unrest in cities across the country revealed African Americans shared a collective experience of being policed, harassed, and subordinated to property laws at the expense of their civil rights.

The circumstances surrounding urban racism seemed less evident to US President Lyndon B. Johnson who commissioned an investigation of the disturbances across the country. The resulting Kerner Report warned, "Our nation is moving toward two societies, one black, one white—separate and unequal." The report concluded, "White society is deeply implicated in the ghetto. White institutions created it, white institutions maintain it, and white society condones it."[58] The report held white society and its institutions responsible for a relation that resulted in the Black "ghetto."[59]

In the wake of the rebellion, Detroiters' alternate vision of self-determination took shape in relation to white flight and the city's increased racial marginalization. Home rule and local control became a reality for Black Detroiters in 1974 when they elected the city's first Black mayor, Coleman Young. He was part of an active political elite, rejected Black subordination to white-dominated institutions, and advocated local community control as "the natural outgrowth of black power."[60] One example of what many journalists considered Young's bold and brash style was reflected in his presentation before the US House Un-American Activities Committee. He corrected a member, Committee Counsel Frank S. Tavenner Jr.: "That word is 'Negro,' not 'Niggra.'" Tavenner apologized, and Young told him to "Speak more clearly." After another exchange, Young explained he resented "the slurring of the name of my race."[61] He suggested Tavenner's Southern background was to blame not only for the mispronunciation, but more generally for the illegitimacy of his authority that kept African Americans from voting. Similar incidents explained why Young remained popular among Detroit voters for five terms: He embodied a city unafraid of speaking out against racism and asserting Black pride.[62]

Young's election expanded the meaning of property ownership beyond individuals and the associated bundle of rights toward collective productions of spaces that explicitly expressed collective possibilities. For example, Detroit Police responded to the 1967 rebellion with a special task force called STRESS (Stop the Robberies, Enjoy Safe Streets). It relied on police patrols and practices that have more recently been referred to as proactive policing. Young disbanded STRESS in 1976 and appointed William Hart as the city's first African American police chief. The changes in policing practices were eventually complemented by a police force dominated by African American officers who lived and worked in a majority Black city.

The meaning of white supremacy and anti-Blackness in metropolitan Detroit was informed by the 1967 rebellion, which Young blamed for decimating the city's tax base. He wrote in his biography that white people's reaction to the rebellion put the city "on the fast track to economic desolation, *mugging the city and making off with* incalculable value in jobs, earnings taxes, corporate taxes, retail dollars, sales taxes, mortgages, interest, property taxes, development dollars, investment dollars, entertainment dollars, tourism dollars, and plain damn money. The money was *carried out in the pockets* of the businesses and the white people who fled as fast as they could."[63] Young explicitly blamed white people who left the city for the theft of its resources. His response to the exodus of people, businesses, and "dollars" was to create a quasi-governmental body in 1978 that could focus on promoting downtown development. The Detroit Economic Growth Corporation (DEGC) was part of his strategic alliance with Henry Ford, the United Auto Workers (UAW), local real estate developers, and private developers. His response indicated the constraints placed on Black governance, even though he claimed to be unlike his predecessors who prioritized investors and ignored the needs of the city's African American population.[64]

Young was a popular mayor, but he was not without his critics. White suburbanites and public officials clearly and consistently implied he was corrupt. Black leftists criticized Young's decisions in ways that mirror the patterned relation between white supremacy, anti-Blackness, and accumulation by dispossession. For example, Kenneth Cockerel Sr. claimed

Young's development policies favored "upscale educated affluent young types who really can make a contribution to the tax base being brought back to eat quiche while the poor are taxed out of their homes."[65] His perspective underscored how space, race, and class compelled the city to cater to outsiders rather than residents. Cockerel was a Black city council member elected as an "independent socialist" and part of the Detroit Alliance for a Rational Economy (DARE) that opposed private property and advocated organizing the "process of production to meet the needs of the people who do the producing."[66] He lamented that Detroit had become a model of urban revitalization designed to promote private-sector profits through tax abatements, tax increment financing, bond schemes, and zoning. These practices were not unlike those currently pursued by many urban development policies.

Mayor Coleman Young recognized the city's demography mapped onto the racialized production of property value. He pointed out that he had "urged city and suburban cooperation in speech after speech and gone out to the suburbs to make the point [about the need for regional cooperation] in person (although I can't recall anybody from the suburbs coming to the city for that purpose)."[67] Young crossed borders into suburban areas but his frustration with the city's "mugging" demonstrated that, rather than a right, bordering practices excluded both the mayor and properties in the city from the region's housing bubble.[68] People leaving the city felt they owned what they took, but their departure was also an abandonment that injured the city. The city they created was subsequently associated with population loss and decay in the regional and national media.

The interests of investors often conflicted with urban residents. Cities depend on investors to finance development, which often conflicts with local, democratic control. This became increasingly true after the 1967 rebellion as Black Detroiters found they did not share the same ability as suburbanites to sell their homes, much less profit from the sale. The value of Black Detroiters' homes eroded as media, politicians, suburbanites, and others produced Detroit narrowly in terms of its racial and spatial difference from white suburban areas. New suburban areas surrounding the city grew in size and value in relation to the borders they erected around the city.[69] The suburban areas they migrated to, including Southfield and Oak Park, had older housing stock, which meant newer Black suburban homeowners spent more than their white counterparts on home maintenance and repair.

Detroiters seemed to gain "a right to the city" after the 1967 rebellion, but the cultural and symbolic rebuilding of the Black city eroded residents' control over their property.[70] For example, when Feikens determined Detroit would pay 83 percent of the cost to develop the water department's infrastructure for suburban homes, a majority Black population in the city subsidized the development, property value, and wealth of majority white suburban areas. This value was secured by suburban leaders who nonetheless expressed their sense of having suffered because they could not control the city's water sewer system.[71]

Young's references to mugging, making off, and carrying money out of the city implied an illegal loss of both tangible and intangible property. This included not only the businesses that left the city, but also the potential returns to the city in the form of tax revenue. Young's assertion also implicated racism as a form of looting because it drained the city of actual and potential resources. Despite evidence of Young's extensive efforts to attract investment and revitalize the city's downtown area, he explicitly recognized how racism undermined development when he observed that "white investors were not too interested in investing into a city where blacks made up both most of the population and city hall. Instead, they opted for the mostly white surrounding suburbs."[72]

White suburbanites and suburban officials resented Young in the decades after the 1967 rebellion; they blamed Detroiters for the city's fortunes. Even Federal Judge Feikens generalized his comments about Young's administration when he characterized 1984 as an era of political development for all Black people. The popular Warren County commissioner and public relations executive Richard Sabaugh concurred: "It's all as one complex—blacks, Coleman Young, crime, drugs, Detroit . . . people feel they've been driven out once, and it could occur again."[73] Sabaugh recasts the decisions white homeowners made to move to the suburbs and the control they had over their lives and property as a *lack* of control over a city they had abandoned. There were many historical examples of the relation that revanchism revealed.

Revanchism also implicates a conceptual inversion that patterns racism. For example, Young was frequently charged with reverse racism against suburban whites. When he died in 1997, Patterson claimed Young had been "hell-bent on . . . getting even" for racism and discrimination and had destroyed Detroit.[74] White suburbanites blamed Young and Detroit's Black population for racism. For example, a suburban educator criticized Young for manipulating "the racism that was rampant within Detroit. There is reverse racism, and Coleman very cynically played black against white for his own ends."[75] Suburbanites imagined they were excluded even as they avoided going into the city or recognizing all the ways it served suburban interests. The projections were echoed by media and law, which elucidated how whiteness is a form of property: White identity politics were profitable and promoted white people's "possessive investment in whiteness."[76]

Summary

A home is to the American Dream what property is to freedom. People born in the United States are socialized to associate security and upward social mobility with suburban home ownership. The American Dream is not what it was in midcentury America. Latino/a/x people who lived in Southwest Detroit struggled to hold onto their homes despite a variety of attacks on their everyday life, including racial profiling, unemployment, increasing rent and declining property values, first mortgage and then tax foreclosure, high car insurance, and closing schools. Latino/a/x people who moved to suburban areas experienced another new set of disadvantages shaped by racism that are not typically associated with social mobility. Latina/o/x youths' experiences contrasted the abstraction of property and demonstrated that belonging was not limited to ownership and value was not always determined by markets. Latina/o/x youth did not define property narrowly in terms of the material ability to control one's life, but instead focused on a sense of belonging to a community, an ethnic "Southwest Pride," and a sense of having paid your dues. They tied the value of property to the experience of contemporary and past community members. They also associated property with time and generational struggles to produce their homes, their neighborhoods, the city, and the nation they were a part of. Detroiters struggled collectively to produce space as a form of individual and collective self-determination.

Law produced abstractions that enabled the transfer of property in the form of land and slaves. As indicated in the case of Detroit, abstractions are also codified through language. Words like "sprawl" and "racism" gained meaning through the population they refer to. For example, Patterson loved sprawl when applied to a suburban county. Applied to Detroit, however, "sprawl" implies a problem for urban intervention and management. Similarly, suburban whites projected their sense of being an object of "racism" despite having the ability and means to leave the city. Their choice to move to the suburbs depended in large part on being white. In this chapter I have referred to the duplicitous nature of these abstractions as conceptual inversions.

4

Big Data, Big Money

Gerrymandering, Bankruptcy, and Demolition

Three cases elucidate how empty abstractions operated as bordering and crossing practices. The first was REDMAP, a gerrymandering project that expanded the use and powers of emergency management. The second was Detroit's bankruptcy, which elucidated how the relation between state and city government was shaped in relation to the production of racial difference and accumulation through dispossession. The city's demolition program was another blow following waves of mortgage and tax foreclosures, state, county, and city land bank auctions, and real estate speculation. The program complemented the production of vacancy as an investment opportunity and played a vital role in producing new demand for real estate.

The Detroit bankruptcy was critical to the other two cases because it marked a coordinated shift in the metropolitan area that was not captured by dominant comparisons to other "naturally" shrinking or legacy cities. It was not inevitable, but the bankruptcy resulted in and coincided with the election of the city's first white mayor in forty years. One outcome of the bankruptcy was a demolition program that furthered a collective sense that "Detroit is being re-everything: revitalized, rebuilt, reborn, renewed, refurbished, revamped, restored, redeveloped."[1] Demolition was a spectacular performance of socio-spatial transformation that depended on the abstraction of abandonment. Difficulties with the rushed demolition program, its lack of transparency, and the lack of accountability underscored that many Detroit neighborhoods and their legacy residents experienced patterned isolation and were further marginalized as stakeholders in the city's future.

There are as many ways of understanding the largest municipal bankruptcy in the nation's history as there are stories about what makes Detroit a national icon. This chapter argues that changes in finance and government bordering practices compelled the city's bankruptcy (2013–2014). The event was something like a "shock doctrine" that caused the city to lose many of its assets and that allowed the state to impose a Financial Review Commission to oversee many of the city's governing structures.[2] Michigan produced Detroit's bankruptcy as a disaster to make Detroit great again for new arrivals who were predominantly white, young urban creatives.

REDMAP

Many scholars have analyzed the role of neoliberal policies in reshaping urban policy. An equally important development have been racist challenges to Black-governed cities and, more generally, racist backlashes to Black leaders' political authority. For instance, following the election of the nation's first Black president in 2010, the Republican Party reconsidered their "dog whistle" strategies that had been successful since the 1970s.[3] Leading Republican strategists used maps and big data to reshape legislative and congressional districts across the United States. Although gerrymandering has a long history in the United States, what came to be known as the REDistricting Minority Project (REDMAP) relied on a variety of novel bordering practices that proved consequential in many state and local elections.

The decennial US Census uses a system of tracts, blocks, and groups to correlate people with property. It is a bordering practice that facilitates some forms of crossing and constrains others. For example, critics claim the census systematically undercounts the Latina/o/x population across the country. The undercount occurs for a variety of reasons, including language barriers, low educational attainment, legal status, large household sizes, and the presumption that all people are tied to a single household. The systematic undercount reflects the population's relative inability to cross administrative borders and be accurately reflected in national numbers. Nonetheless, each Dicennial Census, figures are used to redraw voting districts.

REDMAP followed the 2010 Census and used data and technology to redraw legislative district maps that favored Republican candidates. Drawing gerrymandered districts was a bordering practice used by both parties that traced back to the late 1800s, but it was squarely localized and tied to people and politics located within a particular state or district.

What made REDMAP unique was that it encouraged some forms of crossing: It pulled Republican consultants to redistrict every state legislative and congressional seat in ways that had important consequences for not only the number of seats held by Republicans, but also state and local policies following the census count. It encouraged other forms of corporate crossing. REDMAP benefited from the financial backing of, among others, Walmart, Altria (tobacco), AT&T, and the Koch brothers.[4]

REDMAP illustrated how bordering and crossing practices complemented one another. Republican strategists like Tom Hofeller used maps and a variety of data to create the most partisan map that would maximize Republican votes. The data included census data on a voter's education, income level, race, gender, and age. The analysis predicted how individuals would vote in the future with a strong degree of confidence. The software ran multiple maps to determine the best scenario that would not waste any votes. It either packed Democrats and African American voters into a single district or cracked districts to minimize the impact of both groups. In other words, legislators picked voters and inverted a collective sense of "liberty and justice for all." Republicans not only hijacked the last sentence of the Pledge of Allegiance, but their maps also effectively determined elections, flipping formerly "blue" states and districts (including many in Michigan), even when Democrats cast a greater number of votes. The results were extreme policies that didn't require moderate Republicans to work with conservative Democrats to develop and introduce policies at the national, state, and local levels. Republican politicians worked with corporations instead of voters.

REDMAP was a bordering and crossing practice that relied on abstractive opacity. The maps were drawn using private computers, often far from where they would be implemented. Republicans passed a variety of critical legislation that drastically transformed Detroiters' lives. For example, in 2011, Michigan passed Public Act 4, which redefined an "emergency" and strengthened the authority of emergency managers to take over the authority of elected officials and break collective bargaining agreements with unions. Detroiters joined a statewide, volunteer-driven ballot initiative organized by "Voters not Politicians" to strike down the law. The law was voted down in 2012, but in a lame-duck session, the Republican-dominated Michigan legislature passed a new emergency manager law (Public Act 436) that included new provisions immunizing it from being revoked by referendums. These were the same bordering practices, effected first through maps and voting districts and then through the policies it enabled, that granted Governor Rick Snyder the authority to appoint Kevyn Orr as an emergency manager of Detroit in 2013. "Voters Not Politicians" were able to successfully change the Michigan Constitution in 2018 to create independent citizen redistricting committees.

REDMAP compromised Detroit's influence in the state legislature and reinforced other bordering practices mapped through race. For example, most Detroit Police officers live outside the city.[5] In 2006, the state had passed a constitutional amendment outlawing affirmative action in public employment and education. In 2009, Michigan passed Public Act 563 and transferred control from local to regional authority over what had been known as Cobo Hall and later as the TCF Center and, now, Huntington Place. The City of Detroit had only one representative on the five-member board. These bordering and crossing practices eroded residents' ability to access and use their resources.

White Wealth, Black Debt: Detroit's Bankruptcy

Detroit's bankruptcy proceedings may have officially begun in 2013, but they telescoped a longstanding relation of racializing credit and debt. The event coincided with the improbable election of a write-in candidate for a white mayor of Detroit: Michael "Mike" Duggan. He had recently moved to the city, but nonetheless won against Benny Napoleon, a Black lifelong Detroiter who campaigned with a television ad that repeated, "we must have forgot." Napoleon's campaign ads relied on historical abstractions, like "dream" and "brother," imposed on images of the civil rights movement. Duggan won with a 55 percent margin and ended four decades of continuous Black governance in Detroit. His victory signified, according to one white reporter, "the emergence of a new regime at a critical moment in the city's history."[6] The ways that media and the financial industry contrasted the city's Black and white mayors elucidated how the extension of credit and debt remained heavily dependent on the productive relation between race and space.

The ways we define a problem shape our interventions. Popular narratives about Detroit's bankruptcy relied on abstractions about population loss and a corrupt city government. The emergency management team that negotiated the city's bankruptcy was no different. It blamed the fiscal crisis on "the perceived inefficiency of public sector unions and pension obligations, a bloated municipal bureaucracy and poor and corrupt fiscal management."[7] The team's abstractions about the public sector focused narrowly on Detroit, but alternative narratives about how Detroit's bankruptcy was influenced by debt incurred by providing water service to suburban areas and political decisions made by the Michigan legislature received far less coverage. The abstractions highlighted the unequal relation between the majority Black city and the majority white state: Scholars found that political units with a larger proportion of African American residents were more likely to experience emergency political intervention.[8]

Alternate narratives about Detroit's bankruptcy focused on inequitable development. For instance, banks' predatory mortgage lending practices were particularly marked in Detroit, but they were mirrored across the United States and ultimately caused the 2008 Great Recession. The reality of disinvestment in Detroit meant bankruptcy would not resolve the city's need to increase tax revenues. The proposal for a regional tax base that was promoted during bankruptcy proceedings was nonetheless unsuccessful.[9]

Alternate explanations for Detroit's bankruptcy included the federal government's selective support for banks and the auto industry through loans and bailouts. The Obama administration had only offered Detroit some aid and technical assistance under the "Strong Cities, Strong Communities" program. The federal government favored aid to businesses over Detroit's residents. The explanations also included structural and historical inequalities that misshaped the development of Detroit in relation to the metropolitan area and state. For example, Michigan's Municipal League President Jacqueline Noonan pointed to "the state's broken municipal finance system, under which the Legislature and governor have taken about $6 billion in funds that, by state law, were supposed to go to local governments as statutory revenue sharing, including to the city of Detroit."[10] The double blow meant Detroit lost one-third of its revenue between fiscal years 2011–2013, right after the Great Recession.[11]

Michigan Governor Rick Snyder appointed Kevyn Orr as Detroit's emergency manager in March 2013. The emergency manager's powers superseded that of local elected officials. Orr subsequently filed for Detroit's bankruptcy, which required suspending democracy. First, the Republican-controlled Michigan legislature had passed a revised emergency law in a lame-duck session. Second, Governor Snyder's appointment of an emergency manager concentrated all authority in the city on a nonelected person. Orr gained the attention of a top official in the Snyder administration when he insisted Detroit needed an emergency manager because "elected officials won't get this done. You've been coming this way for sixty years. You just had six and a half years of kleptocracy."[12] He was referring to 2009 conviction of Mayor Kwame Kilpatrick but generalized his judgment to the city's Black officials, four mayoral administrations, and "sixty years" of Black governance that traced back to Mayor Coleman Young. Orr depended on a stereotype about Black people and sameness and disregarded differences between mayoral administrations, priorities, and challenges. Orr filed for bankruptcy and conflated what was considered "essentially a municipal cash-flow problem with an overblown and highly politicized debt crisis."[13]

Looting and Takeovers: The Erosion of Local Control in Favor of Regional Profits

The bankruptcy forced questions about debt and responsibility. For example, why was the city government forced into bankruptcy without the legal ability to negotiate with its creditors? Alternately, financial corporations and bond insurers had extended credit to the city on questionable terms. Were they owed repayment for debts incurred through predatory lending to the city and its residents? The relation between credit and debt, and who owed what to whom, raised critical questions of how debt should be prioritized among creditors that included city pensioners.

Bankruptcy negotiations inherited these social and moral questions about the nature of credit and debt.[14] They pitted pensioners against the city's assets, which included Belle Isle and the Detroit Water and Sewer Department, but media fixed public attention on the Detroit Institute of Art. Orr's law firm used law journals to market municipal debt renegotiation nationally at least two years before Michigan had appointed a review board to consider Detroit's finances. The firm's attorneys used their disciplinary journals to argue "pension woes . . . [were] perhaps the single largest problem facing municipalities today" because municipal pensions were neither regulated by federal law nor "protected by the federal pension guarantee program."[15] The Jones Day lawyers echoed media consensus over New York City's fiscal crisis in the 1970s when they concluded that municipalities had been lax and overly generous.[16] Municipalities have far more freedom than private-sector employers to make their own choices about funding methods and policies. The result has been several decades of increasingly rich benefits packages, often resulting from negotiations with a municipality's collective bargaining unit, coupled with a less-than-rigid fiscal approach to paying for those benefits.[17]

Orr considered public pensions were a product of unregulated municipal concessions to collective bargaining units. The belief implied Detroit mayors favored special interests at the expense of the city's residents, which was confirmed at least for a short time in the years following Mayor Kilpatrick's conviction. The assertions supported the public's impression that pension benefits were too high for public workers. The media, Orr, and his law firm cast Detroit pensioners as another creditor and turned "contractual rights holders [in]to charitable dependents."[18]

Orr claimed that "for a long time the city was dumb, lazy, happy and rich."[19] He related the city's financial difficulties to municipal workers that "had an eighth grade education" and got "30 years of a good job and a pension and great health care."[20] His references to how the city lost wealth because of its workers was an abstraction that obscured how his law firm and its partners benefited from the bankruptcy proceedings. For example, David Heiman of Jones Day billed the city $1,075 an hour and charged $34,000 to go between Detroit and his vacation home in Florida.[21] Orr also hired consultants that extracted millions from the proceedings, including Conway MacKenzie, a firm that collected $27 million in fees "with several individuals earning $400 per hour—or $832,000 annually on a full-time basis."[22] Meanwhile, Orr negotiated a settlement with the city's retirees for a 90 percent cut to their health care benefits.[23] Orr's reference to rich municipal workers was an abstraction that obscured how his actions enriched his social networks and opened the city to a new wave of investors.

There were other ways the Jones Day attorneys associated pensioners with irresponsible municipal spending. In the article they published well before beginning their discussions with Michigan's state government, the attorneys pointed to "credit default swaps—one of the vehicles many claim was a leading culprit of the global financial crisis and the global sovereign-debt crisis."[24] Credit swaps were an important part of Detroit's bankruptcy because of their questionable legality. In 2005, Mayor Kilpatrick was awarded *Bond Buyer's* "Midwest Regional Deal of the Year" for borrowing $1.44 billion in pension obligation certificates of participation (COP). At the time, it was "the largest local-level pension financing in the nation."[25] After the bankruptcy, it was considered "a subprime loan on steroids."[26]

The city was forced to buy credit swaps in part because of the impact that racial segregation had on property values. Michigan law prevents cities from carrying bond debt greater than 10 percent of the assessed value of private property. Detroit was already carrying more than $700 million in bond debt. To buy the credit swaps, the city had to contract a third party to pay the debt, so it set up two shell corporations to sell the COPs to banks that would then sell them to investors. "Though the concept seemed simple, officials said it took the combination of fortunate market timing, knowledge of the 'skeleton' of any bond structure, legal expertise, problems and questions raised and answered, and the expertise of a host of bond professionals to bring the deal together. . . . [It was a] veritable army of professionals that worked to complete the sale."[27] Detroit's expenses preceding the bankruptcy were "a direct result of the complex financial deals Wall Street banks urged on the city," particularly the legacy of the COPs.[28] The deals included interest rate swaps to turn $800 million of variable-rate into fixed-rate COPs that locked the city into the same kinds of high-interest-rate predatory lending that residents faced when the Federal Reserve drove down interest rates in response to the financial crisis. In other words, in the same way that residents faced higher interest rates after the adjustable rate expired on their mortgages, the city was paying higher than market rates on its debt. The Detroit Water and Sewer Department entered similar "predatory interest rate swap agreements" between 1998 and 2006 that made up "one of the largest chunks of bankruptcy-related liabilities for the city."[29]

The problems with the credit swaps came to a head in 2009 when Standard & Poor's Global Ratings downgraded Detroit and the city was faced with termination payments for the swap contracts. To avoid the termination payments, the city pledged future gambling taxes, and the interest rate swaps were restructured in the bank's favor: "Under the new agreement, the banks could cancel the swaps contracts if interest rates rose above 6 percent, but the city could not cancel the deal if rates fell below 6 percent. It was the equivalent of a toxic mortgage that could not be refinanced."[30] Individuals faced foreclosures, which meant starting a life over without equities or assets. Residents faced a comparable restart and a hard reset during emergency management and bankruptcy because they had been locked out of participating in decisions affecting how the city would be restructured. Local elected officials had been divested of their authority.

Bankruptcy was an expedient recapitalization of debt and dispossession and glossed over long-term structural problems. For example, subprime lending and foreclosures had capitalized on racial segregation. Residents were blamed for the city's debt because they were pensioners or failed to pay their utilities (water), property taxes, and mortgages.[31] The city lost revenue from taxes that were shared with the state of Michigan. The circumstances made the city more vulnerable to market fluctuations, including the Great Recession. The bankruptcy and the city's recovery should have focused on the city's residents. Instead, nonresidents recast bankruptcy and recovery as an opportunity for outsiders. For example, Orr pointed out that the bankruptcy was an "opportunity for rebirth . . . [and] to restructure [which] is unique in America."[32] The CEO of JPMorgan Chase, Jamie Dimon, similarly considered Detroit could have "a real renaissance."[33] Chase was involved in the lending that led to foreclosures and the erosion of the city's tax base. Orr had negotiated the terms of bankruptcy. Nonetheless, both men foreshadowed a political slogan that seemed to disconnect the immediate economic past from the city's future when they implied that they could make Detroit, and America, great again.

Producing Detroit as a blighted structure recycled abstractions that diverted audiences' attention from the political decisions leading up to and following Detroit's bankruptcy. One repeated example was lighting. In a November 2019 episode of *60 Minutes*, titled "Jamie Dimon's Data-Focused Investment in Detroit," Lesley Stahl interviewed Mayor Duggan and asked him to describe Detroit when he became mayor. His response began: "Half the streetlights in the city were out. How do you get streetlights fixed?" During the bankruptcy proceedings, Michigan Governor

Rick Snyder asserted the state was doing enough for the city because, among other things, "we [the state] did the public lighting authority."[34] After the city exited bankruptcy, Jamie Dimon proclaimed, "The bankruptcy is over. The streetlights are being turned back on."[35] He later enthused that "less than 18 months after city exited bankruptcy, thousands of new streetlights are lighting the way."[36] Nathan Bomey analyzed the bankruptcy and opened a section of his book by discussing the street-lighting system. He noted it was "one of the simplest public services."[37] Bomey's discussion revealed what Duggan and Dimon had only implied, which was that fixing the city's lighting symbolized "overhauling the entire city."[38] Bomey's analysis associated the "example of dysfunction" with not only a 120-year-old infrastructure but also vandals who had stripped the copper wiring and criminals who could not be seen on unlit streets. He contrasted this depiction with a post-bankruptcy *Detroit Resurrected*, the title of his book, which included a $185 million overhaul of the street-lighting system. Even as late as 2019, Ken Buckfire, who during the bankruptcy had restructured the Detroit Water and Sewer Department as the Great Lakes Water Authority, enthused, "Detroit now after five years has done a great job of restoring services people have new police cars, the buses run, the lights work . . . the basic requirements of living in a city have now been restored."[39] *And then they said "Let there be light" . . . and there was.* Lighting had become a metaphor for the kinds of visible transparency that data measurement and bankruptcy had created. It was an abstraction that facilitated new crossings.

Making Something Out of Nothing: The Demolition Program

What Mayor Duggan institutionalized as the demolition program traced back to the efforts of Mayor Dave Bing and the "ideas emerging from the strategic framework created through Detroit Future City," which targeted some areas of the city for development.[40] Both during and after the bankruptcy, "blight removal" in the form of empty lot clearance and demolition came to mean a variety of things, including making the city livable, governable, and developable.[41] The multiple meanings reflected longstanding tensions between accessing shelter on the one hand and producing space that favored private property ownership on the other. The fundamental question of "productive use" meant prioritizing the practices of developers and investors who held property vacant over residents' needs for affordable housing. In other words, laws allowed the demolition but not the unauthorized occupation of property.

The tension between housing and demolition was a product of national- and state-level priorities. The federal government began the Troubled Asset Relief Program (TARP) in 2010 to "help struggling homeowners avoid foreclosure and preserve homeownership."[42] By June 2013, Michigan had only spent about 19 percent of its award.[43] As Flint's county treasurer, Daniel Kildee had helped Michigan develop its first land bank, but, by 2013, he was a US House Representative who introduced a bill to redirect a quarter of the TARP funds "to tear down and repurpose abandoned properties."[44] This spending came out of one of TARP's programs, the Hardest Hit Fund (HHF). Initially, about a quarter of the funds were used for demolition. The city's bankruptcy made demolition an even greater priority. A *60 Minutes* episode titled "Detroit on the Edge" aired on October 25, 2013. After a brief introduction to "what a city looks like when it's gone bankrupt," the narrator declared Detroit "looks like it has lost a war."[45] National attention and Kildee's legislative initiative lent greater support to the 2013 Detroit Blight Removal Task Force's report that stressed the need "to eradicate the malignant disease of blight" because it was "a cancer."[46] Kevyn Orr delegated the demolition plan to Duggan in 2014, when Duggan became mayor.

HHF was a fund originally established to help homeowners through a state-designed program. In 2016, the Detroit City Council sought to find out whether some of the HHF money couldn't be used to help homeowners avoid tax foreclosure.[47] The legislative policy division director penned an internal city council memo that noted the city administration had allocated $55 million for blight removal, but only $19 million to help homeowners.[48] Federal funds had been redirected away from their intended purpose of helping homeowners and instead directed toward demolition. The Special Inspector General for the Trouble Asset Relief Program identified states that had to wait longer than the average, and found "it took more than a median of 6 months for a Michigan homeowner to gain access to HHF mortgage modification assistance, nearly 5 months for a Michigan homeowner to gain access to HHF loan rescue assistance and more than median of three months for an unemployed

Michigan homeowner to gain access to HHF assistance with their mortgage."[49] Their findings reflected differential crossing ability: Banks and automobile manufacturers received bailouts, but homeowners could not consistently access similar types of debt forgiveness.

The negative impact of redirecting HHF to demolition was only compounded by other changes in the city after bankruptcy. For instance, the memo to the city council pointed out that the "human perspective" would prioritize the original intent of the funds: homeowners and foreclosure prevention. It contrasted a "property values perspective" that focused on blight removal. Both media and Mayor Duggan reiterated that demolition would increase property values and stabilize neighborhoods, but there were at least two problems with the emphasis on property values. First, they obfuscated decades of public disinvestment and public concerns about cleared, vacant land, especially because Duggan didn't have a plan for them. Previous urban renewal projects had displaced residents and fractured communities, but the demolition program lacked the "Keynesian interventionism of urban renewal."[50] Second, Duggan's strategy of targeting some neighborhoods meant others became objects of neglect and disinvestment.

HHF demolitions targeted six neighborhoods: Southwest, Northend, Jefferson Chalmers, Grandmont Rosedale, University of Detroit Mercy–Marygrove, and Morningside–East English Village–Cornerstone. These areas formed an intermediate ring just inside an outer ring that bordered suburban areas. In other words, the HHF demolitions produced a new ring of social and spatial borders. On the one hand, these areas seemed porous because one could walk or drive through them. On the other, these neighborhoods gained new significance after the bankruptcy as the newly formed Department of Neighborhoods created discrete identities for different areas of the city. A *Wall Street Journal* article noted that many residents found Black residents were pushed "into a parallel universe of financing options" as financing flowed toward targeted neighborhoods and further devalued the areas where they lived.[51]

Another problem with the federally funded demolition program follows the same pattern discussed throughout this book, that is, that it produced static space by comparing Detroit's prebankruptcy past to its present. For example, the 2013 *60 Minutes* episode included an interview with the founder of the twenty-five-year-old nonprofit organization, Detroit Blight Busters, who challenged the dominant narrative and explained, "Blight is a very cunning adversary. You eliminate it here and it pops up over there. And it kills everything, so you're constantly battling that enemy." In other words, prioritizing demolition fueled an ongoing need for contractors that could produce a "new" Detroit. As one Reuters article opined, Detroit "seeks to engineer a recovery by tearing itself down."[52] The city council memo referenced a 2015 TARP Special Inspector General report that found "a majority of homeowners have not benefited from the funds originally intended to keep them in their homes.... There is a significant risk of strategically misusing these funds intended to keep people in their homes, by demolishing occupied or potentially repairable homes, thereby potentially increasing blight, poverty and homelessness." Reports produced blight by claiming 78,506 of the city's residential structures needed to be demolished. The report was predictive: Over half of those structures had "indicators of future blight."[53]

There were several federal and city investigations that bolstered residents' concerns about the demolition program. First, both the Federal Bureau of Investigations (FBI) and the US Attorney conducted investigations and found evidence of rigged bidding for demolition contracts. Second, the Office of the Auditor General appeared before the city council in 2020 and identified a series of concerns. The auditor pointed out they had difficulty conducting an audit because of delayed and incomplete documents from city offices, including the amount of payments made by the Detroit Building Authority. He referred to a separate lawsuit against the Detroit Land Bank Authority because of how they reviewed bids. The auditor pointed out that the city had spent at least $5.2 million for costs that were reimbursable by the Michigan State Housing Development Authority, which included gap funding for demolitions costing more than $25,000.[54] In other words, not only had the city borne unnecessary expense, but demolition costs had also spiraled to over double the initial estimate. Third, a 2016 TARP Special Inspector General report confirmed HHF was "significantly vulnerable to fraud, bid rigging, other closed-door contract awards, and overcharging."[55] By 2023, the US Attorney's Office ordered the Detroit Land Bank Authority to pay $1.5 million dollars for paying demolition contractors "unsubstantiated backfill dirt costs."[56]

Residents expressed their concerns at a November 12, 2019, city council meeting. HHF monies had dried up, and Duggan proposed a $200 million bond issue. In one after another ninety-second statement, residents recounted three main problems with the demolition program. First, the city could not prioritize local contractors or workers because HHF was a federally funded program. Second, residents reminded the city council about the need to develop affordable housing and criticized the program that had focused narrowly on demolition rather than renovation. Third, residents protested that their property taxes were already high and continuing the demolition bill would only increase the city's debt. The most alarming testimony came from Auditor General Mark Lockridge, who summarized his audit findings in his November 12, 2019, testimony to Detroit's City Council.[57]

Lockridge began by explaining that the audit had taken three years because his office had not received the documentation it requested. He found demolition costs that weren't covered by federal or state funds had been shifted onto the city. Lockridge said the lack of transparency and delay was the most "egregious" problem, but his audit also identified other problems that included a "lack of documentation to support authorization of payment." Conflicts of interest with contractors posed another set of problems. Many had started work before receiving proper notice, hadn't complied with city policies, and lacked receipts for landfill and backfill charges.[58] Among other things, noncompliance meant that over 75 percent of the time, contractors did *not* ensure resident safety and protection by putting up safety barriers, redirecting traffic, or giving notice to residents, Michigan Department of Environmental Quality (MDEQ), and other agencies for inspection. They also failed to properly dispose of hazardous materials. This failure to comply with city demolition policies meant demolition crews used untested and contaminated backfill and compromised the viability of new development on affected lots. It also meant Detroit residents, including children, were exposed to metals and lead at a higher rate than Flint because of the demolition program.[59]

The "new Detroit" built after bankruptcy implicated a significant crossing of the city's resources. There were the tax foreclosures that dispossessed homeowners, most often in favor of regional investors who bought bundled properties at auction costs and resold them at market value. There were tax subsidies that drew businesses into the city, such as the Ilitch family's Little Caesar's Arena, the Ford Motor Company's purchase and renovation of the Michigan Central Station, and Dan Gilbert's plans that included both a mixed-use building on the former Hudson's Department Store and a Monroe Blocks Project. There were also new forms of crossing, such as the "Transformational Brownfield Redevelopment Plans" that allowed income taxes to be captured and directed to developers. These plans not only undermined some of the state's control over income taxes but also implied developers could exert greater control than cities over some spatial production.

Business and finance capitalized on and crossed the city's borders. For example, the federally funded demolition program created regional growth as it relied on large contractors that could handle multiple demolitions. These contractors were originally based outside of the city, even if they changed their name and purchased a city address to receive correspondence. Detroit residents were also bordered by hiring practices. On publicly funded construction projects, the city's Executive Order 2016-1 required 51 percent of the workforce to be Detroit residents. The city's April 2021 project summary showed less than 14 percent of projects met this requirement.[60] For example, only 15 percent of the total hours worked on the Michigan Central Station project were "qualified employees."

The 2008 foreclosure crisis and the 2013–2014 bankruptcy dispossessed residents of their homes and eroded the power of their vote. Similar bordering and crossing practices had a longer history. For example, following the 1967 rebellion, William Bunge worked with Gwendolyn Warren and other residents to understand how different positions in the metropolitan economy produced one square mile in the city (see figure 4.1.). He published his findings in a book titled Fitzgerald that included several maps, including one focused on money transfers in and out of the city. The lower right-hand side of their map superimposed a cone on a horizontal diagram to indicate that financial flows were not only horizontal and marked by distance from the center of the city, but also vertical and marked by the relatively larger scale of extraction from the slums. It showed a hierarchy in which rental profits were transferred out to affluent suburbs in Wayne, Oakland, and Macomb counties. The mapping also identified extraction in terms of the

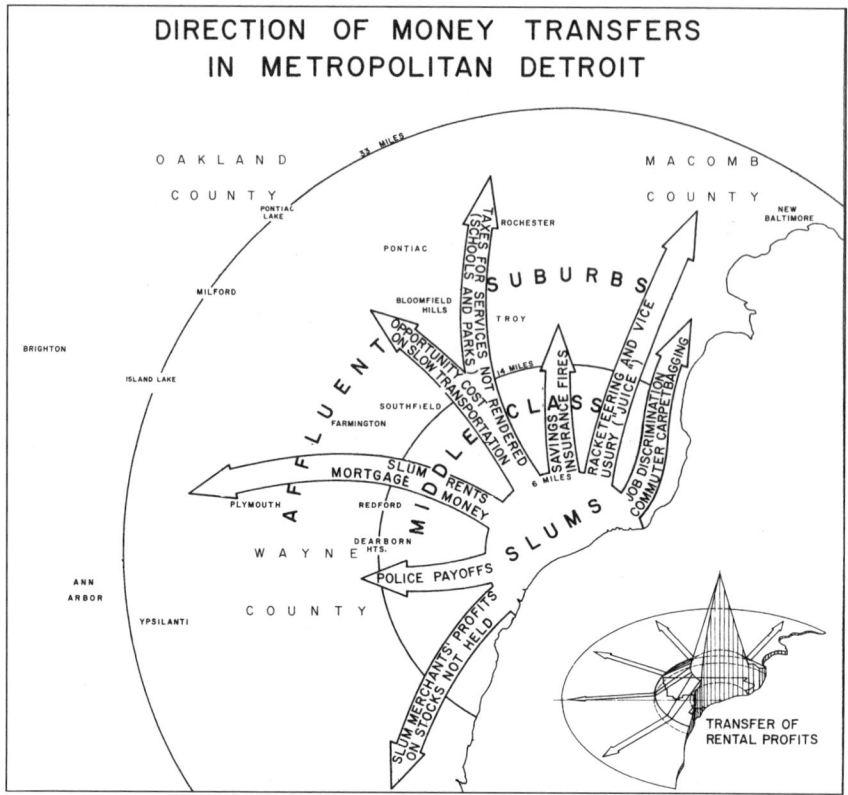

Figure 4.1. Direction of Money Transfers in Metropolitan Detroit (1971)

relation between class and space, including "commuter carpetbagging" by suburbanites who earned income in the city but spent their money in the suburbs. The map's arrows suggested flows like mortgages went well beyond the suburbs. They were reminiscent of the claim Du Bois made in 1899: slums were symptoms of removable causes located "far beyond the slum districts."[61]

Comparing the bankruptcy to the demolition program reveals new ways of thinking about two abstractions: corruption and vacancy. A long and steady criticism of prebankruptcy Detroit centered on corruption. For example, commenting on the city as it exited bankruptcy proceedings, *The Detroit News* editor Nolan Finley said the city was "held mostly harmless from its own mismanagement, incompetence and corruption. . . . Instead of facing its mistakes, those who loaned it money over the years, for reasons good and questionable, paid the price for 60 years of denial and neglect."[62] Finley blamed city workers, many of whom were retired, rather than the armies of legal and financial experts that extended subprime loans on predatory terms. Kevyn Orr was not the only one to generalize a judgment of Detroit's Black mayors to all city officials and to Detroit's history of Black governance. For instance, Kenneth Buckfire "believed that Wall Street investors would extend better bond interest rates to a water authority that did not have the word 'Detroit' in its name."[63] He implied Wall Street was not colorblind.

In a post-bankruptcy Detroit, vacant land was dissociated from the bordering and crossing practices that promoted displacement and dispossession. The metaphor of a "blank slate" that media had repeatedly applied to Detroit became associated with experiments, opportunity, and attracting new residents to the city. Financing followed for targeted neighborhoods. Municipal bond credit ratings increased as financiers became convinced that demolition had not only created a new Detroit, but also that city taxpayers would continue to subsidize private development through new legal instruments like the Transformational Brownfield Redevelopment Plans. Financial industry periodicals encouraged familiar practices as they pointed out that bond issues for continued demolition would nonetheless have junk ratings, which meant that a high-yield paper was in demand among investors.[64] Bond financiers and bond raters used population growth and loss to talk about race and class in ostensibly colorblind language, including credit ratings and interest charges.[65] The new Detroit was produced at a distance as big data, banks, and investors were located outside the city. They abstracted municipal finances and occluded the ways they would reconstitute racial inequities.

Summary

Bordering practices may be relatively stable, as in the case of maps. Bordering practices that rely on a resident's interaction with another resident or on policing practices are more fluid. Crossings are both cause and consequence of bordering practices. What distinguishes the crossing practices discussed in this chapter is that they are products of relatively new or significantly shifting bordering practices.

Each of this chapter's examples demonstrates how different levels of abstraction produce the post-bankruptcy city. REDMAP reorganized and concentrated political power to the detriment of Democrats and African Americans. A Republican governor appointed an emergency manager to declare Detroit bankrupt and clear retired municipal workers, among others, from the city's account sheets. Housing advocates argued that the demolition program not only negatively impacted public health but also eliminated viable housing material. The demolition program produced additional vacancy and reduced housing supply.

This chapter demonstrated how border crossing created selective opportunities for non-Detroit residents. In contrast, to have *created opportunities selectively* would mean crossings had a target, group, or destination. Instead, this chapter demonstrated how crossings are embedded in struggles related to understanding, organizing and experiencing the world from a stable vantage point. The case of public lighting in Detroit followed bordering and crossing practices that were traditionally marked as white, classed, and patriarchal.

The examples of REDMAP, Detroit's bankruptcy, and its demolition program indicated that border crossings undermined African American Detroiters' ability to exercise political influence over the post-bankruptcy city's future. They marked an *other than other*. In other words, rather than marketing to targeted audiences, the bordering and crossing practices in this chapter's examples were selective opportunities that referenced non-Black and nonresident outsiders.

5

Affirmative Action or Reverse Racism?

The African Town Proposal

The Detroit News editor claimed a plan for an African Town in the city belonged on a shelf with Adolf Hitler's *Mein Kampf*. The comparison likened the proposal to a treatise on racial purity and white supremacy. He claimed the plan treated "whites as personae non gratae" and that the city council "might as well hang 'Blacks Only' signs on every entrance to the city."[1] The editor relied on clear examples of racial exclusion to critique a plan designed to promote African American entrepreneurship. His references demonstrated how powerful groups depend on empty abstractions to *do* things, which in this case was to turn white people into the victims of a plan to help African Americans.

The editor implied nonwhite people could not do the same things that white people had done by granting privileges based on race. He assumed that "had a majority white city endorsed such a plan, the US Justice Department would already be serving subpoenas."[2] He assumed differential treatment based on race was illegal but ignored the proposal's main argument: that lenders discriminated against Black entrepreneurs. White people had *not* been systematically discriminated against by lenders. They historically benefited from a variety of ostensibly colorblind practices that consistently demonstrated unequal outcomes. The editor ignored how racial preference and bias operate. His references to the exclusion of white people from the city inverted a historical relation in which African Americans had been segregated in the city and excluded from its suburban areas.

The editor mapped what he saw as the relation between racialized groups. He also demonstrated how white men have historically positioned themselves as spokesmen for what he called "other disadvantaged groups" and "immigrants."[3] He recycled positive stereotypes about the "energy and initiative of risk-taking immigrants," ignoring that these groups often had a different set of challenges and advantages than those facing African American entrepreneurs. He elided the nature of structural discrimination and asserted the "formula followed by immigrant groups is available to African-Americans." His glib and unfounded assertion relied on a long history of culturally based explanations for social mobility and success that presumed Black people lacked the same energy as immigrants, that is, that they were lazy.[4] Immigrants and Latinos echoed the editor's assertions in the weeks and months that followed.

The editorial was important because it reflected several themes that I revisit in this book. First, it demonstrated how media and white men with power depend on empty abstractions to promote a specific set of relations between racialized groups. Second, the editor's references to "Blacks Only" signs and *Mein Kampf* underscored a relation to white supremacy and anti-Blackness that traced back over one hundred years before the African Town proposal. That relation was ignored by the editor, but it underpinned the justifications provided for African Town by the plan's authors, the city council, prominent civil rights leaders, and many city residents. Third, the editorial preceded protests from immigrant and minority groups, which demonstrated how empty abstractions do things: They stimulated or at least offered some measure of legitimacy to the demonstrations that followed.

The Context

The vexing problem of discrimination and blocked social mobility lay at the heart of the civil rights movement. It drove the development of African American residential and business communities, including Detroit's Paradise Valley in the 1920s. African American enclaves were not new, but many were cleared through extralegal, violent massacres led by white mobs. Other Black communities were leveled by government action in the form of urban renewal plans and the expansion of expressways across the city. The struggle for government protection from discrimination made the case of "African Town" a fitting one to elucidate how immigrant community leaders positioned themselves relative to white supremacy and anti-Blackness. It also provided a Black-led development model to compare to the foundation-led one that followed in the years leading up to the city's bankruptcy. The

African Town proposal illustrated the limits of Black urban regimes relative to white urban regimes and marked how the years leading up to and following the bankruptcy were a regime change that many developers now refer to as a "culture shift."[5]

The earliest newspaper reference to "African Town" was in February 2002 when the *Michigan Citizen*, the city's African American newspaper, explained it would be "America's first African-centered retail and entertainment community."[6] There may have been other so-called Black Towns in the United States, but two entrepreneurs in Detroit promoted a desire to inspire and educate people about "African culture" and provide positive images for "our children and our children's children."[7] Dorian Harvey and Terence Willis's plans included a "memorial fountain honoring the 12 million lives lost in the Middle Passage."[8] They said they had "laid the groundwork for the proposal" five years before the article, but it didn't have the Dennis Wayne Archer administration's support even though there was $100 million in federal funds and $1.9 billion in private banking commitments that were targeted for Detroit's Empowerment Zone, and as much as 30 percent remained unspent.[9] Their early conception differed from the proposal that was eventually developed and promoted by the city council and challenged by immigrant groups and local newspapers.

The project gained significant political support only two years later when city council member JoAnn Watson set up a task force. The city council hired Dr. Claud Anderson to develop the proposal. He had advocated for Black self-sufficiency in his 2001 book *PowerNomics: The National Plan to Empower Black America*. He adapted his ideas in a proposal for Detroit that envisioned a space of about two hundred thousand square feet in the city's Empowerment Zone, which meant it would benefit from the same kinds of city and state tax breaks that aided the development of large businesses and corporations. Some claimed African Town would be a national model for Black business ownership and economic advancement. US President George W. Bush declared his support for a new initiative to promote minority entrepreneurship when he visited the city in July 2004, the same month that the city council passed two resolutions supporting African Town.[10] The first affirmed Anderson's claim that African Americans in Detroit were underserved because lenders discriminated against Black entrepreneurs. A second resolution sought to establish a loan fund to develop Black entrepreneurship.

Struggles over Abstraction

Anderson made a significant effort to popularize the idea that African Americans were "underserved." He titled his report to the city council "A Powernomics Economic Development Plan for Detroit's Under-Served Majority Population." Its first sentence indicated the report "was written with the majority under-served population defined as the target group."[11] On the next page, he clearly identified "Detroit's majority under-served population is the Black population." He continued to emphasize the crisis occasioned by a lack of economic power, few services, "a high level of unmet needs," and the majority Black resident population of the city throughout his report.[12] He wrote that Detroit had the potential to be a pan-African capital because it was "a majority Black city, with a Black mayor, Black city council, Black police chief, Black school superintendent, a population that is 86 percent descendants from Africa with a 98 percent Black student body that is centrally located in the heart of urban Black America."[13]

Dr. C. T. Vivian, a well-known civil rights leader who served on Reverend Dr. Martin Luther King Jr.'s executive staff, tied the African Town proposal to a long struggle for civil rights that was also about "economic power and economic rights."[14] Anderson concurred that patterned, systemic discrimination impeded social mobility but thought that segregation could be used to Detroit's advantage. He wrote that the civil rights movement had eroded African Americans' control over their businesses and communities because desegregation had not resulted in integration into the mainstream economy. He considered the concentration of African Americans in the city was a competitive advantage that could translate into buying power and be used for the city's economic development. He suggested residents be reconsidered: Rather than a "crowded inner city neighborhood," Detroit's demographic was a positive if it were viewed as an ethnic niche with "11 billion of disposable income," 95 percent of which left for suburban malls surrounding the city.[15] He encouraged Detroit's majority underserved population to "defend its territory" from corporations that were "joining the gold rush back into Detroit" because they would undermine local interests and "exploit" its population.[16] His emphasis on the flow of dollars outside of the city was reminiscent of William Bunge's map of money transfers out of Detroit and

Du Bois' 1899 claim about the cause of slums being located "far beyond the slum districts" (see figure 4.1).[17] His focus on how residents spent their money outside of the city was later echoed by the 2012 Detroit Future City Strategic Framework and Mayor Mike Duggan.

Anderson's plan emphasized the "majority underserved" residents of Detroit who he considered a "captive consumer base."[18] He explained that the majority underserved shared the fate of Black consumers in other inner cities: They were "untapped gold mines" for "business, political, and economic forces that reside outside of the city."[19] They also provided "capital and resources . . . [for] ethnic immigrants who primarily live in the surrounding suburbs or on the fringes of the urban centers."[20] In other words, urban Black communities were a source of wealth for people who largely lived outside of cities. Financial capital could cross city borders in ways that Black residents of the city could not: "The *stunted* economic status of the majority population [was] reflected in the *stagnant* economic status of the city."[21] Anderson related the city's fortunes to that of its residents and the production of space to race both within and beyond the city's borders.

One abstraction involved in the proposed African Town was government dependency.[22] Media implied the proposal was a new form of welfare. The *Detroit News* editorial claimed there was an "entitlement mentality that continues to hold back African Americans in Detroit."[23] The association of Blackness with public assistance was an empty abstraction that inverted the ways Black residents were subordinated to capital flows in the city. For example, JoAnn Watson pointed out that Detroit residents generated $11 billion in revenue, but 95 percent of it left the city's commercial and retail markets.[24] The city's prominent activist philosopher, Grace Lee Boggs, believed that groups who opposed African Town were threatened by the idea of Black entrepreneurs. She agreed with Anderson that African Americans had been a source of wealth and provided "an outflow of cash that enriches others."[25] The references to others underscored how residents believed people who lived outside the city benefited from the flow of capital out of the city. Outsiders sought to undermine the plan and unduly influenced the city's affairs. Residents' references to outside "others" inverted the "outside agitator" abstraction often used against civil rights protestors.[26]

Another abstraction that circulated in the debates about African Town implicated the meaning of majorities and minorities in terms of numeric and political significance. One of the resolutions indicated the proposal was shaped in relation to local and national debates about immigrants. Hispanics became the largest minority group in 2003, the year before the two resolutions were passed. The first resolution noted that "Black/African Americans" were no longer the *nation's* "majority-minority" group, but that in the *city* of Detroit and in matters related, "contract compliance and minority set-asides . . . the "Black/African American citizenry [would] officially [be] recognized and identified as the 'majority,' as well as the 'majority-minority' and the 'under-served' populations."[27] The proposal responded to concerns that the growth of the Hispanic population would undermine public programs and funding for African Americans.

The idea that the United States is a "nation of immigrants" was an abstraction about the freedom of human movement that obscured how immigrants crossed borders in ways African Americans could not. For example, media reported that the Asian Pacific and American Arab Chambers of Commerce as well as Asian, Hispanic, and Arab business owners opposed the African Town plan.[28] Their reactions indicated they believed ethnic enclaves developed organically by an ethnic group's concentration in a particular geographic area. Their beliefs ignored how space was produced by powerful groups, including employers who recruited Mexican and Mexican American labor through Texas to Southwest Detroit. Planners directed railway lines ending at Michigan's Central Station in Detroit. The Southwestern area of the city was also an enclave produced in relation to chain migration and discrimination in the city's white mainstream housing market. Many factors shaped Southwest Detroit and the United States of America but claims about immigrants' cultural values and self-sufficiency remained empty abstractions that obscured a historical pattern of exclusion that blocked African Americans from the same kinds of freedom that immigration symbolized: Black people had been historically denied the kinds of financing that facilitated border crossing. This reality was magnified when newspapers noted the city council was reviewing contracts "to see how much public money has gone to build up the city's ethnic communities."[29]

The Hispanic Development Corporation and the Arab American and Chaldean Council developed in ways that mirrored the proposal for an African Town. For example, the Arab American population and the Arab American and Chaldean Council were based in Dearborn, an adjoining suburb, but drew funds from the Detroit city government.[30] They gave proof to an assertion Vivian made that opposition to the proposal came from people "who, in most cases, do not live in the city but they do business here."[31] The comment reflected the undue influence of businesses that operated in Detroit but did not share the same material stake in the city's future as its residents.

Prominent civil rights activists supported the African Town proposal, including Boggs, who challenged the conflation of immigrants and African Americans as minorities. She pointed out that she was the daughter of a Chinese entrepreneur and drew on her personal experience of "living for 50+ years in the inner city of Detroit . . . [which made her] very conscious of how relentlessly Black Detroiters have been deprived of opportunities to be productive and entrepreneurial."[32] Her perspective was not just a difference of opinion, but a vantage point shaped in relation to white supremacy and anti-Blackness. She asked a pointed question: "Why do folks feel threatened when blacks [sic] get together?"[33]

Boggs's question indicated non-Black groups relied on the abstractions of threat and exclusion to justify their actions, including mob violence against Black communities. New forms of violence depended on words to do similar work and demolish the plan to develop African Town. For example, several articles quoted Angela Reyes, the executive director and founder of the Detroit Hispanic Development Corporation, for her criticisms of the proposal and demands for a public apology.[34] One article listed her as a protest rally organizer.[35] Another quoted Joseph Reyes, the treasurer of the Hispanic Business Alliance. These references made Hispanic community leaders in general, not just entrepreneurs, seem particularly vocal opponents of the plan. The community leadership's influence was magnified when one article pointed out that "Latino groups" were the ones considering a class action lawsuit against the plan.[36]

Hispanic community leaders positioned themselves and the population they represented in a different relation to white supremacy and anti-Blackness than Boggs. In other words, not all immigrant and native minority groups agreed that the proposal was exclusionary, but Hispanic groups focused on Anderson's report (rather than the city council's resolution) and their own experiences of being treated like immigrants despite their long history in the city. Their claims did not focus on the city's overall development. For example, a Southwest Detroit business owner said her family "built this place up from nothing, with only our own sweat."[37] The narrow focus on her family's effort ignored how Southwest Detroit was produced and benefited from public money. In contrast, other activists emphasized the city's development. Helen Moore, a nationally recognized education activist, spoke to a group that "stormed the Detroit City Council auditorium."[38] She told "opponents of the plan from southwest Detroit" that "there is nothing in this resolution that would discriminate against you . . . I am the granddaughter of a slave. We are demanding a level playing field . . . everyone has a business district; we are the only one [sic] left out."[39]

The Latino community leadership's demands for an apology indicated the struggle between racial and ethnic groups was not only about a competition for material resources or limited to African Town. They also positioned Latinos' relation to anti-Blackness. "Leaders of various ethnic communities" demanded an apology from the city council for references made in Anderson's report.[40] The city council obliged and passed a third resolution in October 2004 that "apologized for the unease the previous two [resolutions] might have caused" the Hispanic, Asian, and Arab communities of the metropolitan area.[41] The city council's deference foresaw a shift in Detroiters' fortunes.

The Hazards of Not Accounting for Race

An important part of the controversy surrounding African Town centered on whether public funds could be targeted to a specific race. The loan fund seemed doomed by its explicit references to African American residents. An article in the *Detroit Free Press* confirmed that the US Department of Housing and Urban Development wrote a letter to the city council warning that "if it planned to use federal dollars to create such a business district, it couldn't use any name that gives the appearance of limiting participation to one race."[42] This did not necessarily affect the private banking commitments or a $38 million dollar minority business fund that would be paid for by Detroit's three casinos. The project survived as a skeleton of its former self and proposed a name change to resurrect a new Paradise Valley. It was dramatically reduced in scale to a four-block area, and instead of developing a large group of entrepreneurs, it focused on a few developers of luxury businesses and apartments.[43]

"African" was subordinated as an abstraction in favor of comparable enclave developments named "Mexicantown" and "Greektown." The distinction is belied because the US Census includes nationalities under the category of race. For instance, it counts as "Asian" any person having origins in Cambodia, China, India, Japan, Korea, Malaysia, Pakistan, the Philippine Islands, Thailand, and Vietnam. In contrast, the Census does *not* include the continent of Africa as a race. There were other important comparisons: The African Town proposed in 2004 involved creating a quasi-public corporation, not unlike the Detroit Growth Development Corporation or the Detroit Land Bank Authority. These two groups did not explicitly refer to race but were nonetheless directed in ways that residents insisted corresponded with white, outsider interests.

Debates over a loan fund for Black entrepreneurs were hotly contested in 2004, but only four years later, amid the national foreclosure crisis, JPMorgan & Chase developed the Entrepreneurs of Color Fund to serve the corporation's interest in promoting positive relations with city residents. It seemed HUD left "economic power and economic rights" in the hands of the same white-dominated corporations that had consistently undermined that power and those rights. JPMorgan & Chase's website subsequently touted that the fund started with Detroit but had been rolled out across the nation: The ideas associated with African Town had become a national model after all.

Summary

The case of African Town is important for several reasons. One of the most significant is that Anderson's proposal struggled to recognize Black Detroiters as an underserved population. The city council's plan to direct public support for the development of an ethnic community was not without precedent, but the city's contracts with Mexicantown and Greektown were directed at organizations rather than individuals. The proposal tried to compensate for racial biases in lending, but the focus on developing Black entrepreneurs threatened non-Black groups located in and outside of the city. Their collaboration and protests against African Town enabled discrimination against Black entrepreneurs to go unaddressed. It also fashioned the relation between these groups: The struggles between white supremacy and anti-Blackness made Latina/o/x community leader protests like a sideview mirror reflected across the country by mainstream media outlets, including *The New York Times*.

The proposal's focus on developing Black entrepreneurs had a longer history whose more recent chapter was tied to President Richard Nixon's use of Black capitalism to placate the demands of the Black Power movement. It was a political strategy that promised everything and cost virtually nothing because Nixon had not dedicated any significant resources to support the mandate. The approach nonetheless foreshadowed the kinds of proposals for Black self-sufficiency that were reflected in the African Town proposals. The city's mayor would face an important corruption scandal in years after the city council backed away from the African Town plan. This turned the proposal into a form of government propaganda for people to place their faith and trust in the private sector to solve social problems. In the years that followed the city's bankruptcy, corporations would rely on media to laud the ways they helped Black businesses even if the support had little measurable impact on developing or expanding Black entrepreneurship. Black capitalism promoted the development of a relation between entrepreneurs and consumers that undermined race cohesion.[44]

The related issue of affirmative action has received similar attacks at the national level, but these criticisms focus narrowly on claims of individual exclusion. The case of African Town demonstrates that an individual's opportunities are largely tied to the places we produce. White people have historically benefited from a variety of colorblind practices that nonetheless demonstrate unequal outcomes, especially when they are tied to residential segregation and its effects on home value and access to a quality education. These are the kinds of relations between people and space that create enduring inequities because we do not take account of race. This was the strategy that shaped public-private partnerships in the years leading up to and following the city's bankruptcy.

6

Public-Private Partnerships

Regime Change and "Some New Form of Management"

It had been thirty-eight years since the New York *Daily News* ran the infamous headline "Ford to City: Drop Dead." The *Detroit Free Press* ran a comparable headline in 2013 that promised the feds were listening but there was no chance of a bailout for the majority Black city. The Obama administration bailed out banks and the automobile industry, but offered the city some computers, technology, and federal personnel. It directed financial aid for Detroit's recovery through a public-private partnership: the Detroit Blight Removal Task Force slated half of the $300 million package of federal, state, and foundation aid to demolish blighted buildings. The Obama administration also appointed an investor to head the task force. Dan Gilbert had moved his company's headquarters to Detroit three years before, but he still lived outside the city and many Detroiters considered him an outsider who benefited from the city at their expense.

The federal government's plan seemed to ignore Detroit's residents. The majority Black city had already experienced significant demolition and displacement after World War II, a trend reflected in James Baldwin's famous quip that urban renewal meant "negro removal."[1] Detroiters came to distrust outsiders because they exercised an outsized influence over the city's economy and politics. Foundation leaders usurped their role, acted as unelected public leaders, imported development plans from other cities, and dismissed legacy residents' immediate needs and concerns. In the years that followed the city's bankruptcy, many working-class and poor Detroiters scorned headlines that proclaimed the city's renaissance while they were dispossessed of their homes and property.

A report out of the US President's executive office summarized the federal response to the bankruptcy. It credited President Barack Obama for his confidence in the city and in American workers. It recognized the federal talent offered the city their assistance and resources for recovery. The report followed its observation that Detroit was not always successful in competing for federal awards and instead offered a "favorite local slogan: Detroit Hustles Harder."[2] The slogan implied the city had an ability akin to underhanded and irregular forms of action that qualified the federal government's relative lack of financial support. In contrast, the auto bailout cost US taxpayers about $80 billion, about four times the amount of the bankruptcy.

The plans that developed before and after Detroit's bankruptcy were not simply another case of urban politicians prioritizing development over people. The conviction of Mayor Kwame Kilpatrick for fraud and racketeering had shaken residents' trust in city government, which was only amplified by Mayor Dave Bing's plans to radically transform the city. A variety of business, civic, and public leaders across the country considered that the public-private partnerships that preceded and followed Detroit's bankruptcy were innovative and instructive for urban areas within and beyond the United States. One professor who participated in the development of the Detroit Future City's (DFC) strategic framework suggested that "the eyes of the nation, the world, are on what Detroit is doing right now because it is unprecedented."[3] Another considered the DFC report to be "arguably the most radical reimagining of a postindustrial city to date."[4] Public-private partnerships like the DFC's strategic framework, the Blight Removal Task Force, and the city and county land banks sought to create real estate markets, but their plans traded on empty abstractions that shifted collective focus from people to property. They undermined democracy as they produced a Detroit that promoted wealth for predominantly white outside investors.

Public-private partnerships dominated the city's purported resurgence. They took many forms that reconfigured the relation that produced race and space in Detroit. Scholars like Kimberley Kinder, Claire Herbert, and Sara Safransky documented how residents struggled to produce space in relation to one another, but Detroiters' collective efforts were undermined by, for example, targeted philanthropic foundation spending, the city and county land banks, and development incentive packages that included transfers of public property and tax increment financing reimbursements. Some bankers, journalists, and scholars credited these partnerships with dramatic improvements after the city's bankruptcy because it meant control over the city's development shifted toward "some new form of management."⁵ Other scholars and many residents complained that public-private partnerships were not transparent or accountable to the city's residents.

Amber Alert: The Increased Importance of Public-Private Partnerships in Urban Development

Public-private partnerships mapped white interests into Detroit's development plans, primarily because they were outsider led and focused. The DFC's framework resulted from two year's work overseen by "a rich, suburban foundation run by a White suburbanite."⁶ Predominantly white corporate and philanthropic foundation leaders used their finances to define development. Their plans were shaped with other nonresident outsiders who were concerned about the legacy of white flight; they sought to attract young creatives to the city. Residents believed development plans could promote racism irrespective of their individual proponent's racial background because the plans were developed in white-majority cities. For example, Rip Rapson came from Minneapolis and was appointed the CEO and president of the Kresge Foundation in 2006. He led Kresge in hiring the urban planner, Toni Griffin, who led "major planning efforts in Newark, New Jersey, and Washington, DC."⁷ Rapson disagreed with residents' demands for plans developed with residents. He considered urban development plans could be transferred between cities and argued outside expertise was exactly what the city needed. Many residents and even planners themselves did not agree that urban development was racially neutral.⁸ When a new white mayor's administration built on public-private partnerships, it nonetheless repeated empty abstractions about responsible homeownership and productive use that were associated with white cultural practices, racial disparities in wealth, and knowledge about laws related to property. In the chapter that follows, I explain how racism also influenced the production of the property fiction through efforts to collect data and monetize Detroit's land parcels.

The DFC's strategic framework complemented the Blight Removal Task Force's report: the former anticipated vacancy and the latter identified indicators of future blight. These definitions did not serve the interests of many legacy Detroiters who found both their homes and neighbors' in the crosshairs of what powerful groups planned for the city. Many undoubtedly wondered if there was a relationship between where they lived, the reports' maps, and the likelihood that they would get a blight ticket that could lead to losing their homes and real property. Many asked who paid for the DFC's bold definition of the city's fifty-year aspirational forecast for the city. If asked, many Detroiters would probably consider that Rapson focused too narrowly on the Kresge Foundation's two-year investment. They might point to the costs borne by US taxpayers who paid for demolitions across the city. Or they might focus instead on the loss of affordable housing that followed in the years after the reports were published. The framework and the report defined development in ways that extended beyond economic markets because they produced a radically transformed relation between race and space.

Philanthropic organizations seem to offer gifts. Indeed, some might say Detroiters looked a gift horse in the mouth. Rapson himself asserted philanthropy was "the sector best able to provide the long-term vision and shorter-term investment of capital the city needs to right itself."[9] His perspective marked an important shift in philanthropy that more explicitly distinguished gifts of charity from their investments in cities. The shift was welcomed by the post-bankruptcy city government, which reflected a trend across urban areas faced with compensating for the reduced support they received from state and federal governments.[10]

The influence of foundations over the city's future was mirrored by Detroit's bankruptcy. Scholars associate philanthropy with the extension of elite control, the concentration of power in the hands of corporate leaders, and the promotion of a new age of inequalities.[11] They note that philanthropic organizations changed the ways they thought about their work and their funding after the 2008 Great Recession because corporations and investors came to believe they could create "shared value" for themselves and for communities.[12] This shift undermined the belief that government leaders, laws, and legal institutions should protect the public from private interests, which was reflected in Rapson's belief that the organization's vision and capital should lead the development of a new Detroit. The shift was also mirrored by Gilbert's support for the Blight Removal Task Force's report. Another outsider's relation to the city was marked by JPMorgan & Chase's (JPMC) CEO, Jamie Dimon, who promoted the multinational financial service firm's investment in Detroit.

The DFC framework, the Blight Removal Task Force, and JPMC depended on corporate influence and big data to produce the property fiction and refashion redlining for the post–civil rights era.[13] The Detroit Future City (DFC) report produced vacancy as an abstraction, which was mirrored by JPMC recycling density in the twenty-minute neighborhood and celebrating it at the 2016 Venice Biennale. JPMC's data depended on the abstractions to shift the terms of inclusion and exclusion away from explicit references to nonwhite residence and toward racially coded indicators of cultural and financial capital, including the number of sit-down restaurants and credit card transactions in a defined area.[14] JPMC's global head of research for corporate and investment banking, Joyce Chang, recognized this coded pattern when she explained: "It's like in investment banking, where you rank an opportunity 'green,' 'amber,' or 'red.'"[15]

The emergency AMBER Alert that shoots across our phones, radio, and television screens means "America's Missing: Broadcast Emergency Response." It signals a child is missing, but it is also a metaphor for reconsidering Chang's reference to amber coding. The reference provided a context to understand Dimon's repeated associations of Detroit with America. He considered the city was a laboratory for the kinds of innovations he believed demonstrated that businesses could develop better, more effective public policy because of their control over big data. He claimed that businesses were free of political ideology. He associated data with JPMC's competitive advantage and emphasized that America's strength lay in its rule of law. This association seemed particularly ironic considering JPMC's role in the 2008 foreclosure crisis and its own experience of being prosecuted by the Department of Justice that considered the resulting settlement the largest with a single entity in American history. Dimon's reference to the rule of law also seemed ironic in the largest Black city in the country because it had been recently punished by reverse redlining, then a wave of foreclosures, and then the largest bankruptcy in US history. Dimon redirected ongoing concerns about trust and lending and inverted the relation JPMC had recently exercised with borrowers in the city in the years leading up to the bankruptcy.

Philanthropic organizations encouraged broad recognition of their role in the city's revival. They made the Grand Bargain and the city's exit from bankruptcy possible. The Kresge Foundation supported the University of Southern California's research on urban revitalization, including a two-day conference that was well attended by national leaders of many philanthropic organizations. Panels focused on topics like "Philanthropy's Catalytic Role," and Rapson was the conference's keynote speaker. Kresge was part of an important trend: Philanthropists, business schools, and investors promoted abstractions like shared value to insist that the increasing concentration of wealth would safeguard the common good. Even Gilbert held to the maxim that one could "do well by doing good."[16] In the years following the bankruptcy, a variety of influential groups similarly lauded JPMC's investment in Detroit.

Philanthropic organizations are invested in what some scholars call philanthrocapitalism. They rely on a much older belief that traces back to Adam Smith's claim that "collective social benefits would naturally accrue as a result of an individual maximizing his own self-interest."[17] Eighteenth century economists similarly promoted the idea that markets followed natural laws and were moralizing, politically civilizing forces.

Philanthrocapitalism informed a variety of powerful groups who traded on abstractions to describe JPMC's investment in Detroit: doing good, inclusive capitalism, shared value, and virtuous circles. Dimon and the various groups who lauded JPMC's investment in Detroit recognized it was an experiment, but continued exposure in mainstream media, industry periodicals, and business schools turned the loans into an object lesson for America and the world. JPMC's investments also produced at least three other realities. First, Dimon relied on Leslie Stahl and an episode of the television show *60 Minutes* to impress audiences with JPMC's use of big data to support Mayor Mike Duggan's efforts to develop twenty-minute neighborhoods. Stahl explicitly compared the company's big data with the US government's and declared JPMC the winner, which seemed ironic. After all, JPMC relied on census data to demonstrate the impact of its investments in Detroit.[18] Second, Dimon celebrated the profit JPMC made on loans to entrepreneurs of color. Although there was little in the way of public disclosure regarding the terms of the loans, research in other cases of philanthrocapitalism identified a consistent pattern: Investors required that they benefit from philanthropy even when the rewards for recipients were unclear or nonexistent.

Some scholars focus on "the gift" to explain the motivation for philanthropic exchanges, which meant the exchanges were not solely economic or narrowly tied to self-interest. The gift echoed Adam Smith's invisible hand: It operated where markets were absent.[19] JPMC's investment in Detroit seemed to be a gift that made "flexible capital" available where credit markets were absent.[20] Dimon emphasized that JPMC's gift was "not the money. This is a very important thing. It was about the advice, the help, the consulting, the ideas, the human capital."[21] The ways Dimon talked about JPMC's investment in Detroit revealed that markets were not natural and JPMC created them through credit.[22] He cast JPMC's initial contribution in 2014 as if it were a gift "to grow the economy. As an American patriot, Detroit is one of the few cities which hasn't had a real renaissance. They can have one here too."[23] Dimon frequently referred to himself as a patriot in the years after the foreclosure crisis, the Great Recession, and the Department of Justice settlement. He also repeatedly associated Detroit with America. His words were empty abstractions that indicated JPMC's relation to multinational financial services, the regulatory frameworks in which the company operated, and his efforts to promote its global leadership. His letters in JPMC's annual reports suggested the company's interest in public policy was intended to reduce repetitive and contradictory regulation in different countries where it operated. JPMC's philanthropic work was tied to broader projects to "drive inclusive economic growth in the U.S. and around the world."[24] It relied on public-private partnerships to promote policy as philanthropy.

When Foundation Funding Outsizes Public Spending

Foundations are often perceived to be independent from both market forces and electoral politics, but "the notion of an independent, charitable, voluntary realm remains one of the country's greatest myths."[25] They had the funds and the staff to shape public-private partnerships that directed the city's strategic plan. This raised at least three important concerns about foundations' interests, particularly for Detroiters. First, foundation leadership concentrated influence in persons and small groups who defined the city's problems and solutions. A related issue was that some foundations' spending priorities were decided by boards that had weak to no relationships with local groups. This meant foundations favored development plans that followed models developed in other cities. Foundations also aligned with dominant ideas in urban planning that Detroit should be restructured, rightsized, and downsized.

Foundations prioritized and directed their funding to nonprofit organizations that aligned with their interests and perspectives. One Latina/o/x interviewee referred to as "nonprofit darlings" to critique the undue influence they had over development in Southwest Detroit.[26] An executive working with a local branch of a national nonprofit pointed out that it was clear among grantees that some nonprofits were favored in the city, which she believed was because one of their CEOs was a white man. Foundations were neither democratic nor accountable to Detroiters and could not substitute for broader social welfare programs. Foundations' involvement in Detroit's development was a decisive example of a public-private initiative, but their funding priorities were consistently directed toward shaping regulation in ways that eroded public governance and that expanded inequities and corporate influence.[27] They nonetheless became a critical influence on Detroit's redevelopment as their spending outpaced federal expenditures. For example, one scholar observed that "from 2005 to 2011, Michigan-based foundations authorized $382.5 million in grants to Detroit nonprofit NPOs [nonprofit organizations] conducting community and economic development activities. Federal community development funding to Detroit through the Community Development Block Grant, Home Investment Partnerships Program, and the Housing Opportunities for Persons with AIDS totaled $367.6 million during this period."[28]

Foundations also had a strong influence on Detroit's development plans. The Knight Foundation set a precedent in 2003 when it increased its awards and their strategy to target six areas of the city for investment. This marked the beginning of targeting areas for place-based investing. Other foundations followed, recapitalizing their investments and taking a more engaged and proactive approach to funding nonprofit organizations. Rapson shifted Kresge's focus from brick-and-mortar buildings to funding nonprofit organizations. Foundations began working with one another. For example, they launched the New Economy Initiative in 2007 that promoted entrepreneurship in Southeast Michigan. Among its target areas, Kresge initially focused on an "eds and meds" approach to development centered on an area that included Wayne State University, Henry Ford Hospital, and the Detroit Medical Center. Rapson wanted employees of these facilities to relocate to Detroit. He called the plan the Lower Woodward Corridor

Initiative. It would build a larger central city core because Woodward Avenue could connect downtown development to the development of an area they called midtown. Several foundations also worked on what was initially called the M-1 rail line and eventually called the QLine, because Quicken Loans bought naming rights. The streetcar is another example of a public-private partnership. It weaves through traffic along Woodward for 3.3 miles. Foundations laud their success in producing people and space. Eight years later, residents continue to give the QLine mixed reviews.

Foundations targeted specific areas of the city to attract predominantly-white migration to the city. For example, the Hudson-Webber Foundation launched "15x15" in 2008 to "to attract 15,000 young, talented households to Greater Downtown Detroit by 2015."[29] Their population-centered approach focused on drawing potential residents that could foster creative development. Place- and population-centered approaches complemented each other. The shared interest in creative development was supported by many urban policymakers because of Richard Florida's research. He was a professor who published books and met with urban leaders to promote his idea that creative classes could drive economic development in postindustrial cities.

The creative development approach was taken up by cities around the world. In a five-part 2012 series on "The State of Detroit," Florida claimed a "creative thing pulsates in the DNA of the city."[30] He credited creative people with the city's "revitalization" because "it was not like there was any big government plan to remake Detroit. In fact, most government plans hurt the city over time."[31] He lent credibility to a skepticism shared among philanthropic and corporate communities about governments' negative influence on urban development. This consensus influenced Detroit's development and reliance on public-private partnerships. By 2017, however, Florida conceded that growing urban inequality, segregation, and poverty had created a "new urban crisis."[32]

Foundation spending was also marked by a shared reliance on bringing outside consultants into the city. This compounded residents' sense that outsiders, like the foundations themselves, had undue influence in setting development priorities. These tensions were reflected in the development of the Detroit Works Project and its successor, the Detroit Future City report.

From Detroit Works to Detroit Future City

The Detroit Works Project reflected the political, economic, and racial tensions facing residents in the years leading up to the city's bankruptcy. Foundations and urban planners sought a concrete plan for the city's future, but controversy centered on the idea of shrinking the city that dated back to the 1990s.[33] Mayor David Bing had been elected in May 2009, and by August of 2010, he began working with the "ideas of reshaping, downsizing and right-sizing Detroit" that "would be revolutionary for a large, urban metropolis," wrote one journalist.[34] Bing was an outsider who had recently moved from an Oakland County suburb to run for public office. His plan seemed further evidence of how ideas developed outside the city were imposed on its residents. It was also reminiscent of the kinds of urban renewal that displaced Black communities across the country. One activist complained they did not like the idea of downsizing the city because Detroit was "a comeback city. The best days are still ahead of us. I don't think we should be planning our demise."[35]

Bing outlined his plan: "Detroit's 140 square miles, much of it vacant or underutilized, is considered by many the largest obstacle facing a city that must become safer, more efficient and more attractive to employers and residents at a time of declining population and financial resources."[36] He announced the plan and explicitly recognized residents had historically been excluded from the city's development plans. The plan remained unpopular among residents who suspected it would include demolishing some areas of the city and relocating them to more populated neighborhoods. Several observers commented on the project's inaugural meeting in September. One noted on the "pent-up demand for citizen engagement" that resulted from "years of isolation from city decision making, frustration with service delivery and neighborhood conditions, excitement over the potential for fundamental change, and mistrust of, or lack of faith in, the city government."[37] Another observed residents were upset because Bing was not present and "small-group breakout sessions devolved into shouting matches. By the time the mayor arrived to close the event with a short speech, scores of residents had stormed out, calling the meeting a sham."[38] Even a *Wall*

Street Journal article noted the confrontational tone of the meeting when it related residents' concerns about the city administration.

The inaugural meeting reflected residents' neglected concerns and continued well after the brief project ended. The initial plan had been to cluster residents in seven to nine neighborhoods and diminish key municipal services to more than 20 percent of the city.[39] Tensions soon followed between the city and the Kresge Foundation that was financing the project. Residents' unease with the project were compounded when Kresge hired Toni Griffin. They criticized her for relying "too heavily on consultants hired by the foundation and for her own data-driven approach, often brushing aside work already done by local groups."[40] Bing emphasized the need to build trust with residents. One city official echoed that residents wanted "to know that their interests are being represented. Someone who doesn't live here can't accurately represent their interests."[41] Neither Bing nor other city officials explicitly referred to racism, but the city's African American newspaper "likened moving neighbors to the 'Trail of Tears' relocation of the American Indians. . . . [it also quoted] Rev. Horace Sheffield III [who] compared it to 'ethnic cleansing.'"[42]

Rapson believed local development required outside expertise. He claimed philanthropy was "the sector best able to provide the long-term vision and shorter-term investment of capital the city needs to right itself."[43] His approach undermined Bing's leadership and compounded residents' sense that Rapson did not take racism in planning seriously. Rapson insisted outsiders, like Griffin, were necessary because local leaders could not meet the challenge of remapping the city. He implied the plan had to be forcefully developed and introduced.

Rapson's approach preceded the Detroit Works Project and centered on promoting data-driven plans. It promoted an empirical blindness to how racism operated in the city. He treated development like a scientific problem, which was a white bias that depended on science to appear neutral. For example, Rapson not only magnified the role of philanthropy in urban development, but he also rationalized targeting investment to specific, "healthier" areas of the city.[44] He contrasted those areas with others that were "ripe for a 'restoration of the natural ecology.'"[45] Similar naturalist contrasts and metaphors have been historically tied to colonization that conflated nature with nonwhite peoples. Perspectives that consider society to be like an organism have been similarly used to obfuscate racist political actions that drive social change. They naturalize social change by noting where people settle, an outcome, rather than identifying the discriminatory policies and incentives that drive the segregation and stratification of populations. The ostensibly race-neutral language that treated Detroit as a natural habitat promoted racial inequity because it was tied to the creation of market scarcity, the valuation of property, and "accumulation by green dispossession."[46]

The Production of Property: From Vacancy to Density

An earlier chapter on neighborhoods introduced Kresge's efforts to fund data collection when it supported the development of Data Driven Detroit by Kurt Metzger. Metzger explained foundations invested in building a data infrastructure, but they replicated grantees' data production efforts.

> They were paying a lot of money to the University of Missouri, to create this platform that was no different than what Grand Valley State was doing.... So it's like, why are we going? Why are you doing this? And where does their information fall within the greater scope? If they're replicating things ... what happened to the work that we were doing? And it it's just indicative of a lot of these organizations kind of going off on whatever seems to be the latest, newest, coolest thing or some friend of a friend, or somebody knows somebody who has that connection.[47]

The data infrastructure supported a broader desire to, in Jerry Paffendorf's words, "monetize" Detroit's property.[48] Paffendorf founded Loveland Technologies and his background provides an illustrative context from thinking about how we produce space, how data creates real estate markets, and how property is a productive fiction. He graduated with a master's degree in Studies of the Future. His first project in Detroit was in 2010. He purchased a vacant lot for $500 and sold one-inch squares for $1 each to people all over the world.[49] News articles celebrated him with headlines that cast the entrepreneur's effort as one to "Save Detroit! One inch, one dollar at a time."[50] After selling all ten thousand one-inch squares, he expanded investment options for "inchvestors" to buy ghost inches that did not refer to a parcel or deed. Paffendorf marketed the ghost inches through Kickstarter, a crowdfunding web-based platform that recorded $1,779 of a $500 "pre-game" and $714 of a "continued" goal had already been pledged by May 2010.[51] The experiment indicated the ways Paffendorf repackaged land at multiple scales through what he considered "the Detroit data movement," which he said sought to democratize data access.[52]

Paffendorf explained the maps needed to "monetize" Detroit because there was no comprehensive sense of the city's parcels or their value. He launched a web-accessible map in 2011 of all tax-foreclosed properties available in the Wayne County tax foreclosure auction. The website was called "Why Don't We Own This?" The maps also indicated occupancy; speculators who lived outside the city used them to identify rental property. This tied the new mapping projects to the practices that resulted in increased evictions and residents' dispossession from their homes. In a city where over one-third of the population lacked adequate access to the internet, Paffendorf's website challenged the broader goal of information justice and open data.[53]

Paffendorf and Loveland Technology were responsible for the Motor City Mapping (MCM) survey completed in 2013, just two months after the city declared bankruptcy.[54] Over sixty days, Loveland Technology's team hired and coordinated two hundred surveyors to collect parcel-specific data across the city's 139 square miles. Surveyors used their phones and tablets to text parcel-specific data and report blight, which became known as "blexting." Loveland also used a cloud-based application that enabled a variety of users to engage in real-time and interactive data collection. Paffendorf claimed the survey data was reliable because of real-time oversight by a quality-control team and because residents could correct information about individual parcels in their neighborhood. The survey was privately funded, but the report that followed brought together state, regional, and federal actors as well as prominent business owners, including Daniel Gilbert, founder of Quicken Loans and Rock Ventures. The concluding report was published in 2014 by the Detroit Blight Removal Task Force. An earlier chapter in this book introduced the report's emphasis on neighborhoods but did not detail the abstractions of blight, mapping projects, and information justice.

The task force report's conclusions were designed to attract federal funds that had been set aside to address the consequences of the 2008 foreclosure crisis. The report emphasized the city's need to demolish what it considered "blighted" structures, which it estimated represented about 22 percent of the city's parcels.[55] They identified these parcels by combining the MCM survey with an additional sixteen datasets, including a parcel survey that had been completed in 2009. The data included utility shutoff records to determine blight, which was a particular concern considering longstanding problems with water affordability and people living in homes without utilities.[56] Paffendorf explained how he created a four point "vacancy index":

> *It would get one point if an in-person surveyor thought it was vacant. It would get one point if the water was shut off. It would get one point if the electricity was shut off. And it would get one point if the US Postal Service said they were not delivering mail there.*
>
> So anything that was a four, you could be almost sure that it was vacant, right? I say almost sure because, you know, particularly in Detroit, there are situations where people move into homes without utilities or anything else, right? It's not the rule, but it's not like . . . You're gonna find it, right? If you go looking you're gonna, you're gonna, you're gonna find it. Um, and that's its own kind of issue. If there's an informal occupant like that.[57]

The report not only quantified and thereby produced blight, but the reissued report in 2013 had 177 pages and repurposed ideas about "broken windows" and visual disorder. Perceptions of neighborhood disorder were strongly influenced by the concentration of poverty and minoritized groups that reside in the area.[58] This influenced data collection by many nonresident surveyors. Kurt Metzger had been involved with earlier surveys as well as the MCM project and recognized surveyors had different conceptions of blight. "You could send out two different teams," Metzger said, "and they would come up with somewhat different results as far as how somebody sees a piece of property or a structure as whether it's, you know . . . how, how you would grade that structure on a scale of one to four."[59] The 2014 Task Force report raised several important questions. Who decided what was considered blight, particularly considering that there was significant poverty and homelessness in the city? Many residents felt they could fix a property that wouldn't meet the US Development of Housing and Urban Development's criterion of "decent, safe, and sanitary."[60] All three words were abstractions. Public consensus followed the bankruptcy and criticized the political prioritization of wide-scale demolition over homeowners assistance. The demolition program raised additional questions about who benefited from the production of blight. Over the following years and into the present, residents continue to compete with investors, the demolition program, and the Detroit Land Bank Authority for city-owned property.

MCM explicitly claimed it wanted to share data broadly. The open data movement refers to this as information justice. Data Driven Detroit worked with the National Neighborhood Indicators Partnership, which professes a belief in democratizing information and access to data. The mapping projects helped foundations target some areas while ignoring the most vulnerable ones. Detroit went from being a city at the heart of the American Dream to one that hosted mapping projects promoting top-down spatial productions objectifying land use and users in favor of "monetizing" the city and market interests. Metzger explained his experience with foundations and nonprofit organizations to me:

> We have seen over time, different organizations take ownership of areas, not necessarily that they were given ownership of areas, but kind of take ownership of areas. We used to try to get organizations to draw the boundaries of what they're responsible.
>
> . . .
>
> *People are loath to designate boundaries, because they don't want to foreclose the possibility of another project that they could be doing just outside their boundaries.*
>
> *And there was discussion around geographic boundaries, you talk about neighborhoods, right? And so we had, that was before the city came up with council districts, but they had a number of other planning districts, they had fire districts, they had a couple other districts, we had zip codes, we had sub communities, we had census tracts, we had a number of initiatives with . . . and so, somebody wanted to figure out how do these things fit?*
>
> . . .

[It] made absolutely no sense. But it was very symbolic of the way the city has operated and the way people in the city and organizations, they just kind of create their own boundaries, and they decide we're going to work over here and, and how does that fit into to a larger framework? or How did these pieces all fit together?[61]

Metzger's frustration with the lack of consistent geographic references and coordination between different groups underscored how foundations competed to fund mapping projects. They produced space through abstractions about boundaries, geographies, neighborhoods, and property.

The Detroit Future City Report

One outcome of the Detroit Works Project was that the Detroit Future City (DFC) report outlined a fifty-year plan, which was "arguably the most radical reimagining of a postindustrial city to date."[62] It chartered a plan to shrink the city's physical footprint where there was no precedent. It built on several foundation-funded citywide parcel surveys and proposed redirecting public resources away from high-vacancy blocks. The report's authors used the surveys to support their claim that the plan was an evidence-based approach to rezoning the city.

Foundations used maps to produce Detroit's most pressing problem: vacant buildings and land. Detroit Future City released a 761-page report in 2012 with maps that emphasized "the critical question of vacant land and buildings . . . [and] abandoned parcels."[63] Seven of twelve "imperative actions" referred to "vacant land," "open space," "densities," "use of land," "areas of the city," "communities," and called for a "regional agenda," which explicitly tied the city's development to land use and outside investment.[64] Despite the report's focus on vacancy, it rationalized further vacating many areas of the future city. The findings intensified residents' concerns that the poor would be displaced in favor of speculators who have preference in acquiring city-owned property.

Critics did not accept the authors' claim of blind empiricism and colorblindness. They challenged the report's assumption that census blocks were homogeneous. They noted the proposed framework zones' contiguous rectangular shapes made their borders seem arbitrarily drawn. Their analyses revealed that the high-vacancy zones were poorer, more isolated, and more likely to have fewer white residents compared to other areas and to the city overall.[65] They also noted that one out of five residents still lived on high-vacancy blocks, which implied a much greater number of Detroiters could be displaced than figures suggested by the press and DFC plan supporters. It was as if DFC had refashioned redlining for the post–civil rights era.

Scholars discuss redlining as a practice used by banks and lenders. They tend to overlook the historical fact that redlining was a public-private partnership that was initiated by the US federal government. President Franklin D. Roosevelt's administration responded to the crises of the Depression and its impact on homeowners by creating the Home Owners' Loan Corporation to refinance existing mortgages that were about to be foreclosed. The Home Owners' Loan Corporation hired real estate agents to appraise properties. The appraisals included valuing the area surrounding the property, which realtors did using color-coded maps that the corporation itself created. The maps coded areas red to signal risk, which was determined by African Americans living there. The area was colored green and signaled a safe investment if it had "not a single foreigner or negro."[66] DFC reinvented the productive fiction that underpinned redlining as it anticipated vacancy, discouraged investment, and ignored the disparate impact that racism had on the city.

There was significant debate on the extent of public participation in the DFC's report. Critics pointed out that the plan's development suffered from a lack of resident feedback. Only 47 percent of those who provided feedback were Black in a city where 82 percent of the population was African American.[67] Several scholars suggested public engagement was an abstraction because the process did not include significant or representative participation and instead consisted largely of presentations. The planning team shared participation figures, but it was not clear how they "translated (or not) into developing a long-term plan, leading to the sense that planners were more invested in the quantification and performance of engagement than in meaningfully including residents in the process."[68] Rapson also wanted organizers to use social media and technology to capture public feedback although almost half the city's population didn't have a computer or an internet subscription in their household.⁶⁹ A member of the report's steering committee claimed, "It wasn't about participation. They were just pushing the participation button to say, 'See? We did it. We had the meeting. All right? Can we get out of here now?'"⁷⁰

The media offered a largely favorable review of the DFC report. A member of the steering committee qualified public commentary on the report on a 2013 episode of the *American Black Journal*, a weekly talk show on Detroit Public Television. She asserted that "those who came to the table . . . they were heard."⁷¹ Stephen Henderson, the show's host, also interviewed John Gallagher, another prominent journalist and author of a celebrated book on Detroit that focused on Detroit's urban and economic redevelopment. Gallagher supported the DFC's strategic framework, and his responses contrasted the actions of city planners and foundations and the concerns of the city's residents about being cut off from city services.

> HENDERSON: This plan doesn't say people will have to move, but it's clear there will be some deprioritization of certain areas and people will be encouraged to move. How realistic is that in a city like Detroit?
>
> GALLAGHER: Not very. Relocating residents voluntarily through incentives has not really worked very well anywhere.
>
> . . .
>
> *We have to understand that we can sort of work around some of the remaining occupants, residents, buildings, commercial activity in some of the most distressed neighborhoods. That's the only way you're going to work.*
>
> HENDERSON: What happens to those people who are still in areas that are mostly depopulated? Where you only have a couple of houses per block?
>
> GALLAGHER: Yeah, I think as the plan is carried out, you'll see some of the vacant lots become orchards, farms, blue infrastructure, you know, retention ponds for rainwater.
> *Now I think they'll probably, to make this go down easier, they'll probably pick the most abandoned areas to start, where there's going to be less push back.*

> *Any place you're going to a lot of push back, because there's still a lot of residents there, you're not going to see that much happening.*[72]

Gallagher's responses indicated the DFC would need a strategy "to make this go down easier." He opined it would have better success by starting in areas "where there's going to be less push back" by residents. Gallagher answered Henderson's question about people by focusing on lots and abandoned areas. He exemplified a more general reasoning that the city should work around residents who didn't want to move because, according to him, incentives had not worked in the past.

Gallagher's dismissive response ignored that many residents of high-vacancy areas lacked the resources to move. His claim was also contradicted by the comparable case of Detroit residents who lived around the proposed Gordie Howe International Bridge. Many of those residents stayed by choice or could not afford another house but they were eventually offered a home from the city's land bank plus renovation costs and moving expenses, up to $60,000 per homeowner. Gallagher lived in Detroit and was ostensibly an insider, but his comments on DFC reflected how his white racial frame worked to promote the exclusion of vulnerable, predominantly Black city residents in favor of blue or green infrastructures.

Concerns about DFC were not limited to residents who would be directly impacted by the loss of services in their areas. Southwest Detroit was targeted by DFC for adjoining the greater downtown area. It also enjoyed the attention of significant funding by other foundations and nonprofits. Felix nonetheless feels philanthropic organizations have had a negative impact on the area because they supplant government and wrest control away from residents in favor of their "nonprofit darlings."

> FELIX: Like the Kellogg Foundation, or like these foundations that give so much money to, like the community like Skillman's and blah, blah, blah. They control how that money is, like what they do with it. So yeah, yeah, you can give somebody a scholarship or something, but it's under the guise of like, rich white people money or like people who aren't part of the community. So more and more, I'm realizing that I need to have the money. If I want to see the things happen, the only change, I'm gonna need to be the actor in that I'm gonna have to

> invest in that, like, I'm gonna have to be the one that makes that happen. Because I don't want to depend on the Kellogg grant that might not come when the recession hits. I don't want to like depend on institutional money. I want to be able to provide, and unfortunately, I don't think there's a job that pays that much money, like in the community. So, like how do you . . . ?
>
> NICOLE: Well, that's a lot of the money that's coming into Southwest now.
>
> FELIX: Yeah. And "nonprofit darlings" I call them, like it's like a guise almost. Like you're, you're . . . supplementing something that the government kind of used to do or whatever now under the guise of like private money, but who's getting this private money? Who has to apply? Like just even applications for grants are dizzying like, "Oh, you have grant experience?" Like, ugh, why do we even have to do grants? So . . .[73]

In the case of Detroit, border crossing produced a white urban core, a bifurcated Black Detroit (one that was targeted for development and another that experienced intensified disinvestment), and Southwest Detroit as a liminal border crossing zone. This meant not only promoting physical movement into and through the neighborhood, which included the Gordie Howe International Bridge crossing and efforts to attract new populations into the area; border crossings also involve the kinds of social and cultural development of new businesses and murals that would support new populations and consumption patterns. In other words, development was centered on creating new markets rather than improving many of the area's existing resources, including problems with schools, traffic, and crime.

"Doing Good While Doing Good Business": The Abstractions of Shared Value, Inclusive Growth, and Virtuous Circles

The federal government's approach to Detroit and the global financial crisis remained important topics of analysis for countless books, theses, and business analysts. This attention nonetheless overlooked a critical shift in the form and significance of public-private partnerships. City governments have become more reliant on public-private partnerships not only for financing, but also for what corporations insisted was a better approach to philanthropy. Some scholars refer to this approach as philanthrocapitalism: "the tendency for a new breed of donors to conflate business aims with charitable endeavors, making philanthropy more cost-effective, impact-oriented, and financially profitable."[74] They point to an "ideological shift" away from a classical liberal belief, dominant in the eighteenth and nineteenth centuries, that there was an intractable conflict between private interest and public welfare.[75] Instead, in ways that reflect Rapson's beliefs that Kresge's vision and capital could save Detroit, philanthrocapitalism implied that corporations and investors could create "shared value" for themselves and for communities.

Philanthropy enabled elite groups to extend their power from the economic to the social and political realms of society. Philanthrocapitalism was distinguished by its shift away from an earlier emphasis on "the need to curb corporate predation through regulation and a fairer redistribution of profits" that characterized corporate responsibility practices.[76] Corporate leaders believed philanthropy meant a passive form of charity. Especially after 2008, they sought to apply their entrepreneurial tools actively and strategically to target their investments and to promote their leadership in public policy design and implementation at national and international levels.

JPMorgan Chase's investment in Detroit is an important example of philanthrocapitalism. The multinational financial services company's work in Detroit was the focus of a *60 Minutes* episode, the basis for its place at the top of *Fortune* magazine's list of companies "Changing the World," and the subject of a three-part case study of "inclusive capitalism" at the Harvard Business School.[77] JPMC considered its work in Detroit an object lesson in "inclusive growth."[78] The case mapped a global significance that implicated a new form of public-private partnership.

JPMC's standard-setting investment came on the heels of being penalized for having conducted business as usual. The Department of Justice reached "the largest settlement with a single entity in American history."[79] The 2013 settlement meant JPMC owed $13 billion dollars to government agencies, homeowners, and distressed areas. It also meant the company publicly acknowledged that it had knowingly bundled toxic loans, made serious misrepresentations to homeowners and investors, and contributed to the 2008 Great Recession. The company's CEO, Jamie Dimon, announced JPMC's investment in Detroit only six months and three days after it reached the settlement with the Department of Justice.

JPMC is the largest lender in the city, but its investment in Detroit was much more than a publicity campaign. Dimon began the company's 2014 annual report by noting he was struck that, "in spite of all the turmoil" that had occurred over the previous seven years, JPMC had become safer and stronger and "never stopped" supporting the growth of both communities and global economies. The annual report's first section boasted that JPMC had "emerged as an endgame winner" that "brought all of [its] resources to bear in a special, coordinated way, which [it] never have done before, to try to help the city of Detroit."[80] JPMC used Detroit to make itself a global innovator.

A prominent 2017 article in *Fortune*, a multinational business magazine, credited JPMC with having performed a "miracle" in Detroit.[81] It illustrated how shared value worked when it wrote Dimon had built a "virtuous circle, where more people with stable incomes foster greater prosperity. If that means more entrepreneurs and would-be homebuyers become creditworthy borrowers, JPMorgan Chase wins too."[82] The article was loudly silent on the kinds of jobs that were created and preserved. The article focused on homebuyers and borrowers, which framed financial development in terms of consumers rather than other market drivers like loan underwriters and business media. It also neglected ongoing critiques about investments that targeted some areas of the city and compounded the neglect of others.

Media, especially business publications, helped Dimon rebrand JPMC after the global financial crisis because of a shared bias. The same *Fortune* magazine article blamed the city and its homeowners for what it described as a "train wreck": "The city took a decisive kick in the teeth from the 2007–09 financial crisis, which not only drove General Motors and Chrysler into bankruptcy but exposed how many Detroit homeowners held subprime mortgages. Some 140,000 Detroit homes were foreclosed between 2005 and 2014, according to research firm RealtyTrac, shredding the city's already decimated tax base and helping precipitate its own bankruptcy."[83] The *Fortune* article ignored the role JPMC played in promoting industry standards and capitalizing on subprime mortgages, which ultimately reduced access to credit and compromised car sales. It instead blamed a majority Black city's homeowners and public officials for not paying their bills and for driving industry (and ultimately itself) into financial ruin. In simplest terms, the article traded on abstractions about the city's past, present and future to imply Black people were primarily or wholly responsible for their collective misfortune.

JPMC's investment was more than a historical coincidence that followed a global financial crisis and the city's bankruptcy. In JPMC's 2014 annual report, Dimon explained that the bank's interest in expanding its commitment to Detroit "was made possible because of our faith in the extraordinary work and talent of Mayor Duggan, Governor Snyder and Kevyn Orr."[84] All three shared important experiences privatizing public resources in ways that directly impacted Detroit's assets.

Dimon's faith in a recently elected mayor who lacked significant experience as an elected official seemed generous because Duggan's most significant professional accomplishment before that time had been to sell the nonprofit eight-hospital Detroit Medical Center (DMC) to Vanguard Health Systems. Dimon's faith and the DMC deal both revealed the limits of shared value. On the one hand, Vanguard prioritized the company's shareholders rather than patients when it considered that it would significantly increase its revenue. On the other hand, the limits of shared value were reflected in the indigent residents who worried about losing medical care. Annual reports showed Vanguard increased its revenue by acquiring DMC, in part through cuts in pay and to the number of its staff and clinics.[85] In other words, the shared value did not include all people who worked at DMC but instead came partly at their expense. Shared value is an abstraction that ties the inclusion of some to the exclusion of others.

Dimon modified the statement about his faith in Duggan with references to coming "together to work toward a common purpose" and "comprehensively and pragmatically attacking the city's enormous problems."[86] Active intervention, cooperation, and work on significant problems were dominant themes that JPMC repeated across subsequent annual reports, press releases, and interviews. They reflected important ideas about how philanthrocapitalism sought to intensify the nature of corporate intervention through governments, foundations, and nonprofit organizations.

JPMC's investment *became* what it was. In other words, over time, Dimon, journalists, analysts, and JPMC representatives offered different explanations for why the company invested in Detroit. At least

Table 6.1. Timeline of JPMC's investment in Detroit	
Year	Timeline: JPMC's investment in Detroit
2017	• #1 on Top 10 *Fortune* magazine's "Change the World" companies
2018	• Harvard Business School released a 3-part case study of JPMC's "Invested in Detroit" (A, B [March], C is a recorded conversation [April]) • 2017 JPMC Annual Report released (April)
2019	• *60 Minutes* episode "Rethinking Banking" (s52, E7) airs on national television

initially, they made the investment an abstraction that was mobilized in relation to other ideas popularly associated with the city, including unions, labor, and innovation. Peter Scher oversaw JPMC's investment in Detroit, which he believed was a result of Dimon's negotiation with the President of the American Federation of State, County, and Municipal Employees.[87] Dimon also vacillated over whether and how Detroit reflected America's (and JPMC's) experience of financial crisis. At the 2014 official announcement of JPMC's investment in Detroit, Dimon hoped that both would recover successfully: "I talk to naysayers who say America is declining. Where is the best place to be born? In America. I hope someday to say Detroit. America still loves to work. America is still innovative. We have a great rule of law."[88] Dimon concluded his discussion of Detroit in the 2014 annual report by noting that Detroit's economic recovery "would be a shining example of American resilience and ingenuity at work."[89] (See table 6.4.)

Five years later, Dimon refashioned the example for an episode of *60 Minutes*. An example of recovery became one of exceptionalism. He explained, "Detroit is probably one of the biggest failures of an American city that we've ever seen. My view is, why can't we make Detroit an example of America's exceptionalism? Have people roll up their sleeves, get together, and change the tide of history. Right there. Right now."[90] This later interpretation contributed to the dominant theme that characterized the investment as a "daring experiment" that had the potential to impact the world.[91] Detroit became an exceptional "laboratory for innovation."[92] Executives and journalists echoed themes associated with scientific intervention, but neither indicated there was any ongoing monitoring of the laboratory experiment to ensure it met ethical guidelines. The nature and the substance of the investment nonetheless generated confusion and skepticism about how JPMC's lending practices in the city had changed.

A problem with how Dimon and Scher talked about JPMC's investment in Detroit is that it initially appeared to finance the ideas and projects that foundations and Duggan had already been working on, but by 2017, JPMC was taking credit for the same ideas and projects. Aside from the money, the company's data, and its ability to use it to support earlier mapping projects, it was not entirely clear what was innovative about JPMC's investment.

Experimenting with The Emperor's New Clothes

The ambiguity surrounding what shared value meant was important to JPMC's investment in Detroit. On the one hand, Dimon repeatedly distinguished the investment from charity. On the other hand, journalists and analysts repeatedly referred to the investment in terms that blurred its relation to a disinterested form of giving. For example, the Harvard Business School professor claimed the company was "rethinking philanthropy" in his case study. The relevance of self-interest to investment seemed blurred even for other business professionals.

JPMC's investment of $100 million in 2014 was initially directed toward workforce and small business development, community development, blight removal, and funding for the M-1 streetcar system. Half of the investment was directed to two Community Development Financial Institutions Funds (CDFIs). Karen Mills, a senior fellow at Harvard Business School, moderated a recorded conversation with Dimon, Duggan, and Scher. She pointed out "some people have criticized that [investing money as loans] because you're making money on money."[93] Sher responded, "someone criticizes everything and it just . . . we don't care."[94] His blithe dismissal signaled his belief that JPMC should not have to justify its lending practices. His approach to public concern recurred when he titled one of his articles "How Detroit Became a Model for Urban Renewal."[95] The title underscored practices that traditionally benefited white investors at the expense of communities that were nonwhite, impoverished, and marginalized. Urban renewal implied the kinds of bordering and crossing practices that have historically led to inequitable development. Scher's use of the phrase and response to Mills implied he enjoyed consensus that the meaning of shared value depended on recasting exclusion as inclusion.

The loans to CDFIs deserved greater consideration because they mirrored similar approaches to risk and responsibility in lending that caused the foreclosure crisis. As JPMC's then-head of community development banking explained in Harvard's case study, "CDFIs can make loans that a traditional bank can't make."[96] JPMC loaned two CDFIs (Invest Detroit and Capital Impact Partners) money that the organizations then used to "on-lend at a higher rate. We [JPMC] allow them to lend the money on terms that we can't. For example, they can lend up to 120 percent loan-to-value ratio or at substantially lower debt yields and coverages and offer an interest-only loan for up to a 10-year tenor. Plus, they can be in deeply subordinated debt positions, which we would never be able to do from a commercial perspective."[97] In other words, the loans to CDFIs tied nontraditional borrowers to significant risk.

The recorded conversation indicated other dimensions of confusion and surprise that mapped the meanings of shared value and JPMC's investment as philanthropy. Scher pointed out that "when we started this, we did not expect to be making any money back anytime soon. By the middle of last year [2017], ten million had been repaid."[98] Later in the conversation, Duggan responded to Mills's question about "what would be your ask" from JPMC. He answered:

> So we went from 50 million to 100 million to 150 million, and they're in the 150 million, and, and the thing is somebody's . . . you, you said, Karen, they were criticized for making money. I want them to make money. Okay? If they make money on the first 100 million, as Jamie was talking about? I said, "Jamie, *if you've made money* on the first 100 million, *it's not really philanthropy*, let's do some more." He came back and went to 150. And I'll give you an example of how much they mean to us. When those 200,000 people cleared out of Detroit. You have these beautiful big brick houses that people just walked away from underwater on their mortgages. You had houses that had sold for $400,000 in 2007, that were sold for 100,000 when I got there. Houses they've been selling for 200,000. We're now selling for 30 or 40. Problem was you couldn't get a mortgage to buy that $200,000 house for $40,000 dollars because

you couldn't get an appraisal. It was crazy. These houses are sitting there empty, they're beautiful homes. And so I went to Jamie, I said, "Here's my problem. I gotta get loans and these appraisals that the feds have and put these restrictions on are killing us."[99]

Duggan's response indicated his confusion about the relationship between philanthropy and profit. It also flagged federal restrictions on appraisals as a problem for Detroit's real estate market.

JPMC's investment allowed Dimon to redirect attention away from the company's contribution to Detroit's foreclosure crisis and subsequent bankruptcy as well as the 2008 Great Recession. In the *60 Minutes* episode the interviewer and narrator Leslie Stahl asked Dimon a pointed question about JPMC's interest in Detroit:

DIMON: Very often these entrepreneurs, they need help in . . . "How do you sign a lease? How do you negotiate with the government? How can I start using a budget? How do you create traffic? How do you do social media? How can I enter the real banking system?" Which is, you know, what the ultimate goal is. So yeah, it may change how we do banking for small business and we're getting better at it.
STAHL: Detroit was in a lot of trouble before the financial crisis. But the financial crisis just did them in 100 percent. That, that was crushing. Do you *feel* in any way that you're *atoning* for the sins of Wall Street when you go and put your effort into Detroit? Is that in your head?
DIMON: Nn . . . I wouldn't use the word atone . . . ? I all think [sic] we owe back to society.
STAHL: But Detroit, specifically? The financial crisis just *decimated* the city.
DIMON: Yeah, and I think that we all have to re-earn our trust a little bit. Because what happened? It's okay to say, "Yeah, we should do better than we did last time." And I think that's true for everybody that was involved in, in the . . . the crisis.[100]

Dimon began his comments with a clearly identified "they," which referred to small business entrepreneurs. He defined JPMC's goal as improving and expanding lending to new borrowers who lacked a basic understanding of business and finance capital. This reproduced the virtuous circle association that tied philanthropy to profit. Stahl asked whether JPMC's involvement meant it recognized its moral responsibility ("atone") for Detroit's fortunes. Dimon's response generalized responsibility. Stahl rephrased her question to emphasize the relationship between the financial crisis and Detroit's bankruptcy. Dimon responded by admonishing that "everyone . . . was involved in the crisis," and suggested they should do better in the future. Dimon recast JPMC's financial responsibility by generalizing it to everyone. This responsibility included the serious misrepresentations JPMC had recognized in the 2013 settlement. Yet Dimon shifted blame onto borrowers for JPMC's discriminatory and predatory lending practices.

JPMC mediated its own risk in ways that furthered questions about its leadership and control over the resources that create shared value. In the *60 Minutes* episode, Dimon explained that "it's not the money. This is a very important thing. It was about the advice, the help, the consulting, the ideas, the human capital."[101] His assertion echoed what the federal government had offered the bankrupt city: computers, technology, and expertise. The *60 Minutes* episode was hosted by Stahl who followed Dimon's assertion about human capital and narrated: "It was about the data that the bank collects and crunches every day, more information about business and consumers than the government collects."[102] Her statement compared the amount of data collected by JPMC versus the federal government and implied the US government was *not* the winner. JPMC's 2014 annual report similarly reinforced the value of its employees and its information when it referred to "our people" and "our top managers." In other words, according to them, JPMC controlled the resources (capital, data, expertise) that could direct a city's recovery.

JPMC's investment created new, proprietary bordering practices. Both Scher and Duggan explicitly recognized that JPMC profited from working with CDFIs to establish who and what could engage in crossings and access the kinds of capital that would enable their participation in the city's recovery. JPMC's resources acted in much the same way as the Detroit Future City maps; they controlled resources and how they were directed in ways that targeted some areas, people, and entrepreneurs and not others. JPMC's investment had not only produced new forms of inequality in Detroit. It also refashioned a legacy of inequity that drove earlier redlining and urban renewal projects. Unlike its predecessors,

JPMC's post-financial-crisis formulation sought to replace the kinds of government oversight and regulation that challenged the way it did business.

One outcome of the Detroit Future City proposal (DFC) had been the production of vacancy as an abstraction; the commensurate philanthropic response for JPMC spending was to produce density. Chase's database shifted the terms of inclusion and exclusion away from explicit references to nonwhite residence and toward racially coded indicators of cultural and financial capital, including the number of sit-down restaurants and credit card transactions.[103] Chase's global head of research for corporate and investment banking recognized this coded pattern when they explained, "It's like in investment banking, where you rank an opportunity 'green,' 'amber,' or 'red.'"[104] Chase used "big data" to reinvent redlining for the post–civil rights era.

The Black Borrower, The Black City, and "Inclusive" Growth

The confusion about JPMC's philanthropy recurred when Mills asked Scher about the company's support for entrepreneurial development. She credited him with implementing the investment but noted, "You've only touched maybe one hundred businesses. How do you measure success in what you're doing?"[105] Earlier in the recorded conversation, Dimon put the figure closer to "forty or fifty loans." JPMC's support for entrepreneurial development was particularly important because it was explicitly directed to the Entrepreneurs of Color (EOC) loan fund and scaled beyond Detroit to several other cities. Scher didn't answer the question. He instead redirected the discussion:

> So Karen, let me say a couple things, and I actually want to try to get a little bit what [sic] the mayor said and where Jamie was going.
>
> If you look at what brought Detroit to where it was before he was elected, it was bad public policy over the course of . . . you know, thirty or forty years. Um, and so part of when we began, as you, when we began to reimagine how we can approach these things, we felt it was important for us to try to be part of the solution to these challenges. And, and where could we bring unique perspective and unique capabilities and unique resources. And so we focused on some key areas.[106]

Scher's response to a direct question about JMPC's impact and success made the interaction seem less of a conversation and more a delivery of prepared arguments. His claim about the period before Detroit's bankruptcy was ironic. He evaded a question about JPMC's success by refocusing the audience's attention on "bad public policy" that he dated to the period between 1973 and 1983, which was the period of Coleman Young's administration. He followed by underscoring JPMC's attempt to "try to be part of the solution" by using its data to support Duggan's development goals. Scher distracted the audience from "what brought Detroit to where it was before he [Duggan] was elected." After all, JPMC had only five years earlier publicly recognized that it had misrepresented its financial products to homeowners and investors.

The way Scher talked about Detroit's Black leadership was a form of colorblind racism.[107] He does not explicitly refer to race, but it mattered to the majority Black city, especially because it explained the disinvestment and lack of capital over the thirty or forty years before the city's bankruptcy. Race also mattered to entrepreneurs of color, their relationship with JPMC, and the success of the EOC initiative. Neither Scher nor Dimon identified what, if anything, had changed about JPMC's lending practices to people of color except that money went through an intermediary. The bundling of money though a CDFI was not entirely unlike the bundling of good and bad mortgages that led to the 2008 foreclosure crisis and the 2013 settlement. There was no way to know whether JPMC's lending practices reproduced similar predatory terms and interest rates. In the past, redlining meant African Americans seeking to buy a home were denied a loan. But the extension of loans on predatory terms brought African Americans into the housing market as owners under disadvantageous terms. Without explicit acknowledgment of how entrepreneurs of color were counseled or the terms of their loans, there was no way to determine that new lending markets did not reproduce earlier patterns of discriminatory lending. These examples illustrate how narratives have consequences and promote colorblind racism.[108]

Scher's response demonstrated how easily racist tropes were uncritically exchanged by corporate leaders at even the most prestigious business schools. Scher claimed Detroit had been governed by "bad public policy" for almost half a century. The period was one in which Mayor Coleman Young created the Detroit Economic Growth Corporation. It was a quasi-public body that engaged in the kinds of experiments that preceded JPMC's investment by fifty years. Young's policies had been sufficiently innovative and sound to promote an investment-grade rating from Moody's, which was "a tremendous feat considering the degree of economic decline affecting Detroit at the time."[109] Scher's general evaluation did not provide any details to identify what was bad about Detroit's public policy before the city's bankruptcy. It displaced blame onto an unidentified cause that left an older, tired, racist, but nevertheless dominant, narrative in place that made Black mayors (and cities governed by a predominantly Black public administration) synonymous with "bad public policy."[110]

The Harvard Business School professor considered JPMC's investment in Detroit to be a case study of inclusive capitalism. His definition relied on Dimon's statements and JPMC's press releases. The term was not explicitly defined in either case. Dimon's statements and JPMC's documents also did not define inclusive growth. They instead listed ways to achieve it. The professor's case study referenced a press release that referred to "inclusive economic growth in underserved Washington, D.C. neighborhoods."[111] Neither the reference to underserved neighborhoods nor the webpage outlined what they lacked. The undefined concept of underserved and inclusive growth nonetheless drove Dimon's goal of making "opportunity available to all Washingtonians no matter the neighborhood they live in."[112] The press release identified two wards, which demonstrated one way that JPMC bordered, targeted, and produced spaces for investment.

Dimon's abstract references to underserved neighborhoods provided a clue to what he meant by inclusive growth. A Google search indicated Wards 7 and 8 were profiled in a *Washington Post* headline that noted they had "long represented poor, Black D.C. neighborhoods."[113] The JPMC press release had also referred to minority small business owners. Dimon and JPMC signaled racial difference but avoided identifying what made a particular neighborhood and its residents underserved. JPMC elided the question of why these communities lacked access to capital and to markets in the first place. JPMC fashioned itself as doing good without explicitly addressing what had changed about how it did business or how it diverged from a historical pattern of the financial industry's racism and predatory lending.

Dimon and JPMC's use of abstract concepts was a form of racism that took place through communication and policy. Many scholars identified the ways racism rationalized inequity through explanations that defaulted to the economic market outcomes of ostensibly colorblind markets.[114] Some scholars noted "there is no neutrality in the racial struggle."[115] This meant antiracism required consistent identification and description of racism as a policy or idea. JPMC and Dimon's refusal to explicitly address racism in their lending practices avoided the kinds of truth and reconciliation that have historically characterized meaningful changes in practice and policy. JPMC used these evasions to reposition itself and shield its reputation.

Another important word that recurred across recorded conversations, television episodes, and quoted statements involving JPMC's investments in Detroit was the word "local." JPMC saw itself as bringing data and expertise (through the Service Corps) to public-private partnerships. It insisted the initiatives could be scaled globally by partnering with government (elected leaders) and nonprofits (local community) and conflated a variety of groups with competing interests. For example, local communities were internally complex and not always effectively represented by nonprofit organizations. JPMC's references to the local often excluded institutions like the Kresge Foundation that had been critical to the EOC initiative. The word "local" served in JPMC press releases as an abstract reference to people and groups where individuals were replaced by other abstract units like "communities." The abstractions did two things. First, they were a way of distancing local actors from JPMC. Second, they enabled JPMC to invert the relation between business, government, and society. If the government had fixed what banks did to *global* societies through bailouts, then JPMC could project itself moving forward into the future and refashioning itself as not only part of the solution for *local* areas, but also the lead author for these solutions. JPMC could fix societies across the world through data and expertise that it deployed locally.

When Dimon and JPMC recognized individuals, they were either white (Duggan) or a generalized "they" who benefited from the company's philanthropy. Dimon claimed JPMC invested in Detroit because he believed in Duggan's leadership, but mayors and city governments were not prominent in subsequent examples of JPMC's investments in other cities. A consistent idea, albeit undefined, was Dimon's claim that the way to solve difficult social problems was not about money but rather about "who's doing it."[116] JPMC and Dimon's references to "they" tied people to place. For example, Dimon explained JPMC was "providing minority-owned, neighborhood small businesses with the capital and advice they need to get off the ground and become engines of growth."[117] His framing produced spaces where people lived and conducted their own businesses. Dimon and JPMC had reimagined what had once been formally segregated spaces as underserved neighborhoods. They imagined residents' desire for spatial mobility would no longer be controlled through policies around segregation because, as Scher explained in the conversation with Mills, mobility could be minimized through data and expertise:

> One of things that data is telling us is how far people have to travel, particularly people in poor neighborhoods, to buy groceries, to go to pharmacies, to get dry cleaning, to go to restaurants. And so we can look in Detroit and understand now, "Where is . . . where are the pockets of money that are being spent on groceries? And what's the access?" And you begin to develop an economic development strategy around that you can fund grocery stores, you can fund pharmacies, you can fund commercial corridors.[118]

The issue of trust and faith is central to understanding the case of JPMC's investment in Detroit. Trust initially surfaced as a matter of concern when Mayor Bing tried to impress upon Rapson what the Kresge Foundation and the Detroit Works Project needed to build with Detroit residents. Bing established that trust referred to racism, or at least residents' concerns about the potential for racial inequity, in plans developed through public-private partnerships led by outsiders. The result of Bing's concerns and Rapson's money and influence meant the latter pushed the former to divide Detroit Works into two components and focus on the short-term components. Rapson and Kresge developed the long-term plan that Duggan inherited as Detroit Future City. It included many of the mapping and targeting projects that JPMC later took credit for supporting. This made JPMC's role in the city's recovery seem greater than it was because many projects had been conceived before the city's bankruptcy.

Dimon expressed his faith that Snyder, Orr, and Duggan could support Detroit's recovery. On the one hand, the 2013 settlement forced the company to acknowledge it had made serious misrepresentations to homeowners and investors and contributed to the 2008 Great Recession. On the other hand, despite it being the city's largest lender, JPMC did not acknowledge it had played a role in bringing the city to where it was before Duggan's election. Dimon instead said borrowers had to reestablish his trust in the *60 Minutes* episode. These statements and events were ironic and operated in the same way as abstractions: They signified the opposite of what they claimed to be. JPMC was not a company that should have the authority to legitimately establish a basis for trust and faith, but trust was fundamental to the extension of credit.[119]

Dimon valued JPMC's expertise in ways that resonated with Felix's criticism: Gatekeeping institutions created and assigned value to human capital. Felix referred to universities while Dimon's experience and influence were value-producing institutions in themselves. In other words, value was a product of faith and expectation about who influenced markets. JPMC created value through the data that consumers provided and through its own consulting. Its work with Detroit was not directly accountable to the public or minoritized groups. The limited transparency mirrored the terms of the 2013 settlement with the Department of Justice. The settlement's monitor reviewed documentation on each of the five agreements that were referred to collectively as the Chase Residential Mortgage–Backed Securities (RMBS) Settlement. Its details were likely cryptic to the average consumer. The monitor tried to account for the details over email and explained that settlements with financial services firms "were developing art forms in 2013 and got more granular in later settlements. Chase was in early and got the most lenient deal."[120]

Dimon considered JPMC's most significant investment in Detroit was the "human capital" that he believed the city, its residents, and its entrepreneurs lacked. Dimon and Scher repeated that they were part of the solution but, besides Duggan, they only credited their own data and expertise for what *Fortune* magazine considered a miracle. Dimon repeated the successes of JPMC and rolled the EOC fund out to other cities but, at least on its own website, the company rarely profiled individual entrepreneurs. One illustrative exception named an entrepreneur in a sentence clause before reporting that the company promoted federal policy changes.[121] JPMC presented public-private partnerships in ways that centered almost exclusively on itself, which demonstrated an unequal relationship. Dimon was not an elected official and was only accountable to his shareholders, most of whom lived outside of Detroit.

Trust was undoubtedly a critical public issue following the 2008 financial recession. Different surveys attempted to measure what many journalists and scholars referred to as a "trust deficit," which referred the distrust that people across the world had for business. For the Harvard Business School professors who coined the idea of shared value, the lack of trust extended more broadly to capitalism itself. For example, Michael Porter and Mark Kramer wrote about created shared value in the *Harvard Business Review* and argued businesses had to consider corporate responsibility to be competitive.[122] Dimon echoed some of these ideas in JPMC press releases and the recorded conversation, but he shifted blame for social problems onto ideology, party affiliations, and politicians. He repeated that the Detroit example had been successful because of the kind of politician Duggan was: "People trust him."[123]

In both an undated press release and the recorded conversation with Karen Mills, Dimon identified both party affiliations and ideology as sources of ineffective and irrational public policy. Mills referred to 2017 JPMC's annual report and observed it began with a "very long" letter from Dimon in which almost twenty pages talked about public policy. He responded that businesses needed to be more broadly involved in developing public policy.

> MILLS: You spend a lot of this annual report talking about how we are going to do things like get our country on its feet, get Detroit on its feet and prospering. So, here's the question for you. Why is it, is it business's job to engage in public policy? How should business be engaged? What are the boundaries, if there are any?
> DIMON: I think public policy or business and society are inextricably linked. And so you can look at any country and you can have examples of great countries and bad countries and great cities and bad cities and great states and bad states. And it's all around public policy. Poorly designed policy leads to terrible outcomes.
> I make a list in there. And I think if you're an American citizen, you should read this list. It's on one page, it's very discouraging . . .

> ... our tax system, workforce, small business formation, wages, medical care, infrastructure...
>
> ... our inner-city school kids don't graduate kids, which means you know, there might be a *Barack Obama* in that group, there might be an Albert Einstein. So, we're not providing opportunity to our people....
>
> Business has to be involved. 150 million people work in America. 130 million work for private enterprise. 20 million work for, for cities, schools, states, etc., and we hold in high regard, but *we've got to get the country doing a better job* for all of our Americans. It's all around public policy.
>
> There are groups that do it well.... I think business does get involved, there are limits... there are *things that you the citizens of the world are going to decide*. And there are things that businesses are very good at.[124]

Dimon's three-minute response identified five important ideas that were echoed not only in the letter included in the 2014 annual report, but also in subsequent annual reports and JPMC press releases. They indicated Dimon believed JPMC's data and employees produced more public policy more effectively than politicians, residents, or citizens.[125] His response to Mills also illustrated that Dimon also believed public policy was the expression of the relationship between business and society. Second, Dimon considered the government's role in mediating that relationship later in his response when he implied that the twenty million people who work in the public sector could do a better job. Third, the breadth of policies that Dimon believed JPMC should inform extended beyond his response. In addition to the ones in the quote just given, he subsequently responded to an audience member's question about the trade-off between taxes and "these social ills: these human capital problems, these physical capital problems."[126] Dimon added immigration to the list of issues that JPMC could "attack" more effectively with specific policies that would "actually get at the heart of it, and not just yelling and screaming each other because it doesn't work."[127] Earlier in his response to the audience member, he had referred to socialists and Democrats, which reinforced the conclusion that Dimon had positioned JPMC as more effective at developing public policy than politicians. Finally, his reference to "citizens of the world" supported his framing of political parties and ideology as having a negative impact on public policy.[128]

Dimon positioned JPMC's investment as an alternative to the welfare state and public spending. The idea was repeated across press releases that repeatedly contrasted the company's work in Detroit with political ideology and partisanship. Like the idea of shared value, they shifted explanations for urban poverty away from the loss of manufacturing jobs toward assertions that JPMC was "doing good" by fostering loans and providing "businesses with the skills to pay the bills with interest."[129] JPMC's press releases asserted its philanthropic spending promoted development more effectively than local, state, or federal governments. For example, it claimed it could more effectively close the gap between lower-skilled workers and jobs "by fostering small businesses and training workers."[130]

The ways JPMC saw itself replacing public functions raised important questions about accountability. For example, Felix's understanding of opportunity was focused squarely on questions of racial disparities over the control of financial resources. In other words, it was precisely the fact that private money was part of vertical philanthropy controlled by "rich white people" that meant he and his community were further removed from government oversight that he could hold accountable for public needs.

The ways that Dimon believed JPMC could use its data and expertise to drive public policy reforms were also troubling because the federal government has historically promoted the kinds of civil rights reforms that lessen the impact of structural racism. Dimon's reference to Obama in his response to Mills demonstrates why his arguments for expanding JPMC's role in public policy was a problem. Dimon was a corporate leader whose advice extended to other businesses, which was evidenced by the attention given to JPMC's work in Detroit. Dimon juxtaposed two conflicting associations. He referred to inner-city school kids, which implied urban areas of concentrated poverty that are most often dominated by minority or minoritized immigrant groups. Dimon also referred to the possibility that Obama could be one of those kids, but the former president of the United States attended private, elite schools. Dimon associated Obama's Blackness with inner-city schools to argue they do not provide opportunity for African American students. It reflected the association of inner cities with Blackness and failure. This example of colorblind racism indicates the limits to Dimon's inflated sense of the role JPMC should play in developing public policy.

Dimon's approach to its investment in Detroit had a history that preceded and followed the city. JPMC worked with The Brookings Institution in 2011 to develop the Global Cities Initiative that promoted the economic integration of US metropolitan areas in global markets. JPMC credited its work in Detroit for expanding similar work to Chicago and Washington, DC. In 2018, JPMC announced the AdvancingCities initiative would promote similar work around the world. Scher oversaw JPMC's philanthropy and efforts to influence public policy across the globe through PolicyCenter. Dimon referred to JPMC's investment in Detroit as an example of American exceptionalism. He saw JPMC's leadership in the United States as a model for the world.

Summary

Millions of homeowners experienced foreclosure during the Great Recession, but it was banks and the automotive industry that the federal government deemed "too big to fail."[131] Detroit was not a model of neoliberal governance that relied on privatizing public functions, but instead one that marked a new approach to public-private partnerships in which corporations and foundations led city, state, and federal governments in designing urban reform. This approach only further entrenched cities' dependence on ostensibly colorblind markets, but also naturalized whiteness through data and related abstractions about urban vacancy and shared value.

Conclusion

Getting Past the Overlay to the Underplay

Writing this book was about more than penning another book about Detroit. A diverse audience of scholars, journalists, tourists, investors, and recently settled residents saw the city as a laboratory and considered its residents part of an experiment.[1] They largely missed the city's most important lesson: how we produce race and space. Two examples show what I mean. The first happened in a class I taught in 2009 on social problems. My students seemed up to date on the twinned crises of foreclosures in the city and the automotive industry bailouts that affected the metropolitan region. I wanted to know what they thought about the city at that point in time, so I asked them to free write about how they would describe it to someone who had never visited. I asked them to indicate whether they lived in or outside the city.

I coded thirty-nine responses and found a discrepancy between Detroiters and nonresidents. Almost half (46 percent) of students who lived in the city used words or phrases like "love," "fun," "unique," "amazing," and "great city" to describe Detroit. Most students (54 percent) did not live in the city. Some of their descriptions referenced possibility, segregation, or a desire to make greater use of the city, but most were emotional reactions to the way the city "looks." These descriptions used words or phrases, like "filth," and "lack of care." When I asked students to think about the difference between the responses, one nonresident student who presented as white suggested Detroiters exaggerated the city's positive attributes. He opined that Detroiters' descriptions were intended to help them "feel better" about the city.

I'm not sure how students who lived in the city thought about the difference in responses because no one else wanted to answer. The student who had delivered a partial truth about the city's misfortunes ended the discussion when he dismissed the experiences of his classmates who lived in Detroit. He hadn't considered they might be telling the truth about how they experienced their lives in the city. All that mattered to him was what we could all agree, must agree, was true, because it had been reported to us in our newspapers, on the radio, and in countless news reports over the television. It was mirrored in countless examples, including the MacArthur Fellowship ("genius grant") recipient Camilo José Vergara who had similarly insisted that Detroiters denied an "obvious" reality that their downtown buildings were ruins.[2] At the same time, the white student likely took advantage of inexpensive housing and probably shared the sense he was doing something good for the city. He was like the philanthrocapitalist who felt they were doing good while doing good business.

A second example and important point of comparison happened much later in July of 2024. I attended an event intended to improve research relations between residents and a globally recognized university that was about a forty-five-minute drive away from the city. Over the years I learned Detroiters felt they were a laboratory for the university's research, but at this event, the researchers presented summaries of their community-engaged projects, including community violence intervention programs. The question-and-answer period allowed the audience to reframe the issues that the researchers had discussed. For example, they distinguished crime as a matter of public perception "manipulated by the police and media" from the "violence that is happening all the time to us."[3] One person posed the matter directly. Eugene ("Gene") Cunningham was an older Black gentleman that had been sitting in the back of room. He explained:

> Some of your efforts are in the wrong direction. Maybe you should broaden your study to the city administration and some of the stakeholders in the economic development of how we got here in the first place. I'd like you to understand that in a lot of these areas, the city is an active agent behind perpetrating some of the inequalities that they claim they want to address.
>
> Let me give you two big examples. [He talked about tax increment finance areas, subsidies for developers, and property tax overassessments.]
> . . .

The city had a homeownership program that was based around urban homesteading, a law that has been on the books for forty years that they refused to implement that involved home ownership and home repair that was engendered by a city council from forty years ago.

And that most of the money that they spent was actually going toward demolition of a lot of properties that could have been saved.

So, the people that you're engaging with, they tell you that they want to solve these problems [another audience member says "exactly"] should themselves be researched by you [another audience member says "allright"] as to why they are the perpetrators of the problems that they *claim* [emphasis his] that they want to address. [two audience members say "mm hmm," and "yes"] And if you're successfully able to do that [audience member chortles], then you can come to the public at large and find out, "Well, why is this happening?" [several audience members say, "problem solved," "that's right," and "yes"].[4]

There were several notable features of the older gentleman's comments. First, he complained about what he felt were unjust practices carried out by the current city administration and developers. Many of those bordering practices were discussed in this book. Second, he distinguished a homeownership and repair program that was "engendered by a city council from forty years ago." He referred indirectly to Mayor Coleman Young's administration and a relatively long period of Black governance when he referred to "forty years ago." Finally, many audience members punctuated his comments and indicated their support and agreement with his claim that the poverty solutions researchers were studying the wrong population.

Cunningham's comments recalled a question that Du Bois posed over 120 years earlier: "How does it feel to be a problem?"[5] Du Bois revealed the doubleness of abstraction: The problem was the person producing his racial difference, even if they did not ask him their question. Audience members commented during the question-and-answer period, but scarcely addressed the content of the researcher's projects. Instead, they focused on what the researchers had missed about the relationship between the city's residents and a variety of groups that profited from them, at their expense. They talked about land and tax dollars that had been redirected from public use to "stadium development." Another audience member reflected, "It's like we're paying for our own demise." One pointed out that "in the city of Detroit it is hard for people of color to get their initiatives off the ground, but we look around and people that are white that come in, they get whatever they need." The theme of audience members' comments was that recent development initiatives did not benefit legacy Detroiters.

The student's observation in 2009 and the audience members' comments in 2023 reflected a pattern: Detroiters felt they had been so frequently studied, and yet they were still so little understood. Most researchers and commentators considered their questions to be about Detroit and its residents rather than their own relation to white supremacy. The students who lived in Detroit clearly had a different perspective than the white student whose ideas were shaped by media rather than experience. He had recently moved to the city and felt he was part of a wave of new, young people who were moving to the midtown and downtown areas and making the city "better." He felt legacy resident students shouldn't exaggerate the city's positive attributes, but inflated his own role in contributing to the city's resurgence. This inversion exemplified how a powerful group (young, white, college-educated men) claimed authority over describing the city to others. He naturalized his whiteness. In contrast, audience members felt the problem was another powerful group, the city government and developers, rather than legacy residents because violence was "happening all the time to us." One of the researchers eventually recognized that what he called "invisible violence," which included things like community centers being closed in the city, were not a part of his study on community violence.

Detroit has been largely defined by outsiders who do not reflect on their own relation to what they consider its problems. This was repeatedly reflected by mainstream news outlets who used their international audience to define Detroit's main problem: too much (square miles), too little (population size), too late (decades). Influential figures echoed the idea that the city's leadership had been stagnant for over forty to sixty years even though at least five different mayors during that time faced different challenges and had different priorities. Kevyn Orr claimed elected officials had been "coming this way for sixty years" and were to blame for leading the city to bankruptcy.[6] Scher similarly distinguished

Duggan from the "bad public policy over the course of . . . you know, thirty or forty years."[7] The theme was repeated in the days leading up to 2013 election when Stephen Henderson asked Dan Kinkead, director of Detroit Future City's Implementation Office, what he needed to see from a new mayor and a new city council. Kinkead responded: "We need to make sure leaders are embracing innovation here, you know, the thought process we need to have around Detroit's future needs to be one that isn't tied to decision making that's gone on in the last 20 to 30 years."[8] The patterned judgements against Black governance disregarded the challenges of disinvestment, predatory lending, and state preemption. They also reflected a tired stereotype about Black people and sameness. They inverted Mayor Dave Bing's innovation: He began what became Detroit Future City, but people like Kinkead took credit for envisioning a new future for the city. This demonstrated the advantage that powerful groups had in realizing their dreams for the city's future.

The problem of outsiders' anti-Blackness extended well beyond Detroit's borders. For example, another MacArthur Fellowship ("genius grant") recipient, the sociologist Loïc Wacquant, found that the concept of an underclass gained credibility as it circulated among "academic, political-policy-philanthropic and journalistic fields."[9] His analysis illustrated it was a consequential classification that impacted urban reality, but revealed more about those who used the term than those who it ostensibly designated. In other words, underclass was another empty abstraction that revealed a relation between powerful groups and the people they claimed to represent.

The doubleness of abstraction encouraged this book's focus on two themes. First, it denaturalized what we take for granted about the relationship between race and space. These were the kinds of phenomena shared by the student and the researchers in the examples given. Both the Detroit resident students and the audience members felt space was produced through human action and their experiences of the city, but the white student and the researchers took the conditions they were studying for granted and naturalized their experience of "the world from a stable (white, patriarchal, Eurocentric, heterosexual, classed) vantage point."[10] The problem with the container theory of space was also reflected in my analysis of other abstractions that operated as partial truths and deceptive mystifications, including "sprawl," "blight," "vacancy," "tipping points," "broken windows," "twenty-minute neighborhoods," "responsibility," "virtuous circles," and "shared value." One of the most important insights of this analysis was that urban scholars, planners, philanthropists, and politicians reverted to natural imagery and blind empiricism to substitute for clear analyses. These reductions promoted white supremacy.[11]

Second, this book used cases of abstraction to reveal the relation between white supremacy, anti-Blackness, accumulation, and dispossession. The relevance of these cases was confirmed by the older gentleman's comments and the audiences' reaction in the 2023 university–community engagement event: The abstractions were related to experiences that mattered to Detroiters. For example, one audience member objected to the distribution of resources in the city in which new white residents "get whatever they need." Another protested the disparities in funding between grassroots and corrupt nonprofit organizations. My examples of Southwest Solutions and "nonprofit darlings" underscored the problems with the nonprofit industrial complex, particularly because they reinforced the relation between white supremacy and anti-Blackness through their Latina/o/x clients.[12] My analysis focused on the role of philanthropic organizations in encouraging the nonprofit industrial complex and eroding local, grassroots, democratic control over development and social services.

Felix, Fausto, Mireya, Jorge, and Luisa's lived experiences contrasted empty abstractions around property, real estate, and neighborhoods. These abstractions were perhaps most colorfully illustrated in Jerry Paffendorf's case: He created the possibility of investing in ghost inches of real estate that were untethered from physical land or a deed. The 2012 Detroit Future City's Strategic Framework similarly insisted "Detroit must be welcoming to all, including those moving in from neighboring cities [and] those who are originally from other countries," which implied the city was not already welcoming and that attracting new residents was its priority. The Framework also inverted the relation in which the predominantly white suburban ring was not welcoming to majority Black Detroiters; drivers along the 8-mile-border were heavily profiled and ticketed by suburban police. Abstractions about property and potential residents enabled powerful groups to recast the majority Black city after its bankruptcy to be a diverse one with 209 neighborhoods. Other powerful groups followed the Department of Neighborhood's example, including Vergara, who believed people of the future were rebuilding the post-bankruptcy city and negotiating its identity online, beyond the city's borders, by outsiders, and no longer spatialized along the Black-white color line. These examples telegraphed how individual experiences of dispossession were shared by a city that lost control over its assets, including the Detroit Institute of Arts, Belle Isle, and the Detroit Water and Sewer Department.

Residents' experiences of being secure in owning their homes, struggling to hold onto property, becoming insecure after losing their property, and then being forced to accept their new status as a renter undermines our taken-for-granted assumptions that belonging is narrowly tied to ownership and property rights. There were multiple ways that Detroiters lost their homes in the years leading up to the city's bankruptcy, including mortgage and tax foreclosure. These experiences were compounded by other forms of extraction, including high car insurance, water bills, and property taxes, over assessed property taxes, and interest penalties on tax bills. At the same time, the Detroit Future City Strategic Framework and the Blight Removal Task Force engaged in the kinds of speculation that commodified land. Dan Gilbert's leadership of the task force illustrated how financial entities like Quicken Loans and Rocket Mortgage used abstraction to create a problem and then define themselves as its solution. The state worked with the city and federal governments to use Hardest Hit Funds, and then eventually issued bonds, for demolition rather than construction. This new debt was speculative: It shrunk supply and raised market rates for real estate and housing. At the same time, the Hardest Hit Funds were public funds that had been redirected away from people who needed homes. They complemented the role of foreclosures and demolition and helped financial entities turn a city of owners into one of renters. Powerful groups tied to finance not only produced but also financialized space. Investors could bundle parcels and buy them through tax foreclosure auctions, then either leave them empty or rent them, allowing the property to either become blighted, resold for a higher price, or, in many cases, returned to another tax foreclosure auction to repeat the cycle.

The financialization of space depended on public-private partnerships that transferred desirable public property located in the downtown area to Gilbert, the Ilitches, and the Marouns, among others. These speculative investments complemented other quasi-public organizations, like the Detroit Economic Growth Corporation and the Detroit Land Bank.

These public-private partnerships reflected the kinds of governance that Jamie Dimon idealized because they promoted the role of businesses like JPMorgan Chase in developing public policy. He exported the model through the Global Cities Initiative.

Other abstractions like "trust" mapped how the production of race and space changed in the years leading up to and following the bankruptcy. Mayor Dave Bing emphasized the need for the Kresge Foundation to build trust with Detroit residents so that the Detroit Works Project would be successful. Tensions between Bing and Rip Rapson, Kresge's CEO, forced a division of labor between short and long-term planning. Rapson insisted philanthropy was "best able to provide the long-term vision . . . the city needs to right itself."[13] He privileged other outsiders, including the urban planner they hired, and plans they developed in other cities. Perhaps the strongest criticism of what became the Detroit Future City Strategic Framework, besides that it intensified inequality, was that it failed to adequately represent the city's residents. Bing associated Detroiter's lack of trust with anti-Black racism, a trend repeated in the case of JPMC's investment in Detroit. Dimon emphasized that Detroiters had to gain his trust after JPMC settled with what the Department of Justice in what it considered the largest settlement in US history. He also explained that his trust in Mayor Mike Duggan justified JPMC's support for Detroit's recovery. This trust drastically contrasted with the distrust that a variety of outside investors had in Detroit's Black governing structure, which Mayor Coleman Young recognized had impacted the city in the decades after he was elected.

Rapson was like Emergency Manager Kevyn Orr in that both believed Detroit's turnaround depended on outsiders. Rapson trusted them to provide a vision aligned with ecology and nature, which depend on empty abstractions that have historically furthered racism in urban planning and development. Orr insisted that Governor Rick Snyder should hire Jones Day because elected officials would not make the kinds of structural changes that he (Orr) believed the city needed, notably undermining pensioners who earned much less than the lawyers hired to negotiate the city's bankruptcy. The assumption that outsiders were better custodians of the city's future indicated that they believed Detroit belonged to outside investors and its potential new residents. Orr also traded on the abstraction that underpinned the presumed relation between race and action when he claimed that "for a long time the city was dumb, lazy, happy and rich."[14] He related the city's financial difficulties to municipal workers that "had an eighth grade education" and got "30 years of a good job and a pension and great health care."[15] His references are part of a long history in which the abstraction of laziness has been used to dispossess Black and Latina/o/x populations of property. In this immediate case, Orr's reference to the city's workers was also an abstraction that obscured how his law firm and its partners benefited from the bankruptcy proceedings. For example, David Heiman of Jones Day billed the city $1,075 an hour and $34,000 to go between Detroit and his vacation home in Florida.[16] Orr also hired consultants that extracted millions from the proceedings, including Conway MacKenzie that collected $27 million in fees "with several individuals earning $400 per hour—or $832,000 annually on a full-time basis."[17] Meanwhile, Orr negotiated a settlement with the city's retirees for a 90 percent cut to their health care benefits.[18] Orr's reference to rich municipal workers was an abstraction that inverted how his own actions enriched his social networks.

Cunningham's first example in his comments at the 2023 university–community engagement event were tax increment finance areas; it was an empty abstraction that he used to reveal the relation between the development of the predominantly white downtown and midtown areas of a majority Black city. This development was largely the product of the bankruptcy, the city's first white mayor in forty years, mapping efforts in the Detroit Future City's Strategic Framework, Paffendorf's "Why Don't We Own This?" website, the Motor City Mapping survey, the Blight Removal Task Force's report, and JPMorgan & Chase's efforts to support Duggan and the development of twenty-minute neighborhoods with big data. Powerful groups depended on abstractions about value, trust, responsibility, and risk that were informed by racial difference. They refashioned redlining for the post–civil rights era but insulated them from public scrutiny. Where the Home Owners' Loan Corporation used redlined maps to refinance existing mortgages, the mapping efforts leading up to the city's bankruptcy were informed by how powerful groups anticipated vacancy and indicated future blight. The predictive measures were productive fictions about a future that monetized the city's real estate, financialized the city, and facilitated accumulation by dispossession. Targeting areas for investment has heavily impacted the city's development and Detroit activists continue to struggle against the extractive redirection of property taxes for downtown, midtown, and luxury development.[19]

I described the Latina/o/x experience in Detroit as a sideview mirror and used the metaphor to name what I observed: Rather than a static racial identity, Latina/o/x youth struggled for social and spatial mobility in relation to a majority Black city and the predominantly white suburban ring that surrounded it. Their experience looked forward to financial security and freedom that seemed concentrated in the richest and whitest areas of the metropolitan region. Latina/o/x youth consistently felt that white suburbanites were free to come into the city for a variety of reasons, including entertainment and to dump trash or make graffiti. These freedoms were tied to white supremacy because, as they explained, white kids could simply leave the city when they were done and did not have to live with the consequences of their actions. In contrast, the Latina/o/x youth I spoke with did not feel they had the same kinds of freedom of movement. They also did not want to experience the same kinds of exclusion and discrimination that seemed an important part of the Black experience in the nation's largest Black city. For example, Latina/o/x youth who I thought were dark skinned said they were "brown" and "brown . . . and white" when I asked how they saw themselves.

Vergara's writings, his status as an outsider, and his influence on discussions about the city reflect an increasingly important dimension of the Latina/o/x experience in the United States. He is Chilean and mirrors the growth of the South American immigrant population in the United States and Southwest Detroit. Many of these immigrants come with human capital in the form of college degrees. The increasing diversity erodes the Latina/o/x population's cohesion around an identity as a historically marginalized group. It also sharpens the utility of the sideview mirror metaphor because it reflects how the population's fortunes are tied to the *longue durée* of struggles between white supremacy and anti-Blackness. The militarization of police underscored this reality for interviewees like Mireya and Jorge who worry about racial profiling. They also influenced residents who joined the Black Lives Matter protests during the summer of 2020.

Interrogating empty abstractions proved instructive. For example, the authors of the broken windows theory admitted at the time they first published their ideas that there was no empirical basis to support their thesis. The abstraction nonetheless encouraged police to escalate their use of brutal force. Andrea Ritchie is a lawyer who represented many nonwhite people who have been negatively impacted by broken windows offenses. She thought broken windows policing was not about reducing crime, but instead about "assuaging white fears, however irrational or racist, of poor and homeless people, Black people, people of color, and queer and gender-nonconforming people."[20] I similarly analyzed Richard Florida's 2012 series on "The State of Detroit" and critiqued his naturalization of the city's DNA. By 2017, Florida conceded that his promotion of creative development resulted in growing urban inequality, segregation, poverty, and had created a "new urban crisis."[21] A more recent example of how using empty abstractions to identify inequitable relations was evidenced by the most famous proponent of the tipping point. Malcolm Gladwell recently admitted he was wrong, but his acknowledgment offered no reparative compensation and came too late for the millions of nonwhite people whose lives were negatively impacted by the stop and frisk policies that resulted from his ideas.[22]

A colleague who read a draft of my manuscript said that, upon reflection, "it's all abstraction." To a certain extent, I imagine he's right: All language and thought depends on abstraction, but he missed the point. He naturalized the historical origin and use of categories and accepted their formality and emptiness. He neglected the social nature of abstractions, which are often hidden and taken for granted in human relations. His comment reminded me of Mack at the bottom of the stack of turtles in Dr. Seuss' story. Mack knew it wasn't an infinite number of turtles all the way down, but many academics are like King Yertle at the top of the stack who depend on formal, empty abstractions for their authority.[23] Formal, empty abstractions are modeled on white experiences of the world; they impoverish life. Detroiters engaged in unauthorized occupations and used public property without authorization, including for art and for gardening. Their collective cation demonstrated how concrete abstractions could be realized through struggle, including movements for inclusion, equality, justice, and democracy.

ACKNOWLEDGMENTS

Detroit has been called a "movement city" and I am grateful for all the wonderful people I have met here. They taught me life lessons that extend well beyond the city's boundaries. Elena Herrada was one the first Detroiters I met. She subsequently became a friend and patiently explained the dynamics of the city's struggles. I especially appreciate all the lessons I've learned from her work "showing up" for the people of Detroit.

I am also grateful to my students who motivated the questions for this project almost as soon as I arrived in the city. My students in the Center for Latina/o and Latin American Studies were foundational to establishing my early concern for how we would weather the rocky years leading up to the bankruptcy. Thank you for sharing your strength and joy as you created new, beautiful lives for yourself in and beyond the city.

Thank you to community members who helped me understand Southwest Detroit and its residents. Wonderful people like Raquel Castañeda-Lopez, Amelia Duran, Antonio Cosme, Sacramento Knoxx, Mayte Penman, Laura Chavez-Wazeerud-Din, and Robert Dewaelsche helped me map the area's challenges, its relation to the city, and residents' ongoing struggles surrounding development and against colonization and gentrification.

My colleagues at Wayne State University have been especially generous with their time and interest in thinking about the city's changes. My conversations with David Fasenfest, Steven Winter, Andy Newman, Janine Lanza, Patrick Cooper-McCann, Eric Bettis, Andrew Guinn, George Galster, Alex Hill, David Goldberg, Peter Hammer, John Mogk, and Krysta Ryzewski were particularly helpful. Thank you especially to Eric for helping me create multiple census tract maps to help the reader envision Southwest Detroit. Their contributions to our collective understanding of "what's going on" are precious and inspiring examples of how we make our work and lives matter. I am also thankful for their time in reading my work and sharing their ideas with me. Thank you also to Heidi Gottfried, Prudence Cumberbatch, Jack Blaszkiewicz, Ariel Helfer, Janine Lanza, Lauren Duquette-Rury, David Merolla, and Zachary Brewster for reading over and giving helpful feedback on chapters and sections of the book. Thank you also to my colleagues at University of Michigan who shared helpful insight into their university's relationship with Detroit's development, including Margaret Dewar and Peter Draus.

Kidada Williams deserves special recognition for helping me move beyond university distractions to focus on my research. Her advice about writing and publishing was invaluable. I am especially grateful for her ongoing engagement with "the literature" and her continual encouragement to think about the audience and the craft of writing.

This book would have been impossible without Lisa Anderson's daily support as my writing partner. Thank you for being such a good colleague and friend. I am also such a fan of my other writing partner: Teresa Gonzales, whose support as I finished the manuscript was invaluable. She along with other colleagues helped me think about book workshops and I am especially grateful to her participation, along with that of Vanesa Rosa, Louise Seamster, and Carlos Hernandez. Our work together will remain an inspiration for an alternate way of doing scholarship that leans into more engaged, thoughtful, and generous support from colleagues who are truly committed to good work and a better world. I am also thankful to the Race and Space research group that came out of that interest in working collaboratively and for the productive support of colleagues like Zawadi Rucks-Ahidiana, Angela Simms, Ana Villareal, Sarah Mayorga, and Amaka Okechukwu.

I was also fortunate to spend some time with Detroiters for Tax Justice. Thank you for the lessons about the underplay!

Thank you to anonymous reviewers for their feedback and support of the book's project. I am also fortunate to have worked with such a wonderful team at New York University Press that included co-editors of the Latina/o Sociology Book Series: Pierrette Hondagneu-Sotelo and Victor Rios. I am especially grateful for my editor, Ilene Kalish, for her helpful advice and support for this project. Thank you also for your careful and patient support: Associate Production Editor Ainee Jeong, Editorial Assistant Priyanka Ray, and Copy Editor Ann Boisvert. I also thank the rest of the wonderful team: Publishing Director Eric I. Schwartz; Cover Designer Brady McNamara; Design and Production Manager Charles Hames; Publicist Jenny Rossberg; and Marketer Ingrid Xu. Thanks also to Arc Indexing.

I would not have had the time and funds to collect and analyze my data, much less write the manuscript, without the generous support of the Humanities Center, the Office of the Provost, and the Wayne Academic Union at Wayne State University. I especially appreciate the helpful support of Walter Edwards, Jamie Goodrich, and Sara Kacin.

Thank you to Enrique for his daily support that made our family and our lives productive and joyful. Liani and I are grateful for how he drove this project forward.

My daughter Liani once asked me to write a dedication to her for my previous book. At some point or other I wrote some notes about how guilty I felt for taking time away from paying more attention to her toddler years to finish it. I still remember she was in first grade when she asked when I would be done with this book so I would have more time with her. Now that she's completing eighth grade, it looks like I'm right on time for high school! Thank you for your patience on weekends and on vacation when I took time to plug along at this manuscript. *Eres me principio y fin.* You will always inspire creativity, joy, and wonder! Thank you for coming into my life and being you.

APPENDIX I

Bordering Practices

Table A.1. Examples of prominent bordering practices

	Positions/Agents	Rules
Maps and Measurement	· Foundations · Universities · Speculators (investors)	· Data-Driven Detroit (D3) · Motor City Mapping (MCM)
Administrative Boundaries	· Federal and State Government · Districts · Zip codes · Census Tracts	State retains significant authority. Can · undermine local control over cities (Home Rule, Dillon's Rule) · roll back civil rights gains in Black-governed cities.
Legal status	· Law · Politicians · Interest Groups · Department of Homeland Security Officers · Local and State Police	· Politicians build political capital by promoting immigration enforcement. · Business interests related to enforcement promote (a) expanding (interior) enforcement, (b) increasing technological development (surveillance). · Local police and jails to partner with ICE · Policing and deportations split families and increase housing insecurity.
Surveillance/Policing	· Federal Government · Businesses	· Green Light Project (facial recognition)
REDMAP	· Republican strategists · Politicians/voters	
Zoning	· City Government · Builders/developers · Politicians/voters	· From Harlan Bartholomew to Zoning Analytic 2020
Neighborhoods	· Block Clubs · Neighborhood Maps	

APPENDIX II

Methods

The data I collected helped me outline the relation between race and space. They indicated a predominantly Black population was repeatedly deprived of their ability to govern the city, particularly under state-mandated emergency managers. The city's experiences with emergency managers were not limited to Kevyn Orr who handled the bankruptcy but began much earlier in 2008 when the state began appointing emergency managers to oversee Detroit Public Schools. These lived experiences of "when democracy disappears" were only compounded by a variety of private and publicly funded data collection efforts that preceded the bankruptcy and that endeavored to monetize its land parcels.[1] Many city residents associated those efforts with the tax foreclosures and dispossession that followed. Their concerns reflected a patterned problem for social scientists who struggled to recruit marginalized populations in their research. These populations included people with minoritized racial identities, the poor, the homeless, and the illiterate. A significant percent of Detroit residents occupied one or more of these identities. There was significant evidence that they were excluded from urban planning and development. These factors indicated *Detroit Never Left* should consider alternate data sources in its analysis.

My interviews indicated that group boundaries changed as respondents compared their experiences to other racial and ethnic groups. For example, an interviewee might say she was "Mexican" when I asked, "What do you say when people ask 'What are you?'" By the second interview, the same interviewee would explain why their experience was unlike that of a white suburbanite. The labels they used for themselves shifted from a national identity to a racial one when their narrative focused on how they saw themselves as a Detroiter. The strategies they developed to make sense of and maximize their opportunities in the city, in the area they considered Southwest Detroit, in the metropolitan area, and in relation to Mexico indicated the ways they distinguished themselves from others based on race, class, and location. Respondents' choices encouraged a shift in my analysis toward a broader set of practices that they used to produce the spaces they could access and the struggles they experienced trying to cross the borders they faced.

In the introduction to the book, I mentioned my regret over not being able to share all the painful stories that interviewees shared with me. This regret is not because I minimized or, alternately, wanted to capitalize on their suffering. Instead, all the Latino/a/x youth I spoke with shared stories that paralleled one another's struggles to create opportunities in their lives. For example, Maya talked about her struggles to split her time between work and school. This was the most significant theme in interviews with Latino/a/x youth between the ages of 20 and 24 because there was a consistent tension between being able to afford college and being able to attend college. Transportation and freedom of movement was an inextricable part of that struggle. Many youth held multiple jobs. For example, one of Maya's jobs was to work with a group that connected the internet locally to people who lived within Southwest Detroit. Most Latina/o/x youth I spoke with struggled to attend college, but they also shared a desire to improve Southwest Detroit and contribute meaningfully to the lives of youth "like them" who did not go to college. These struggles overlapped, such as when Fausto spent most of his time working, going to school, and coaching soccer.

Another important and consistent theme involved the ways that youth navigated race as they moved within and beyond the city's borders and tried to make sense of non-Latino groups. These were deeply personal experiences that mapped their friendships and romantic experiences. For example, Concha talked about how her darker-skinned baby was treated differently by her family. Her intimate struggles with color seemed just as real for her as they were for lighter-skinned youth who did not want to be considered white because they felt it would mean rejecting their families. They also complemented darker-skinned interviewees who did not believe color had made a significant difference in their lives.

The intimacy of color and movement within and beyond the city was perhaps most marked when youth struggled without their parents. Flor's experience losing her in-laws and their house to foreclosure paled in comparison to Julieta's struggles to adapt to life in Mexico. She was a teenager when her parents were deported and after many traumatizing experiences there, came back to Detroit and struggled amidst poverty, home foreclosure, and housing insecurity with her aunt and cousins. Deportation was a familial experience that continued to have devastating and long-term impacts on her life and her extended family. This was not unlike Jorge who was also burdened by his family's mixed legal statuses and his distance from his beloved mother and grandmother who had returned to California.

All of these stories came together to create the sense that, as Marx had explained, abstractions were being made real "behind the backs of the producers."[2] The youth knew that life in Southwest Detroit was changing rapidly, but they did not understand why. They knew they struggled to hold onto property, but they could not make the connection that legal status was not only an individual condition that undermined their ability as an individual to work and go to school. They knew that color and their residence in Detroit made questions fraught and unanswerable about who they were like, and who they were becoming. These questions pushed my analysis to understand what shaped the quality of secondary education in Southwest Detroit and their ability to attend schools of choice in the adjoining suburbs. It pushed hard questions about emergency management and why the Detroit Public School Board was ultimately disbanded. It pushed questions about democracy and how much they were to control about their lives beyond simply informing each other about the latest immigration raid that might affect a workplace in Southwest Detroit. Questions that begged explanation included why Cano was able to buy his family's home back from a county tax foreclosure auction while other interviewees were not. They forced identifying the powerful groups who produced abstractions that demolished their struggles to mark their walls and produce their space.

Although this book could not do justice to their stories, I wanted them to know their time and experiences drove my analysis. I refer to our conversations below in gratitude for their time and for sharing memories about their most important struggles.

FIELD INTERVIEWS

Vito Valdez, face-to-face interview by Nicole Trujillo-Pagán, Detroit, MI, January 6, 2019.

Luz Meza, Deputy Director of Economic Development Division, face-to-face interview by Nicole Trujillo-Pagán, Detroit, MI, October 10, 2019.

Mari, community resident, telephone interview by Nicole Trujillo-Pagán, October 10, 2019.

Kurt Metzger, Zoom interview by Nicole Trujillo-Pagán, December 9, 2020.

Carrie Lewand-Monroe, Zoom interview by Nicole Trujillo-Pagán, January 8, 2021.

Jerry Paffendorf. Zoom interview by Nicole Trujillo-Pagán, February 2, 2021.

Carmen (pseudonym), Former LISC Program Officer, telephone interview by Nicole Trujillo-Pagán, March 25, 2021.

John Van Camp, telephone interview by Nicole Trujillo-Pagán, July 19, 2023.

Tahirih Ziegler, LISC Chief of Staff and Senior Vice President, Phone interview by Nicole Trujillo-Pagán, July 21, 2023.

Ira Goldstein, Reinvestment Fund, telephone interview by Nicole Trujillo-Pagán, August 23, 2023.

Faith in Action, face-to-face interview by Nicole Trujillo-Pagán, Date Unrecorded.

John (pseudonym), CDFI owner (formerly an official at another prominent CDFI), face-to-face interview by Nicole Trujillo-Pagán, Detroit, MI, May 1, 2025.

SEMI-STRUCTURED INTERVIEWS

Alicia, face-to-face interview by Nicole Trujillo-Pagán, Detroit, MI, December 20, 2018

Alicia, face-to-face interview by Nicole Trujillo-Pagán, Detroit, MI, December 28, 2018

Alicia, face-to-face interview by Nicole Trujillo-Pagán, Detroit, MI, January 12, 2019

Alicia, face-to-face interview by Nicole Trujillo-Pagán, Detroit, MI, February 23, 2019

Antonio, face-to-face interview by Nicole Trujillo-Pagán, Detroit, September 28, 2019.

Antonio, face-to-face interview by Nicole Trujillo-Pagán, Detroit, October 5, 2019.

Antonio, face-to-face interview by Nicole Trujillo-Pagán, Detroit, October 20, 2019.
Ariel, face-to-face interview by Nicole Trujillo-Pagán, Detroit, MI, January 4, 2019.
Ariel, face-to-face interview by Nicole Trujillo-Pagán, Detroit, MI, January 18, 2019.
Ariel, face-to-face interview by Nicole Trujillo-Pagán, Detroit, MI, January 29, 2019.
Blanca, face-to-face interview by Nicole Trujillo-Pagán, Detroit, MI, November 19, 2019,
Blanca, face-to-face interview by Nicole Trujillo-Pagán, Detroit, MI, December 19, 2019.
Blanca, face-to-face interview by Nicole Trujillo-Pagán, Detroit, MI, December 26, 2019.
Cano, face-to-face interview by Nicole Trujillo-Pagán, Detroit, MI, March 4, 2019.
Cano, face-to-face interview by Nicole Trujillo-Pagán, Detroit, MI, March 6, 2019.
Cano, face-to-face interview by Nicole Trujillo-Pagán, Detroit, MI, March 8, 2019.
Central American Woman, face-to-face interview by Nicole Trujillo-Pagán, Detroit, MI, Date Unrecorded.
Concha, face-to-face interview by Nicole Trujillo-Pagán, Detroit, MI, December 21, 2019.
Concha, face-to-face interview by Nicole Trujillo-Pagán, Detroit, MI, December 27, 2019.
Concha, face-to-face interview by Nicole Trujillo-Pagán, Detroit, MI, May 22, 2019.
Fausto, face-to-face interview by Nicole Trujillo-Pagán, Detroit, MI, September 20, 2018.
Fausto, face-to-face interview by Nicole Trujillo-Pagán, Detroit, MI, October 4, 2018.
Fausto, face-to-face interview by Nicole Trujillo-Pagán, Detroit, MI, October 24, 2018.
Felix, face-to-face interview by Nicole Trujillo-Pagán, Detroit, MI, December 23, 2018.

Felix, face-to-face interview by Nicole Trujillo-Pagán, Detroit, MI, December 29, 2018.
Felix, face-to-face interview by Nicole Trujillo-Pagán, Detroit, MI, January 2, 2018.
Felix, face-to-face interview by Nicole Trujillo-Pagán, Detroit, MI, July 14, 2019.
Flor, face-to-face interview by Nicole Trujillo-Pagán, Detroit, MI, February 23, 2019.
Flor, face-to-face interview by Nicole Trujillo-Pagán, Detroit, MI, July 16, 2019.
Flor, face-to-face interview by Nicole Trujillo-Pagán, Detroit, MI, July 23, 2019.
Gabi, face-to-face interview by Nicole Trujillo-Pagán, Detroit, MI, December 1, 2019.
Gabi, face-to-face interview by Nicole Trujillo-Pagán, Detroit, MI, February 9, 2019.
Gabi, face-to-face interview by Nicole Trujillo-Pagán, Detroit, MI, February 23, 2019.
Gabi, face-to-face interview by Nicole Trujillo-Pagán, Detroit, MI, March 2, 2019.
Guillermo, face-to-face interview by Nicole Trujillo-Pagán, Detroit, MI, August 31, 2018.
Guillermo, face-to-face interview by Nicole Trujillo-Pagán, Detroit, MI, Date Unrecorded.
Guillermo, face-to-face interview by Nicole Trujillo-Pagán, Detroit, MI, September 26, 2018.
Luisa, face-to-face interview by Nicole Trujillo-Pagán, Detroit, MI, December 17, 2018.
Luisa, face-to-face interview by Nicole Trujillo-Pagán, Detroit, MI, January 7, 2019.
Luisa, face-to-face interview by Nicole Trujillo-Pagán, Detroit, MI, February 9, 2019.
Luisa, face-to-face interview by Nicole Trujillo-Pagán, Detroit, MI, February 23, 2019.
Luisa, face-to-face interview by Nicole Trujillo-Pagán, Detroit, MI, October 3, 2019.

Jorge, face-to-face interview by Nicole Trujillo-Pagán, Detroit, MI, October 8, 2019.
Jorge, face-to-face interview by Nicole Trujillo-Pagán, Detroit, MI, November 5, 2019.
Jorge, face-to-face interview by Nicole Trujillo-Pagán, Detroit, MI, December 1, 2019.
Julieta, face-to-face interview by Nicole Trujillo-Pagán, Detroit, MI, September 27, 2019.
Julieta, face-to-face interview by Nicole Trujillo-Pagán, Detroit, MI, October 6, 2019.
Julieta, face-to-face interview by Nicole Trujillo-Pagán, Detroit, MI, October 19, 2019.
Maria, face-to-face interview by Nicole Trujillo-Pagán, Dearborn, MI, October 6, 2019.
Maria, face-to-face interview by Nicole Trujillo-Pagán, Dearborn, MI, Date Unrecorded.
Maria, face-to-face interview by Nicole Trujillo-Pagán, Dearborn, MI, Date Unrecorded.
Maya, face-to-face interview by Nicole Trujillo-Pagán, Detroit, MI, January 7, 2019.
Maya, face-to-face interview by Nicole Trujillo-Pagán, Detroit, MI, Date Unrecorded.
Maya, face-to-face interview by Nicole Trujillo-Pagán, Detroit, MI, Date Unrecorded.
Mireya, face-to-face interview by Nicole Trujillo-Pagán, Detroit, MI, September 2, 2018.
Mireya, face-to-face interview by Nicole Trujillo-Pagán, Detroit, MI, September 23, 2018.
Mireya, face-to-face interview by Nicole Trujillo-Pagán, Detroit, MI, October 6, 2018.
Mirta, face-to-face interview by Nicole Trujillo-Pagán, Detroit, MI, September 28, 2019.
Mirta, face-to-face interview by Nicole Trujillo-Pagán, Detroit, MI, October 5, 2019.
Mirta, face-to-face interview by Nicole Trujillo-Pagán, Detroit, MI, October 19, 2019.

APPENDIX III

An Example of How a Street Sign Is an Abstraction

Abstractions are not only words spoken and written in books. Figures A.1 and A.2 compare a light pole near 518 Wabash in 2009 and 2019. The puzzling sign appeared sometime after the city's bankruptcy in an area between Southwest Detroit and downtown. Corktown mirrored other explicit attempts to attract new urban professionals to the city, the most notable being Ford's development of Central Station. The sign directed potential parking to a few blocks away but adjoined a fenced lot. It announced itself as a "Warning" but shared a block with businesses that invented tradition and manufactured authenticity when they branded themselves using signs from the 1950s.

The sign complemented other recent residents' efforts to brand the city's grit and resilience. It shared a block with a business owner who called on "conquistadors" to conquer the area, which sparked distain among many legacy residents because the area was already densely occupied. The reference to conquest was reminiscent of a nation founded on land theft and forced removal. Legacy residents also felt the email reflected a more general disdain that new residents had for them. He

Figure A.1. No Warning, 518 Wabash (2009)

Figure A.2. "Warning: Car Break-In Area" (2019)

also used a Spanish term at a time when Spanish-speaking people were being pushed out of the border city. Terrorist groups claimed Mexicans were engaged in a *reconquista* to reconquer parts of the United States.

The word *conquista* demonstrated how abstractions can be reflected in direct physical violence: A recent resident (Steve DiPonio) beat a legacy resident (Charles Duncan) "repeatedly with a baseball bat, tied his feet with a rope and pulled him toward the truck, threatening to drag him to the river."[1] Pastors who served the area pointed to the doubleness of abstraction when they explained the area was a home to people who did not own or rent property. New arrivals nonetheless considered people like Duncan "homeless."

NOTES

INTRODUCTION

1. Jill Blickstein in Blickstein, McCarthy, and Simon 2016.
2. MacDuffie, Smetters, and Cohen 2018.
3. Council of Michigan Foundations 2022.
4. *USA Today* 2023; *USA Today* 2025a; *USA Today* 2025b.
5. Saulny 2010; *The Economist* 2013a; Cassidy 2013; Katz and Bradley 2009; Muller 2010.
6. Davey 2011, A1.
7. See, for example, *The Economist* 2013a and Muller 2010. The reference to "too much, too little, too late" draws from a 1978 love song by Johnny Mathis and Denice Williams.
8. Kellogg 2010a; Frey 2021.
9. Seelye 2011, A1; Davey 2013, A1.
10. MacDuffie et al. 2018. For a discussion of the "Detroit Is Dead," see Tabb 2015.
11. The county and city land banks have been controversial because they have been associated with the eviction and dispossession of legacy residents.
12. US Census Bureau 2022. In 2022, the poverty rate in Detroit was 31.5 percent; in the United States, 12.5 percent. The same year, the median income in Detroit was $37,761; in the United States, $105,833. Regarding the ongoing foreclosure crisis in the city, see Safransky 2023; Akers and Seymour 2019; and Atuahene 2020.
13. Altavena 2025; Lupher 2024; Sroka 2024.
14. Coates 2011. See also Farley 2015.
15. For critiques of the shrinking cities literature, see, for instance, Berglund 2020a; Audirac 2018; Akers 2015.
16. Zunz 1982.
17. The concept of a "world city" preceded the first reference to Detroit as a global city in 1943. See Clark 2016.
18. The wave of civil unrest across northern cities have more commonly been referred to as urban riots, but Kurashige (2017) explained the broader (national and international) context shaping the "rebellion." See also H. Thompson 2017.
19. Kurashige 2017.
20. Hedman and Pendall 2018.
21. Martin 1993.
22. Sugrue 2014; Farley, Danziger, and Holzer 2000.

23 The Black middle class and the poor who moved into public housing were distinguished by class status, but this book overlooks these distinctions to focus on the persistence of racial inequality in the period leading up to and following Detroit's bankruptcy. In part to ameliorate the analytic consequences of this choice, I focus on the interviewees who had owned home in the suburbs in chapter 3 on poverty.
24 Latina/o/x includes people with Latin American ancestry and who identify themselves as Latina, Latino, Latinx, or LatinX.
25 This compares to East Harlem where rapid development and social transformation occurred along with residents' continued poverty. See Dávila 2004.
26 Brown-Saracino 2019; Berglund 2020b; Evans 2025; Howell 2019.
27 This approach has dominated the way sociologists think about space, urban areas, and residential segregation. It led Gans (2002) to ask whether space was cause or consequence of the social. Examples of attempts to address this question include Gieryn 2000; Galster and Sharkey 2017; Logan 2012; Löw 2016; Small and Adler 2019; Wacquant 2023.
28 Lefebvre 1984. Scholars who focus on real abstractions consider they correspond with lived experience. In contrast, Jay (2023) argues abstractions are not all dominating or violent, just as concreteness is not inherently liberating. He also points out that abstractions are more than mere reflections of reality and they can play a role in realizing freedom, reason, justice, and truth.
29 An example of how media conglomerates control publications would be the publicization of smoking hazards. See, for example, Milov 2019; Herman 2021.
30 Saulny 2010, A16.
31 Saulny 2010, A16.
32 Saulny 2010, A16.
33 See, for instance, Kinney 2016; Vergara 1995b and 1999; Draus and Roddy 2018. On the social construction of nature, see Vogel 1996.
34 Kellogg 2010b, A3.
35 Saulny 2010, A16; Kellogg 2010b; *The Economist* 2013b.
36 The issue of whether the city could or should solve its own problems was especially marked in *The New York Times*. See, for instance, Davey 2011, 2013a, 2013b, 2013c, 2013d, 2014a, and 2014b.
37 Renn 2009. For other examples of the frontier association, see Safransky 2014; Kinney 2016. For the association of the frontier with revanchism and something to be conquered, see Smith 2005.
38 Davey 2011, A1.
39 Bomey and Gallagher 2013, 12A.
40 Bomey and Gallagher 2013, 1A.
41 Bomey and Gallagher 2013, 12A.
42 Bomey and Gallagher 2013, 1A.
43 Bomey and Gallagher 2013, 15A.
44 Reed 1999; Seamster 2018. There is a voluminous literature that considers how Black communities are colonized, which means relegating Black people to second

class citizenship and undermining their self-determination. White peoples' concern that Black people were unable to govern themselves was reflected in Federal Judge John Feikens's claim that Black people were "still in an era of development." Feikens in Brown 1984, 1A. He had been appointed to oversee the Detroit Water and Sewer Department.
45 C. Young 1997, 37.
46 Akers 2013; Atuahene 2025; Kahrl 2024.
47 Lefebvre 1984; Safransky 2022; Blomley 2004.
48 McKittrick 2006, xiii, and 2011; Rucks-Ahidiana 2022; Dinzey-Flores 2017.
49 Combs 2022.
50 See, for instance, Alexander's (2010) discussion of the origins of police departments in slave patrols.
51 Du Bois 1899, 4, 6; Oeur and Rucks-Ahidiana 2024.
52 Du Bois 1899, 6. Du Bois writes "a slum is not a simple fact, it is a symptom, and that to know the removable causes of the Negro slums of Philadelphia requires a study that takes one far beyond the slum districts."
53 Lefebvre 1984, 94.
54 Polanyi 2001, 75.
55 Ghertner and Lake 2021; Mele 2017.
56 Ghertner and Lake 2021. For examples of the literature on speculative urbanism see, for instance, Goldman 2023; Fields 2023.
57 Feagin 2020, 11. For other examples of how narrative framing promotes inequitable community development, see, for instance, Gonzales 2022.
58 Rosa 2023.
59 Feagin, Vera, and Batur 2020, 4.
60 Bonilla-Silva 2006, 2.
61 Mele 2017, 6.
62 Campbell et al. 2020; Montgomery 2016.
63 Gonzales (2021) refers to this as collective skepticism.
64 Tax increments and increased property tax revenues result from rising property values. Other examples include how legacy and new residents are treated differently. Berglund 2019 and Herbert 2021. See also debates about neighborhood reputation in Korver-Glenn and Mayorga 2024.
65 Du Bois 1920, 15. Du Bois suggested this method when he wrote he saw "in and through" whiteness as "the ownership of the earth." The doubleness also traces to Marx. For example, Sorentino (2019) underscores the double freedom of wage labor to suggest the distinction between labor and slavery, between free and unfree labor, might be united on a continuum of coercion. Polanyi (2001) wrote about the double movement of history. Hartman (2022) identifies the two freedoms implied by emancipation: the freedom from bondage and the freedom to starve. These forms of double movement are grounded in action, which represents a development from the twoness of consciousness identified by DuBois 1903.
66 Lefebvre 1984. See also Soja 1980 and Merrifield 2002.

67 Lefebvre 1984.
68 Quijano 2007; Mignolo 2011; Connell 2020; Lowe 2015; Harvey 2014a; Zuberi and Bonilla-Silva 2008. Lefebvre (1984) in particular criticized Aristotle, René Descartes, and Immanuel Kant.
69 Lefebvre 1984, 28, 39.
70 Lefebvre (1984) used a variety of adjectives to describe abstractions that underscore their centrality to his analysis and the production of space. In addition to formal and pure, he also used the terms "philosophical," "empty," "theological," "lethal," and "verbal" to refer to the kinds of abstractions he critiqued. He used other words to describe their form, including "fascinating," "spectacular," and "fetishized." His preoccupation with describing these abstractions underscore their importance to the production of space. Marx referred to inversion in his discussion of ideology: "Men and their circumstances appear upside-down as in a *camera obscura*" (1978a, 154). In the *Grundrisse*, he clarified that rational abstractions allowed economists to present production as natural and independent of history, thereby "smuggling" bourgeois relations in as "inviolable national laws" (Marx 1973, 19). The shift in his conception meant he no longer considered abstraction a substitute for reality but instead an action in which powerful groups misrepresented social relations. A similar conception is reflected in the literature on controlling images. See, for instance, Rucks-Ahidiana 2024.
71 Marx 1973; Lefebvre 1984; Sohn-Rethel 2020; Bhandar and Toscano 2015; Sorentino 2019. Moore (2016) distinguishes between violent abstractions that obscure relations in the interest of narrative and theoretical coherence, empty abstractions that are chaotic conceptions, and dialectical abstractions that are grounded in historical movement.
72 Marx 1973, 100.
73 Marx, 1973, 100.
74 Lefebvre 1984, 64. Londoño (2020) draws on this insight.
75 Harvey 2014b, 8.
76 I use monetize and commodify interchangeably.
77 Lefebvre draws on Marx in his writing on mystification. See also Mezzadra and Neilson (2013, 35), who recognize a map as a productive abstraction that "replicates the appropriation of the commons that establishes private property as well as the colonial conquest with its global geography of genocide and extraction." They consider that maps fabricate the world. See also Lewis and Wigen 1997; Piper 2002; Lepore 2018.
78 Brady 2002 and Scott 2008.
79 Franco Farinelli in Mezzadra and Neilson 2013, 29.
80 Safransky 2014, 244.
81 Marx 1973, 101.
82 Lefebvre 1984, 9. Lefebvre also explained and developed Marx's conception of concrete abstractions: Space was both a product to be used, and thereby consumed, but it was also, and simultaneously, a means of production. He echoed

Marx's insistence on historical determinism and considered space a "motor" of history that was "inherent to property relationships (especially the ownership of the earth, of land) and closely bound up with the forces of production (which impose a form on that earth or land)." Lefebvre 1984, 85, 275. This made Lefebvre's insights both theoretical and methodological. He recognized abstraction was "necessary at first," but scientists unwittingly participated in "the abuse of reductionism" when they failed to restore what had been temporarily set aside for analysis. "Reduced models are constructed-models of society, of the city, of institutions, of the family, and so forth-and things are left at that. This is how social space comes to be reduced to mental space by means of a 'scientific' procedure whose scientific status is really nothing but a veil for ideology." Lefebvre 1984, 106.

83 Logan and Molotch 2007.
84 McKittrick 2006, 16.
85 Michele Spanò in Bhandar and Toscano 2015, 10.
86 K. Taylor 2019, 6. Taylor focuses on how public-private partnerships benefited brokers, bankers and builders at the expense of African American homeowners and neighborhoods. See also Rucks-Ahidiana 2023 and J. Robinson 2021.
87 Korver-Glenn 2021, 3.
88 Londoño 2020, 7.
89 Kelley 2020, xv.
90 Block 2001, xxiv.
91 This distinguishes my analysis from the legacy of the "race relations cycle" (Park 1950). Omi and Winant (2015, 125) conceive of these projects as occurring "at varying scales . . . at the macro-level of racial policy-making, state activity, and collective action, but also at the level of everyday experience and personal interaction." They also define white supremacy as an evolving project that takes different forms over time. This distinguishes my use and focus on dominant abstractions from other references to white supremacy that emphasize expressions of prejudice, such as the ideas underpinning hate speech and the beliefs of white supremacist organizations. On formal abstraction and white supremacy, see also Mills 2019. On white supremacy as a relational racial project, see HoSang and Molina 2019. My reference to white supremacy emphasizes that empty, formal abstractions are outcomes of action and not only of thought. Marx (1978, 311) explained they are made real "of the producers." This means that a person need not occupy a body racialized as white to participate in the relation between white supremacy and anti-Blackness. Mayorga (2023) explains that white people are also exploited and dehumanized by white supremacy. See also McMillan 2024.
92 Harvey 2003a, 141, 144. On the relation of urban growth and decline, see also Murray 2021. Hackworth and Dantzler (2024) note scholars neglected groups that benefit from racial capitalism. On the role race plays in shaping economic alternatives, see Bledsoe, Welch, Sigelman, and Combs 1995.
93 See, for instance, Carruthers and Ariovich 2004; Herbert and Orne 2021; Kelly 2020, xv. In contrast, Cedric Robinson (2020) associated the pursuit of property

with mass violence. He observed that a Black movement could be traced from the sixteenth century to the present that preserved "the ontological totality granted by a metaphysical system that had never allowed for property" (C. Robinson 2020, 168). He also considered this experience exceeded racial capitalism, slavery, and colonialism. There is a significant literature on "racial capitalism" that traces its origins to Robinson 2020. Gilmore referred to Robinson's work and argued "racial capitalism is all capitalism" (2019, 15).

94 Purifoy and Seamster 2021; Krippner 2011; Quinn 2019; Peck 2010; Davidson, Lukens, and Ward 2020; Sassen 2008. Gibson, Legacy, and Roger (2023) distinguish neoliberal governance from "hybrid urban governance reconfigurations" that rely on public-private partnerships.
95 Peck and Whiteside 2016.
96 Harris 1993, 1,714.
97 Harris 1993, 1,725.
98 Bhandar 2018 and 2014. See also the scholarship following Sylvia Wynter's (2003) analysis of the human and nonhuman, such as Weheliye 2014. See also Pattillo's (2021) call to turn research on race (Black people) on its head.
99 A state is "a compulsory political organization with continuous operations . . . its staff successfully upholds the claim to the monopoly of the legitimate use of force in the enforcement of its order." Weber 1978, 54.
100 Lefebvre 1984, 306.
101 Lefebvre 1984, 289; see also Fields and Raymond 2021; McKittrick 2013; Bledsoe and Wright 2018; Bledsoe 2019.
102 Henry Ford Hospital (Robert Riney), the Detroit Institute of Arts (Salvador Salort-Pons, born in Spain), and Wayne State University (Kimberly Andrews Espy).
103 Kickert 2019.
104 K. Taylor (2019) points out that cultural conceptions of citizenship and belonging were tied to homeownership.
105 Lenders' risk assessments drive higher interest rates. Ponder and Omstedt 2019.
106 For a comparable relational analysis, see, for instance, Ponder 2023.
107 Massey and Denton 1993.
108 See, for instance, Dinzey-Flores 2013; Novak 2017; Heyman 2017; Villarreal 2021.
109 Hackman 2015.
110 Moynihan 1967, 494.
111 Wacquant 2001. See also Ruth Wilson Gilmore (2007, 16), who talked about how households stretched "from neighborhood to visiting room to courtroom, with a consequent thinning of financial and emotional resources." See also, Shabazz 2015.
112 Embrick and Moore 2020; W. Moore 2008 and 2020; E. Anderson 2022; Hawthorne 2019. Purifoy and Seamster (2021) and Seamster and Purifoy (2020) demonstrate how the development of white space is related to Black towns. Scholars who work on Latino urbanism emphasize the ways that culture shapes the ways

residents adapt urban spaces through the creative use of, for instance, murals, parks, and sidewalks. See, for instance, Diaz and Torres 2012; Sandoval-Strausz 2019.

113 Mezzadra and Neilson 2013, 38. See also Mayorga-Gallo 2014.
114 Sheller 2017; Sheller and Urry 2006.
115 Woods 2017a and 2017b; Hunter and Robinson 2018; Lipsitz 2011; Duneier 2016; Roane 2023.
116 Woods 2017b.
117 Hartman 2019.
118 McKittrick 2021, 33.
119 Summers 2019, 19.
120 Summers 2019, 4. See also Moskowitz 2018 and Okechukwu 2024.
121 Summers 2019, 3.
122 Summers 2019, 20.
123 Vergara 2016. Emphasis mine.
124 Adorno 2006, 11.
125 See, for example, Farley, Danziger, and Holzer 2000; Sugrue 2014; Thomas 2013; Dewar and Thomas 2013.
126 For a useful evaluation of these trends, see Darden 2023.
127 Du Bois 1903, 9. See also Du Bois' discussion of agency in Itzigsohn and Brown 2020.
128 This number is based on a search of social science titles published between 2010 and 2021 on Detroit.
129 Apel (2015) refers to this as ruin porn in *Beautiful Terrible Ruins*.
130 Howes 2004, 1D.
131 Black 2015.
132 The saying "Buscando Trabajo Rogando a Dios no Encontrarlo" was also the title of a book. It implies a belief that unemployment is the result of the lack of individual will to work.
133 On the relationship between trust and investment, see Gonzales 2021 and Quinn 2019.
134 Dunning 2022, 15. On the relation between nonprofit and grassroots organizations, see Gonzales 2017 and Silverman 2005. J. Robinson (2020) distinguishes grassroots from community-based groups.
135 John van Camp, telephone interview by the author, July 19, 2023.
136 These experiences echo scholars who examine the social isolation produced by residential segregation. See, for example, A. Young 2004; Rendon 2019; Boccagni and Hondagneu-Sotelo 2023.
137 Brenner 2019.
138 Marx 1978b, 311.
139 Bebow 2002, A6.
140 See, for instance, Long-Bey 2003.
141 We the People of Detroit Community Research Collective 2016.

142 Vergara 2016, 297.
143 Florida 2012b.
144 Svoboda 2014, A3.
145 Kelley 2015, 334; H. White 2020; Quizar 2019; Combs 2022; Myers 2022.
146 Gold and Rappeport 2024.
147 Gordon 1997, 63. See, for instance, Hernández 2022; Jiménez Román and Flores 2010; Torres-Saillant 1998; Pattillo, Rico, and Guevara 2021.
148 Braudel 1982.
149 DeGenaro 2007. There is an important scholarship that distinguishes how Latina/o/x people see themselves from how they believe other people racialize them and how this distinction affects their life chances. See, for instance, López and Hogan 2021; Vargas et al. 2021.
150 Hartigan (1999) demonstrates how whiteness is produced in relation to space and class. Halvorson and Reno (2022) explain how global white supremacy is a racial project tied to the Midwest and America. Treitler (2013) examines how ethnic groups position themselves in relation to the US racial hierarchy.
151 Aguilar 2022; Cruz 2014; Nicolaides 2024; Simms, forthcoming.
152 US Department of Justice 2013.
153 JPMorgan Chase & Co. 2019. See also Porter and Kramer 2002.
154 White saviors are criticized for not examining themselves or the conditions that cause suffering.
155 Loughran (2015) 252, similarly observes that Du Bois's analysis of Philadelphia's Seventh Ward found residents were "bound up in global processes of capitalism, racialization, industrialization, and migration." These processes involve actors in recasting places that promote displacement and gentrification. See also Silverman et al. 2019.
156 Safransky 2023; Herbert 2021; Kinder 2016, 34–64.

CHAPTER 1. THIS BRIDGE CALLED MY 'HOOD
1 Moraga 2021, xv.
2 Grabar 2016.
3 Cooney, Phillips, and Rivera 2019.
4 Feltner and Heller 2015; Federal Insurance Office, US Department of Treasury 2017.
5 The Michigan Department of Insurance and Financial Services (2024) estimates that sixty percent of Detroiters drive uninsured.
6 WXYZ-TV 2025.
7 Metro Times Editorial Staff 2020.
8 Korver-Glenn 2021; Howell and Korver-Glenn 2018; Perry 2020.
9 Hernández 2022.
10 Mireya, face-to-face interview by Nicole Trujillo-Pagan, Detroit, MI, September 2, 2018. The transcription retains the original language so that the reader can have the experience of a bordering practice. In this case, impeding automatic transla-

tion acts as a bordering practice. Mireya translated: "Yes. And this has happened to me, now that I think of it, but I don't know if it was, I wouldn't be able to directly say it was because of discrimination."

11 The quote in the text is a shortened version of what she said, which was: "Well, I have been stopped. The police have stopped me, um . . . I was on the way to, um . . . when I had time I liked to run. But where I would go was in (nearby suburb). I was with a friend and the point was we would run together in a track . . . (suburb), something. It's (suburb). Suburb high school they have like a open track? And on the way the police stops me. It was, it was at night. He said: 'Oh, do you know why I'm stopping you?' I told him 'no.' 'Oh, because your headlights are, are off.' And I'm like 'But my headlights don't turn off.' They literally, it's one of the cars that the headlights don't go off, but he couldn't find anything to excuse himself and then he said: 'Let me get your license and registration.' In other words, I don't know. I think, I feel that he was looking to see if there was another reason to stop me. Aside from him being incorrect and not even, not even. My lights don't go off. That's when I felt it was a form of discrimination."
12 "Like, what was I doing in that city?"
13 "Aside from what he said?"
14 "Yes."
15 "For me it was that, 'What is this girl doing here, at this time, at this hour, going to a park . . . to run?' In other words, I had to explain to him that 'Oh, I'm going to go running.'"
16 "No. I think it was for my color."
17 Maggio 2021; Menjívar 2013.
18 Sampson 2008.
19 Neavling 2020a.
20 Benjamin 2019.
21 Smith and Walters 2018; Foster and Newell 2019.
22 Bond 2020; Arthur and Passini, 1992.

CHAPTER 2. PRODUCING NEIGHBORHOODS

1 The phrase is a riff on the famous line from the movie *Field of Dreams*: "If you build it, they will come."
2 Talen 2018; Bledsoe et al. 1995.
3 US Census Bureau 2018. Up until that time, the US Census Bureau also collected data on wards and block number areas.
4 Pardo and Donnelly 2013, A3.
5 Trujillo-Pagán 2019.
6 The idea of a twenty-minute neighborhood was preceded by a long history of scholarship on urban space that traces at least to the 1929 regional plan for New York. It emphasized the number of minutes required for pedestrians to reach locations, including public transit. The idea was revived during the 1990s. Hebbert 2003.

7   Many of the stories and references to diversity were subsequently taken down from the website after the storyteller's role was absorbed by the city's Media Services Department. The neighborhood map remained on the Department of Neighborhood's website.
8   Talen 2018.
9   Du Bois 1899, 4.
10 Park and Burgess 1925, 7. For a discussion of the differences between Du Bois and Park and Burgess, see Morris 2015.
11 Sampson, Morenoff, and Gannon-Rowley 2002, 210; Sampson 2012; Galster 2019.
12 Du Bois 1899; M. Hunter 2013.
13 Go 2023; Beardall, Rocha, and Lewis 2024.
14 Lewis 1966.
15 Wilson 1980 and 2012.
16 Vergara 1995b; Kinney 2016; Wacquant 2010.
17 Wilson and Kelling, 1982, 29.
18 Wilson and Kelling 1982, 29.
19 Wilson and Kelling 1982, 34, 35.
20 Alexander (2010) traces the development of police to patrols and militias that rewarded white people with protection as it policed slave labor in *The New Jim Crow*. See also Burton 2015; Pickett, Graham, and Cullen 2022; D. Gordon 2022; Harcourt 2009; Okechukwu 2021; Krinks 2024.
21 Kurashige 2017.
22 Wilson and Kelling 1982, 31–32.
23 Z. Jackson 2020; Bennett 2020.
24 Wilson and Kelling 1982, 38.
25 Grodzins 1957.
26 Urban Institute 2017.
27 Scher 2019.
28 The Detroit Blight Removal Task Force credited "activists Marcus Pollock and Ed Rutkowski" for coining the concept of "tipping point" in 1998, but it described "rising vacancy" in "diverse, formerly stable neighborhoods" (2014, 86). The report's authors referenced the activists to legitimize the concept but obscured that the term had a longer history. The report also repeated a new association of tipping points with crime, which exemplified how the Task Force's symbolically acknowledged activists' protests and created an illusion that it accommodated disagreement.
29 Wilson and Kelling 1982, 34.
30 National Academies of Sciences, Engineering, and Medicine 2018.
31 Smith 2001, 69.
32 R. Taylor 2018, 6.
33 Cooper-McCann 2016, 149.
34 Marchiel 2020.
35 K. Taylor 2019, 4.
36 Hackworth 2019.

37 Mitchell Sviridoff in Kohler 2007a, 154.
38 Hoffman 2012, 27–28.
39 Peter C. Goldmark Jr. in Kohler 2007b, 218.
40 Laskey and Nicholls 2019; Shaw and Spence 2004.
41 Knight Foundation 2008.
42 Locker 2013.
43 Foley 1970.
44 Knight Foundation 2008.
45 Knight Foundation 2005.
46 Ramsey 2006.
47 Walsh 2006, A1.
48 Diggs 2009.
49 Henderson 2008. Henderson wrote in the context of Kilpatrick's trials that disrupted plans for the NDNI.
50 Kurt Metzger, Zoom interview by Nicole Trujillo-Pagán, December 9, 2020.
51 City of Detroit 2009, appendix C.
52 Detroit Future City 2012, 14.
53 Dixon 2018.
54 Detroit Future City 2012, 22.
55 Detroit Future City 2012, 451.
56 Detroit Future City 2012, 455.
57 US Federal Housing Administration 1938, 1,360–63.
58 Gregory 2012; Campbell et al. 2020; Herbert 2021; Ryzewski 2021; Helps and Hwang 2024; Safransky 2017; Stovall and Hill 2016.
59 Gallagher 2013b, 18A.
60 Gallagher 2013a, 22A.
61 Walsh and Gallagher 2014.
62 Dixon 2019.
63 Detroit Blight Removal Task Force 2014, 4. C. Gordon (2004) explains that increasingly broad definitions of blight are adopted by municipalities as a way to promote economic development through state tax increment financing.
64 Detroit Blight Removal Task Force 2014, 4.
65 Quizar 2020; Abowd 2024; Bender 2010.
66 Detroit Blight Removal Task Force 2014, 92. See also Pacewicz's (2016) discussion of how municipal leaders stretched the definition of blight and its elimination to generate revenue and contribute to place entrepreneurs' enrichment.
67 Helmore 2017.
68 Bloomberg Cities 2018.
69 The Neighborhoods, n.d.
70 Embrick 2011; Mayorga-Gallo 2019.
71 The other neighborhoods included Southwest, Hubbard Richard, Hubbard Farms, West Side Industrial, Michigan-Martin, Chadsey Condon, Claytown, Springwells, Delraym and Oakwood Heights.

72 Journalists and other commentators interpreted his reference in a variety of ways that included race and equitable participation in the city's future. DeVito 2014.
73 Ryssdal and Velasco 2017.
74 Ikonomova 2018; Clarke 2018.
75 Montgomery 2016.
76 Kurashige 2017, 103; Zukin 2010.
77 Neavling 2020b.
78 Detroit LISC 2008, 4.
79 Knight Foundation 2003.
80 JPMorgan Chase & Co. 2017b.
81 Detroit LISC 2008, x.
82 Camp 2014.
83 Carmen, telephone interview by Nicole Trujillo-Pagán, March 25, 2021.
84 John van Camp, telephone interview by Nicole Trujillo-Pagán, July 19, 2023.
85 Welch 2017. Emphasis mine.
86 John van Camp, telephone interview by Nicole Trujillo-Pagán, July 19, 2023.
87 DeVito 2015.
88 *Crain's Detroit Business* 2005.
89 Begin 2006.
90 G. Hunter 2019, A3.
91 Gross 2019.
92 Welch 2019.
93 Du Bois 1899, 4.
94 I relied on the city's Strategic Neighborhood Fund to identify the census tracts that were targeted for Southwest Detroit.

CHAPTER 3. "WHERE YOU FROM?"

1 Harris 1993.
2 Humphrey 1943; M. E. Rodriguez 2011.
3 Vargas 1993; M. S. Rodriguez 2011.
4 Gordillo 2010.
5 An effective tax rate is the property tax payment as a percentage of market value. Lincoln Institute of Land Policy (2020) tracks the rate for different types of properties across one hundred US cities. Both owner-occupied (median home value) and commercial Detroit property tax rates were among the highest in the United States.
6 Eisenberg, Mehdipanah, and Dewar 2020.
7 Atuahene 2020, 107.
8 Freund 2010.
9 Bocian, Ernst, and Li 2008.
10 Benjamin 2019.
11 Carruthers and Ariovich 2004, 24.
12 Underkuffler 1990, 129.

13 Harris 1993, 1,734.
14 Ronald Reosti in Wylie 1989, 75.
15 J. Jackson 2010; Jacobs 1961.
16 Safransky 2017; Davy 2020.
17 Flor, face-to-face interview by Nicole Trujillo-Pagan, Detroit, MI, February 23, 2019.
18 Zukin 2010.
19 Shachar and Hirschl 2007.
20 Dávila 2008; Devos and Banaji 2005; Feagin 2020; Feagin and Cobas 2008; Flores-González 2017.
21 Balderrama and Rodríguez 2006.
22 Gabi, face-to-face interview by Nicole Trujillo-Pagán, Detroit, MI, February 23, 2019.
23 Hedman and Pendall 2018.
24 Afana 2022; Neidert, Reynolds, and Morenoff 2025.
25 City of Detroit, n.d.
26 Mr. Kruger, fieldnotes taken by Nicole Trujillo-Pagán, Detroit, MI, July 19, 2019.
27 Augé 1995, 94.
28 Alarcón and Larsen 2015.
29 Perkins and DeVito 2019.
30 Crain 2012; Gallagher 2017; Moskowitz 2015.
31 Kang 2020.
32 Eisenberg, Mehdipanah, and Dewar 2020; Atuahene 2020; Atuahene and Hodge 2018; Atuahene and Berry 2018; Pacewicz and Robinson 2021.
33 Atuahene 2020, 110.
34 Akers and Seymour 2018.
35 K. Taylor 2019; Faber 2013; Engel and McCoy 2008.
36 Kurashige 2017, 47.
37 Immergluck 2008.
38 Bocian, Li, and Ernst 2010.
39 Reid et al. 2017; Rugh 2015; Steil et al. 2018.
40 Rugh and Hall 2016.
41 Hall et al. 2018.
42 Hall, Crowder, and Spring 2015; Hall et al. 2018.
43 Faber and Ellen 2016.
44 Seymour and Akers 2019.
45 Seymour and Akers (2024) distinguished higher odds of failure for large contract sellers. See also Seymour and Akers 2021 and Desmond 2017.
46 The most common code violation in Southwest Detroit was an owner's failure to obtain a certificate of compliance, which includes property maintenance and registering a property as a rental.
47 Mari, telephone interview by Nicole Trujillo-Pagán, October 10, 2019.
48 Herbert 2021.

49 Balderrama and Rodríguez 2006.
50 Gonzales, Rosaldo, and Pratt 2021.
51 Molotch 2012.
52 Williams 2014.
53 Kornberg 2016, 269.
54 We the People of Detroit Community Research Collective 2016, 8.
55 John Feikens in Brown 1984, 1A.
56 We the People of Detroit Community Research Collective 2016, 6.
57 See discussion of state preemptions in DuPuis et al. 2018.
58 US National Advisory Commission on Civil Disorders 1968, 1.
59 US National Advisory Commission on Civil Disorders 1968, 112.
60 Sugrue 2008, 471.
61 US House Committee on Un-American Activities 1952, 2,879.
62 Thomas 2013; Lewis-Colman 2008.
63 Young and Wheeler 1994, 179. Emphasis mine.
64 C. Young 1997; Reed 1999.
65 Kenneth Cockerel in Lighthill 1980.
66 Lighthill 1980.
67 C. Young in Young 1997, 37.
68 Martin 2011.
69 Farley, Danziger, and Holzer 2000.
70 Harvey (2003b, 939) writes that "the right to the city is not merely a right of access to what already exists, but a right to change it."
71 Ponder and Omstedt 2019.
72 C. Young 1997, 37.
73 Richard Sabaugh in Chafets 1990.
74 Brooks Patterson in McGraw 2018, A2.
75 John Telford in Gallagher 1991, 22.
76 Lipsitz 2018, xxii.

CHAPTER 4. BIG DATA, BIG MONEY
1 Jay and Conklin 2020, 11.
2 Klein 2007.
3 Haney-López 2014.
4 Daley 2016.
5 Livengood and Frank 2020.
6 Mahu and Thompson 2014, 115.
7 Phinney 2018, 612.
8 Breznau and Kirkpatrick 2023; Lee et al. 2016; Fasenfest and Pride 2016.
9 Bomey 2016.
10 Jacqueline Noonan in Westbrook, 2013.
11 Turbeville 2014.
12 Bomey 2016, 35.

13 Desan 2014, 126. See also Turbeville 2014 and Hackworth 2002.
14 Graeber 2014.
15 Ellman and Merrett 2011, 368.
16 Phillips-Fein 2017.
17 Ellman and Merrett 2011, 368.
18 Hyman 2020, 633.
19 Kevyn Orr in A. Finley, 2013.
20 Kevyn Orr in A. Finley, 2013.
21 Snell 2014.
22 Ferretti 2016, 14.
23 Bomey 2016, 202.
24 Ellman and Merrett 2011, 367.
25 Carvlin 2005.
26 Bomey 2016, 22.
27 Carvlin 2005, 28A.
28 Turbeville 2013, 5; Turbeville 2014.
29 Ponder and Omstedt 2019, 4, 5.
30 Bomey 2016, 28.
31 Phinney 2018; Ponder and Omstedt 2019.
32 Stech 2014.
33 Greenwood 2014a, B4.
34 Detroit News Editorial Board 2013.
35 JPMorgan Chase & Co. n.d.a.
36 Dimon 2015.
37 Bomey 2016, 95.
38 Bomey 2016, 97.
39 Livengood 2019, 1.
40 Detroit Blight Removal Task Force 2014, 23.
41 Koscielniak 2020; Herstad 2017.
42 US Government Accountability Office 2020.
43 Schultz 2013.
44 Schultz 2013, A1.
45 Simon 2013.
46 Detroit Blight Removal Task Force 2014, 15.
47 Whitaker 2016.
48 Whitaker 2016. In the period between 2013 and 2015, $102.3 million in HHF funding was directed to demolition. Dynamo Metrics, LLC, 2015.
49 US Special Inspector General for the Troubled Asset Relief Program 2016, 92. The US Special Inspector General for the Troubled Asset Relief Program was a federal agency created to oversee expenditures and reported delays in accessing HHF funds.
50 Hackworth 2015, 766
51 Day 2020.

52 McKinney 2015.
53 Detroit Blight Removal Task Force 2014, 15.
54 Lockridge 2020.
55 US Special Inspector General for the Troubled Asset Relief Program 2016, 40.
56 US Attorney's Office, Eastern District of Michigan, 2023.
57 Detroit City Council 2019.
58 Office of the Auditor General, City of Detroit 2019.
59 Stafford and Tanner 2020; Rector 2022.
60 ArcGIS Dashboards, n.d. The requirement is measured in terms of hours worked, but reports included Detroit Skilled Trades Program (STEP) participants among "qualified employees." STEP participants are union and/or Joint Apprentice Training Committees (JATC) that participate in STEP. They are not necessarily Detroit residents. This not only means the numbers overestimate the impact on the employment of Detroiters, but it also provides further evidence of border crossing in the public financing of private development.
61 Du Bois 1899, 6.
62 N. Finley 2014.
63 Bomey 2016, 183.
64 Shields 2020 and 2021.
65 Jenkins 2021; Norris 2023.

CHAPTER 5. AFFIRMATIVE ACTION OR REVERSE RACISM?

1 Detroit News Editorial Board 2004, 14A.
2 Detroit News Editorial Board 2004. Kidada Williams turns questions about affirmative action on their head when she asks "do you want to talk about the affirmative action of the past sixty, or the past 400 years?"
3 Detroit News Editorial Board, 2004, 14A. On white men as spokesmen, see, for instance, Spivak's (2023) reference to white men saving brown women from brown men.
4 See, for instance, Bogle 2016 and Goings 1994.
5 On Black urban regimes, see Reed 1999; on white urban regimes, see Seamster 2018.
6 Bukowski 2002, A1.
7 Bukowski 2002.
8 Bukowski 2002.
9 Bukowski 2002.
10 Bush 2004.
11 C. Anderson 2001, 1.
12 C. Anderson 2001, 2.
13 C. Anderson 2001, 39.
14 B. Thompson 2004b, A1.
15 C. Anderson 2001, 2, 20.
16 C. Anderson 2001, 10, 11.

17 Du Bois 1899, 6.
18 C. Anderson, 2001, 7.
19 C. Anderson, 2001, 7.
20 C. Anderson 2001, 8.
21 C. Anderson 2001, 8. Emphasis mine.
22 Berman 2004, 1D.
23 Detroit News Editorial Board, 2004, 14A.
24 Watson 2004.
25 Boggs 2004a, C1.
26 King 2018; D'Arcus 2004.
27 A Majority Black Resolution was approved by a vote of seven to two on July 15, 2004.
28 Kinzer 2004.
29 Bello 2004b
30 Bello 2004b, B4.
31 B. Thompson 2004b, A1.
32 Boggs 2004b, A6.
33 Boggs 2004a.
34 Bello 2004a; B. Thompson 2004a; N. Moore 2004.
35 Bello 2004a; B. Thompson 2004a; N. Moore 2004.
36 N. Moore 2004, 1C.
37 Kinzer 2004, A24.
38 B. Thompson 2004b
39 Helen Moore in B. Thompson 2004b, A1.
40 Bello 2004a, B1.
41 B. Thompson 2004a, A1.
42 Bello et al. 2006, B3.
43 Reindl 2020, A1.
44 Baradaran 2017.

CHAPTER 6. PUBLIC-PRIVATE PARTNERSHIPS
1 Baldwin 1963.
2 Executive Office of the President 2016, 3.
3 Dan Pitera in Gallagher 2011, A7.
4 Safransky 2014, 238.
5 Gallagher 2019.
6 Thomson 2019, 562, and 2012.
7 Thomson 2019, 561.
8 See, for instance, Thomas, 2022 and 2013.
9 Dolan 2011, A1.
10 See, for instance, McGoey 2012.
11 Haydon, Jung, and Russell 2021; Maclean et al. 2021.
12 Porter and Kramer 2011.

13 Safransky 2020.
14 Heimer 2017, 101.
15 Heimer 2017, 101.
16 Austen 2014, 25. On altruism as profit-generating developer strategy, see Hyde 2022.
17 McGoey 2012, 191.
18 JPMorgan Chase & Co. press releases focused on general changes, such as "loans to Black households." The measure could have multiple causes. JPMC marketed the value of its data, but it did not use its data to qualify the "meaningful progress" that Detroit's economy made in JPMorgan Chase & Co. 2023.
19 Douglas in McGoey 2012, 193.
20 Bower 2019.
21 Stahl 2019.
22 Krippner 2005. See also Pacewicz (2016, 264), which explains how municipal leaders also create markets.
23 Greenwood 2014a, B4.
24 JPMorgan Chase & Co. n.d.b.
25 Dunning 2022, 3.
26 Felix, face-to-face interview by Nicole Trujillo-Pagán, Detroit, MI, January 2, 2018.
27 McGoey 2012 and 2016; Guilhot 2007; Haydon, Jung, and Russell 2021; Maclean et al. 2021.
28 Thomson 2019, 556.
29 Conlin 2011, 6.
30 Florida 2012a.
31 Editors 2012.
32 Florida 2017.
33 Safransky (2023, 151) notes the proposals "were so incendiary that they were shelved for nearly twenty years."
34 Hackney and Patton 2010, A6.
35 MacDonald and Nichols 2010, A1.
36 Hackney 2010, A8.
37 Thomson 2019, 561.
38 Safransky 2023, 153.
39 Dolan 2010, A1.
40 Dolan 2011.
41 Dolan 2011.
42 MacDonald, 2010.
43 Dolan 2011, A1.
44 Dolan 2011, A1.
45 Dolan 2011, A1.
46 Safransky, 2014, 244. See also Montgomery, 2020.
47 Kurt Metzger, Zoom interview by Nicole Trujillo-Pagán, December 9, 2020.

48 Jerry Paffendorf, Zoom interview by Nicole Trujillo-Pagán, February 2, 2021.
49 Arieff 2016.
50 Bostwick 2010; Hulett 2010.
51 Paffendorf, 2010a and 2010b.
52 Jerry Paffendorf, Zoom interview by Nicole Trujillo-Pagán, February 2, 2021.
53 US Census Bureau 2017. Thirty-five percent of households had no internet access in Detroit city (89,230 out of 258,471 households).
54 Motor City Mapping 2014.
55 Detroit Blight Removal Task Force 2014, 48.
56 We the People of Detroit Community Research Collective 2016; Kinder 2016.
57 Jerry Paffendorf, Zoom call with author, February 2, 2021.
58 Sampson and Raudenbush, 2004 and 2005.
59 Jerry Paffendorf, Zoom conversation with author, February 2, 2021.
60 United States Housing Act of 1937, 42 U.S.C § 1437a.
61 Kurt Metzger, Zoom interview with Nicole Trujillo-Pagán, December 9, 2020.
62 Safransky 2014, 238.
63 Detroit Future City 2012, 12, 22.
64 Detroit Future City 2012, 15.
65 Clement and Kanai 2015.
66 Rothstein 2017, 64. See also Winling and Michney 2021.
67 Detroit Future City 2012, 717; US Census 2012.
68 Safransky 2023, 160.
69 US Census Bureau 2014. Thirty-eight percent of households had no internet access in Detroit city (95,825 out of 253,490 households).
70 Anonymous committee member in Markus and Krings 2020, 1146.
71 Henderson 2013b.
72 Henderson 2013b. Edited for length.
73 Felix, face-to-face interview by Nicole Trujillo-Pagán, Detroit, MI, January 2, 2018.
74 McGoey 2012, 185. See also McGoey 2016.
75 McGoey 2021, 392.
76 McGoey 2021, 392.
77 Stahl 2019; Heimer 2017; Bower 2019.
78 JPMorgan Chase & Co. 2019.
79 US Department of Justice 2013. Dimon considered JPMC had been unfairly penalized for the toxic assets other banks had acquired.
80 JPMorgan Chase & Co. 2014, 15.
81 Heimer 2017.
82 Heimer 2017, 97.
83 Heimer 2017, 96, 98
84 JPMorgan Chase & Co. 2014, 15.
85 Greene 2014.
86 JPMorgan Chase & Co. 2014, 15.

87   Bower 2019.
88   Greenwood 2014b.
89   JPMorgan Chase & Co. 2014, 15.
90   Jamie Dimon in Stahl 2019.
91   Heimer 2017, 96.
92   Scher 2019.
93   Dimon, Duggan, and Scher 2018.
94   Dimon, Duggan, and Scher 2018.
95   Scher 2019.
96   Bower 2019. A businessperson affiliated with a CDFI explained they have a variety of strategies for being able to offer these loans, but even those that have above-market interest rates should not necessarily be considered high or predatory because the loan would not otherwise occur. They recognized above-market rates were common in the years following the bankruptcy but pointed out that ten years after the bankruptcy, there still are many underserved areas beyond those targeted by CDFIs. The areas are not only those in the city but also include ones throughout Wayne County that are not dominated by white residents, including the historically Black suburb of Inkster.
97   Priscilla Almodovar in Bower 2019.
98   Peter Scher in Stahl 2019.
99   Michael Edward Duggan in Stahl 2019. Emphasis mine.
100 Stahl 2019. Emphasis original. On the relation between trust and development, see Gonzales 2021; Carruthers 2022; Quinn 2019.
101 Stahl 2019.
102 Stahl 2019.
103 Heimer 2017, 101.
104 Heimer 2017, 101.
105 Dimon, Duggan, and Scher 2018.
106 Dimon, Duggan, and Scher 2018.
107 Bonilla-Silva 2006.
108 Gonzales, Thissell, and Thorat 2022.
109 Hackworth 2002, 722.
110 Hackworth 2002. Hackworth points out that city leaders were fiscally conservative well before their counterparts in Philadelphia and New York. Mainstream press outlets nonetheless projected their own racism when they characterized Young as preoccupied with racial antagonism. Young had spoken publicly about how racism undermined investment in the city.
111 JPMorgan Chase & Co. 2017a.
112 JPMorgan Chase & Co. 2017a.
113 Weil 2021.
114 Bonilla-Silva 2006.
115 Kendi 2023.
116 See, for instance, Dimon's response in Stahl 2019.

117 Dimon 2015.
118 Dimon, Duggan, and Scher 2018.
119 Quinn 2019.
120 Joseph Smith, personal communication by email, November 17, 2021.
121 JPMorgan Chase & Co. 2021.
122 Porter and Kramer 2011.
123 Dimon, Duggan, and Scher 2018.
124 Dimon, Duggan, and Scher 2018. Emphasis mine.
125 Dimon writes that "our government institutions are stuck in the mud-too slow and inadequate for the job at hand." JPMorgan Chase & Co. 2017c, 34.
126 Dimon, Duggan, and Scher 2018.
127 Dimon, Duggan, and Scher 2018.
128 Dimon, Duggan, and Scher 2018.
129 Heimer 2017, 97.
130 Heimer 2017.
131 Stern and Feldman 2004.

CONCLUSION

1 Some scholars, like Beauregard (2003), Davidson (2020), and Brenner (2003), warn of extrapolating to urban areas from a single case, but others signal Detroit as an important case to study urban decline and transformation. See, for instance, Silver 2015; Schindler 2014; Kinkead 2016; Dewar et al. 2015. Residents explained they felt like experimental subjects for the world-renown university located about forty-five minutes outside of the city. Both Dimon and Scher referred to Detroit as a laboratory and an experiment. Paffendorf's sale of inches in Detroit was similarly an experiment. Journalists and scholars similarly suggested that "the eyes of the nation, the world, are on what Detroit is doing right now because it is unprecedented." Don Pitera, a professor at Detroit Mercy, in Gallagher 2011, A7. The scholarship on ruin porn indicates Detroit attracted an international audience that fetishized the physical decline of the city's buildings.
2 Kinney 2016, 59.
3 Kling, Nothaft, and Stragand 2024.
4 Eugene Cunningham quoted in Kling et al. 2024.
5 Du Bois 1903, 1.
6 Bomey 2016, 35.
7 Dimon, Duggan, and Scher 2018.
8 Henderson 2013a.
9 Wacquant 2022, 34.
10 McKittrick 2006, xiii, and 2011.
11 The concept of white supremacy has its limitations, but it underscores the salience of whiteness is that it is based on consequential human action.
12 Felix, face-to-face interview by Nicole Trujillo-Pagán, Detroit, MI, January 2, 2018.

13 Dolan 2011, A1.
14 Kevyn Orr in A. Finley 2013.
15 Kevyn Orr in A. Finley 2013.
16 Snell 2014.
17 Ferretti 2016, 14.
18 Bomey 2016, 202.
19 See, for instance, Lupher 2024.
20 Ritchie 2017, 57. See also New York Advisory Committee to the US Commission on Civil Rights 2018.
21 Florida 2017.
22 Gladwell 2024.
23 Seuss 1958.

APPENDIX II
1 Seamster 2018.
2 Marx 1978b, 311.

APPENDIX III
1 Wylie-Kellermann 2010.

BIBLIOGRAPHY

Abowd, Thomas. 2024. "Scarcity Amid Abundance: Navigating the Waters of Neoliberal Austerity in Detroit." *City & Society* 36 (2): 91–101. https://doi.org/10.1111/ciso.12492.
Adorno, Theodor W. 2006. *History and Freedom: Lectures 1964–1965*. Malden, MA: Polity Press.
Afana, Dana. 2022. "Filing Says People of Color are Undercounted." *Detroit Free Press*, September 21.
Aguilar, Louis. 2022. "In Detroit, Gentrification. But Downriver, Let's Call it 'La Gente-Fication.'" *Outlier Media*, March 23. https://outliermedia.org.
Akers, Joshua M. 2013. "Making Markets: Think Tank Legislation and Private Property in Detroit." *Urban Geography* 34 (8): 1070–95.
Akers, Joshua M. 2015. "Emerging Market City." *Environment and Planning A* 47 (9): 1842–58.
Akers, Joshua, and Eric Seymour. 2018. "Instrumental Exploitation: Predatory Property Relations at City's End." *Geoforum* 91:127–40.
Akers, Joshua, and Eric Seymour. 2019. "The Eviction Machine: Neighborhood Instability and Blight in Detroit's Neighborhoods." Working Paper No. 5-19, Poverty Solutions at the University of Michigan, July. https://poverty.umich.edu.
Alarcón, María Arquero de, and Larissa Larsen. 2015. "Mapping Delray: Understanding Changes in a Southwest Detroit Community." In *Mapping Detroit: Land, Community, and Shaping a City*, edited by June Manning Thomas and Henco Bekkering, 115–142. Detroit: Wayne State University Press.
Alami, Ilias. 2023. "Racial Capitalism, Uneven Development, and the Abstractive Powers of Race and Money." *Environment and Planning A: Economy and Space* 56 (4): 1304–10.
Alexander, Michelle. 2010. *The New Jim Crow: Mass Incarceration in the Age of Colorblindness*. New York: New Press.
Anderson, Claud. 2001. *PowerNomics: The National Plan to Empower Black America*. Bethesda, MD: Powernomics Corporation of America.
Anderson, Elijah. 2022. *Black in White Space: The Enduring Impact of Color in Everyday Life*. Chicago: University of Chicago Press.
Apel, Dora. 2015. *Beautiful Terrible Ruins: Detroit and the Anxiety of Decline*. New Brunswick, NJ: Rutgers University Press.
ArcGIS Dashboards. N.d. "EO 2021-2 Project Metrics August 2024." https://detroitmi.maps.arcgis.com.

Arieff, Allison. 2016. "Mapping Detroit, Inch by Inch." *New York Times*, July 20. https://www.nytimes.com.

Arieff, Allison. 2017. "A Model of Recovery for America's Cities." *Politico Magazine*, May 18. https://www.politico.com.

Arthur, Paul, and Romedi Passini. 1992. *Wayfinding: People, Signs, and Architecture*. New York: McGraw Hill.

Altavena, Lily. 2025. "Michigan Students' Scores Stagnate: Reading, Math Numbers Continue to be Concern." *Detroit Free Press*, January 29.

Atuahene, Bernadette. 2020. "Predatory Cities." *California Law Review* 108 (1): 107–82.

Atuahene, Bernadette. 2025. *Plundered: How Racist Policies Undermine Black Homeownership in America*. New York: Little, Brown.

Atuahene, Bernadette, and Christopher Berry. 2018. "Taxed Out: Illegal Property Tax Assessments and the Epidemic of Tax Foreclosures in Detroit." *UC Irvine Law Review* 9 (4): 847–86.

Atuahene, Bernadette, and Timothy R. Hodge. 2018. "Stategraft." *Southern California Law Review* 91 (2): 263–302.

Audirac, Ivonne. 2018. "Shrinking Cities: An Unfit Term for American Urban Policy?" *Cities* 75:12–19.

Augé, Marc. 1995. *Non-Places: An Introduction to Supermodernity*. London: Verso Books.

Austen, Ben. 2014. "The Post-Post-Apocalyptic Detroit." *New York Times Magazine*, July 13.

Bachelor, Lynn W., and Bryan D. Jones. 1981. "Managed Participation: Detroit's Neighborhood Opportunity Fund." *Journal of Applied Behavioral Science* 17 (4): 518–36.

Balderrama, Francisco E., and Raymond Rodríguez. 2006. *Decade of Betrayal: Mexican Repatriation in the 1930s*. Albuquerque: University of New Mexico Press.

Baldwin, James. 1963. "A Conversation with James Baldwin." In *Perspectives: Negro and the American Promise*, edited by Kenneth Bancroft Clark. Boston: WGBH Educational Foundation.

Baradaran, Mehrsa. 2017. *The Color of Money: Black Banks and the Racial Wealth Gap*. Cambridge, MA: Harvard University Press.

Beardall, Theresa Rocha, Rahim Kurwa, and Demar F. Lewis IV. 2024. "Mended Windows, Not Broken Windows: A Du Boisian Analysis of Urban Policing." *City & Community* 23 (4): 320–40.

Beauregard, Robert A. 2003. "City of Superlatives." *City & Community* 2 (3): 183–99.

Bebow, John. 2002. "Users Circumvent City Water Shutoffs." *Detroit News*, September 3.

Begin, Sherri. 2006. "Southwest Solutions Takes Over Housing-loan Nonprofit." *Crain's Detroit Business*, June 5.

Bello, Marisol. 2004a. "Ethnics Protest Detroit's Plan for African Town: Members of Other Minorities Say District Shouldn't Exclude Them." *Detroit Free Press*, September 29.

Bello, Marisol. 2004b. "Michigan News Briefs." *Detroit Free Press*, October 14.

Bello, Marisol, Niraj Warikoo, Naomi R. Patton, and Zlati Meyer. 2006. "Wayne Briefs." *Detroit Free Press*, May 14.

Bender, Steven W. 2010. *Tierra y Libertad: Land, Liberty, and Latino Housing*. New York: New York University Press.

Benjamin, Ruha. 2019. *Race after Technology: Abolitionist Tools for the New Jim Code*. Cambridge: Polity Press.

Bennett, Joshua. 2020. *Being Property Once Myself: Blackness and the End of Man*. Cambridge, MA: Harvard University Press.

Berglund, Lisa. 2019. "Excluded by Design: Informality Versus Tactical Urbanism in the Redevelopment of Detroit Neighborhoods." *Journal of Cultural Geography* 36 (2): 144–81.

Berglund, Lisa. 2020a. "Critiques of the Shrinking Cities Literature from an Urban Political Economy Framework." *Journal of Planning Literature* 35 (4): 423–39.

Berglund, Lisa. 2020b. "'We're Forgotten': The Shaping of Place Attachment and Collective Action in Detroit's 48217 Neighborhood." *Journal of Urban Affairs* 42 (3): 390–413.

Berman, Laura. 2004. "Africa Town Plan Will Hasten Detroit's Demise, not Stem the Tide." *Detroit News*, September 23.

Bhandar, Brenna. 2014. "Property, Law, and Race: Modes of abstraction." *UC Irvine Law Review* 4 (1): 203–12.

Bhandar, Brenna. 2018. *Colonial Lives of Property: Law, Land, and Racial Regimes of Ownership*. Durham, NC: Duke University Press.

Bhandar, Brenna, and Alberto Toscano. 2015. "Race, Real Estate and Real Abstraction." *Radical Philosophy* 194 (November/December): 8–17.

Black, Ariel. 2015. "'Say Nice Things about Detroit' Creator Helps Carry on Message." *Crain's Detroit Business*, August 26. https://www.crainsdetroit.com.

Bledsoe, Timothy, Susan Welch, Lee Sigelman, and Michael Combs. 1995. "Residential Context and Racial Solidarity among African Americans." *American Journal of Political Science* 39 (2): 434–58.

Bledsoe, Adam, Willie Jamaal Wright. 2018. "The Anti-Blackness of Global Capital." *Environment and Planning D: Society and Space* 37 (1): 8–26.

Bledsoe, Adam. 2019. "The Primacy of Anti-Blackness." *Area* 52 (3): 472–79.

Bledsoe, Adam, Willie Jamaal Wright. 2022. "Theorizing Diverse Economies in the Context of Racial Capitalism." *Geoforum* 123 (June): 281–90.

Blickstein, Jill, George McCarthy, and Ariel Simon. 2016. "Enabling Environments and Timelines for Change." Moderated by Carol Coletta. Panel at Drawing on Detroit, May 4, Posted June 2, 2016, by University of Southern Carolina Price. YouTube, 1:23:25. https://www.youtube.com/watch?v=uIUzjMCov3Y&list=PL0ABA7EFC361 16EEC.

Block, Fred. 2001. Introduction to *The Great Transformation: The Political and Economic Origins of Our Time*, edited by Karl Polanyi. Boston, MA: Beacon Press.

Blomley, Nicholas. 2004. *Unsettling the City: Urban Land and the Politics of Property*. New York, NY: Routledge.

Bloomberg Cities. 2018. "How Detroit's 'Chief Storyteller' Is Crafting a New Narrative for His City." *Medium*, April 25. https://bloombergcities.medium.com.

Boccagni, Paolo, and Pierrette Hondagneu-Sotelo. 2023. "Integration and the Struggle to Turn Space into 'Our' Place: Homemaking as a Way Beyond the Stalemate of Assimilationism vs Transnationalism." *International Migration* 61 (1): 154–67.

Bocian, Debbie Gruenstein, Keith S. Ernst, and Wei Li. 2008. "Race, Ethnicity and Subprime Home Loan Pricing." *Journal of Economics and Business* 60 (1–2): 110–24.

Bocian, Debbie Gruenstein, Wei Li, and Keith S. Ernst. 2010. "Foreclosures by Race and Ethnicity." CRL Research Report, June 18. https://www.mvfairhousing.com.

Boggs, Grace Lee. 2004a. "Living for Change; African Town: Threat or Promise?" *Michigan Citizen*, October 31–November 6.

Boggs, Grace Lee. 2004b. "Living for Change; An African Business District in Detroit?" *Michigan Citizen*, October 16.

Bogle, Donald. 2016. *Toms, Coons, Mulattoes, Mammies, and Bucks: An Interpretive History of Blacks in American Films*. New York: Bloomsbury Academic.

Bomey, Nathan. 2016. *Detroit Resurrected: To Bankruptcy and Back*. New York: W. W. Norton.

Bomey, Nathan, and John Gallagher. 2013. "How Detroit Went Broke: The Answers May Surprise You—and Don't Blame Coleman Young." *Detroit Free Press*, September 15, 1A, 12–15A.

Bond, Michael. 2020. *Wayfinding: The Art and Science of How We Find and Lose Our Way*. London: Picador.

Bonilla-Silva, Eduardo. 2006. *Racism Without Racists: Color-Blind Racism and the Persistence of Racial Inequality in the United States*. Lanham, MD: Rowman & Littlefield.

Bostwick, William. 2010. "Save Detroit! One Inch, One Dollar at a Time." *Fast Company*, March 8. https://www.fastcompany.com.

Bower, Joseph L. 2019. *JPMorgan Chase: Invested in Detroit (A), (B), and (C)*. Harvard Business School Teaching Note 919-407, January. Cambridge, MA: Harvard Business School.

Brady, Mary Pat. 2002. *Extinct Lands, Temporal Geographies*. Durham, NC: Duke University Press.

Braudel, Fernand. 1982. *On History*. Chicago: University of Chicago Press.

Brenner, Neil. 2003. "Stereotypes, Archetypes, and Uses of Superlatives in Contemporary Urban Studies." *City & Community* 2 (3): 205–16.

Brenner, Neil. 2019. *New Urban Spaces: Urban Theory and the Scale Question*. New York: Oxford University Press.

Breznau, Nate, and L. Owen Kirkpatrick. 2023. "Urban Fiscal Crisis and Local Emergency Management." *Race & Society* 11 (Spring): 9–47.

Brown, Peter. 1984. "Feikens Assesses Mayor Young, Vista, Sewage Cleanup." *Detroit Free Press*, August 26.

Brown-Saracino, Japonica. 2019. *How Places Make Us: Novel LBQ Identities in Four Small Cities*. Chicago: University of Chicago Press.

Bukowski, Diane. 2002. "African Town: Retail Dream Nears Reality." *Michigan Citizen*, February 9.
Bunge, William. 2022. *Fitzgerald: Geography of a Revolution*. Athens: University of Georgia Press.
Burton, Orisanmi. 2015. "To Protect and Serve Whiteness." *North American Dialogue* 18 (2): 38–50.
Bush, President George W. 2004. "President Emphasizes Minority Entrepreneurship at Urban League." Remarks by the president to the 2004 National Urban League Conference. The White House, July 23. https://georgewbush-whitehouse.archives.gov.
Camp, John Van. 2014. "How Do You Rebuild a City?" *Politico*, September 10. https://www.swsol.org.
Campbell, Linda, Andrew Newman, Sara Safransky, and Tim Stallmann. 2020. Introduction to *A People's Atlas of Detroit*, edited by Linda Campbell, Andrew Newman, Sara Safransky, and Tim Stallmann. Detroit, MI: Wayne State University Press.
Carruthers, Bruce G. 2022. *The Economy of Promises: Trust, Power, and Credit in America*. Princeton, NJ: Princeton University Press.
Carruthers, Bruce G., and Laura Ariovich. 2004. "The Sociology of Property Rights." *Annual Review of Sociology* 30:23–46.
Carvlin, Elizabeth. 2005. "Detroit Uses COPs to Shift Pension Burden and Set a Few Records." *Bond Buyer*, December 29.
Cassidy, John. 2013. "Motown Down." *New Yorker*, August 5.
Chafets, Ze'ev. 1990. "The Tragedy of Detroit." *New York Times Magazine*, July 29.
City of Detroit. N.d. *Census Data Map*. Detroit: City of Detroit. https://detroitmi.gov.
City of Detroit. 2009. *Master Plan of Policies*. Detroit: City of Detroit. https://detroitmi.gov.
Clark, Greg. 2016. *Global Cities: A Short History*. Washington, DC: Brookings Institution Press.
Clark, J. H. Cullum. 2022. *Immigrants and Opportunity in America's Cities*. Dallas, TX: George W. Bush Institute. https://www.bushcenter.org/.
Clarke, Kinsey. 2018. "Inside the Real Time Crime Center, DPD's 24-hour Monitoring Station." The Neighborhoods Channel, City of Detroit. https://lsa.umich.edu.
Clement, Daniel, and Miguel Kanai. 2015. "The Detroit Future City: How Pervasive Neoliberal Urbanism Exacerbates Racialized Spatial Injustice." *American Behavioral Scientist* 59 (3): 369–85.
Coates, Ta-Nehisi. 2011. "The Other Detroit." *Atlantic Monthly*, April.
Combs, Barbara Harris. 2022. *Bodies Out of Place: Theorizing Anti-blackness in US Society*. Athens: University of Georgia Press.
Conlin, Jennifer. 2011. "Detroit Pushes Back with Young Muscles." *New York Times*, July 3.
Connell, Raewyn. 2020. *Southern Theory: The Global Dynamics of Knowledge in Social Science*. New York: Routledge.
Cooney, Patrick, Elizabeth Phillips, and Joshua Rivera. 2019. "Auto Insurance and Economic Mobility in Michigan: A Cycle of Poverty." University of Michigan Poverty Solutions, March 1. https://poverty.umich.edu.

Cooper-McCann, Patrick. 2016. "The Trap of Triage: Lessons from the 'Team Four Plan.'" *Journal of Planning History* 15 (2): 149–69.
Council of Michigan Foundations. 2022. "Detroit Named One of the World's Greatest Places of 2022." August 29. https://www.michiganfoundations.org.
Crain, Keith. 2012. "Detroiters are Living a Tale of Two Cities." *Crain's Detroit Business*, June 4.
Crain's Detroit Business. 2005. "Innovation, Expansion a Hit." December 19.
Cruz, John. 2014. *Metro Detroit's Foreign-Born Populations*. N.p.: Global Detroit. https://globaldetroitmi.org.
Daley, David. 2016. *Ratf**ked: The True Story Behind the Secret Plan to Steal America's Democracy*. New York: Liveright.
D'Arcus, Bruce. 2004. "Dissent, Public Space and the Politics of Citizenship: Riots and the 'Outside Agitator.'" *Space and Polity* 8 (3): 355–370.
Darden, Joe. 2023. *Detroit After Bankruptcy: Are There Trends Towards an Inclusive City?* Bristol: Bristol University Press.
Davey, Monica. 2011. "Looking Up, Detroit Faces a New Crisis." *New York Times*, December 24.
Davey, Monica. 2013a. "Review Moves Detroit Nearer Emergency Oversight." *New York Times*, February 2.
Davey, Monica. 2013b. "Michigan Naming Fiscal Manager to Help Detroit." *New York Times*, March 2.
Davey, Monica. 2013c. "A Private Boom Amid Detroit's Public Blight." *New York Times*, March 5.
Davey, Monica. 2013d. "Financial Crisis Just a Symptom of Detroit's Woes." *New York Times*, July 9.
Davey, Monica. 2013e. "Big Dreams, but Little Consensus, for a New Detroit." *New York Times*, September 3.
Davey, Monica. 2014a. "A Picture of Detroit Ruin, Street by Forlorn Street." *New York Times*, February 18.
Davey, Monica. 2014b. "Needing Residents, Detroit Sends Some Packing," *New York Times*, June 27.
Davidson, Mark. 2020. "From Big to Small Cities: A Qualitative Analysis of the Causes and Outcomes of Post-Recession Municipal Bankruptcies." *City & Community* 19 (1): 132–52.
Davidson, Mark, David Lukens, and Kevin Ward. 2020. "The Post-Great Recession Geographies of US Municipal Borrowing and Indebtedness." *Professional Geographer* 73 (2): 1–14.
Dávila, Arlene. 2004. *Barrio Dreams: Puerto Ricans, Latinos, and the Neoliberal City*. Berkeley, CA: University of California Press.
Dávila, Arlene. 2008. "Latino Spin: Public Image and the Whitewashing of Race." In *Latino Spin*. New York: New York University Press.
Davy, Benjamin. 2020. "'Dehumanized Housing' and the Ideology of Property as a Social Function." *Planning Theory* 19 (1): 38–58.

Day, Brian. 2020. "Dearth of Credit Starves Detroit's Housing Market." *Wall Street Journal*, October 29. www.wsj.com.

DeGenaro, William. 2007. "Eight-Mile and Woodward: Intersections of Difference and the Rhetoric of Detroit." *JAC* 27 (1/2): 135–61.

Desan, Mathieu Hikaru. 2014. "Bankrupted Detroit." *Thesis Eleven* 121 (1): 122–30.

Desmond, M. 2017. *Evicted: Poverty and Profit in the American City*. New York: Broadway Books.

Detroit City Council. 2019. "Detroit City Council Formal 11-12-2019." November 12. https://detroitmi.gov.

Detroit Future City. 2012. *2012 Detroit Strategic Framework Plan*. Detroit: Detroit Future City. https://detroitfuturecity.com.

Detroit Local Initiative Support Corporation (LISC). 2008. "Southwest: Strategic Investment Area Initiative." *Neighborhoods Now*. In the possession of the author.

Detroit Blight Removal Task Force. 2014. *Every Neighborhood Has a Future . . . And It Doesn't Include Blight*. Detroit: Detroit Blight Removal Task Force. https://datadrivendetroit.org.

Detroit News Editorial Board. 2004. "Council Embraces Racism as a Development Strategy." *Detroit News*, September 22.

Detroit News Editorial Board. 2013. "Gov. Rick Snyder Talks About Detroit." *Detroit News*, December 20.

DeVito, Lee. 2014. "George N'Namdi Talks 'Psychological Gentrification.'" *Detroit Metro Times*, July 23. https://www.metrotimes.com.

DeVito, Lee. 2015. "Welcome to 'Springwells Village'—A Southwest Detroit Neighborhood Most of Its Own Residents Have Never Heard Of." *Detroit Metro Times*, January 7. https://www.metrotimes.com.

Devos, Thierry, and Mahzarin R. Banaji. 2005. "American=White?" *Journal of Personality and Social Psychology* 88 (3): 447–66.

Dewar, Margaret, and June Manning Thomas. 2013. "Introduction: The City After Abandonment." In *The City After Abandonment*, edited by Margaret Dewar and June Manning Thomas, 1–16. Philadelphia: University of Pennsylvania Press.

Dewar, Margaret, Matthew Weber, Eric Seymour, Meagan Elliott, and Patrick Cooper-McCann. 2015. "Learning from Detroit: How Research on a Declining City Enriches Urban Studies." In *Reinventing Detroit*, edited by Michael Peter Smith and L. Owen Kirkpatrick, 37–56. New York: Routledge.

Diaz, David R., and Rodolfo D. Torres. 2012. Introduction to *Latino Urbanism: The Politics of Planning, Policy, and Redevelopment*, edited by David R. Diaz and Rodolfo D. Torres. New York: New York University Press.

Diggs, Douglass J. 2009. *Neighborhood Stabilization Program Plan*. N.p.: City of Detroit. https://detroitmi.gov.

Dimon, Jamie. 2015. "Why Detroit Matters." In *Sparking Economic Opportunity: 2015 Corporate Responsibility Report*. N.p.: JP Morgan Chase. https://www.jpmorganchase.com.

Dimon, Jamie, Mike Duggan, and Peter Scher. 2018. "Invested in Detroit." Moderated by Karen Mills. Panel, April 11, Posted April 19, 2018, by Institute of

Politics Harvard Kennedy School. YouTube, 1:02:44. https://www.youtube.com/watch?v=wpQBTDUZZN0.

Dinzey-Flores, Zaire. 2013. *Locked In, Locked Out: Gated Communities in a Puerto Rican City*. Philadelphia: University of Pennsylvania Press.

Dinzey-Flores, Zaire Z. 2017. "Spatially Polarized Landscapes and a New Approach to Urban Inequality." *Latin American Research Review* 52 (2): 241–52.

Dixon, Jennifer. 2018. "A Free Press Investigation Has Found That Dead Bodies, Wild Dogs, Unauthorized Occupants are Scattered Through Detroit in Houses Owned by the Government." *Detroit Free Press*, July 22.

Dixon, Jennifer. 2019. "Gilbert Promised, City Delivered: Experts: Usual Real Estate Procedures Not Followed." *Detroit Free Press*, September 8.

Dolan, Matthew. 2010. "Less Than a Full-Service City; Plan for Detroit Would Pull Resources—and Population—From Blighted Districts." *Wall Street Journal*, December 11.

Dolan, Matthew. 2011. "Revival Bid Pits Detroit vs. Donor." *Wall Street Journal*, July 2.

Draus, Paul, and Juliette Roddy. 2018. "Weeds, Pheasants and Wild Dogs: Resituating the Ecological Paradigm in Postindustrial Detroit." *International Journal of Urban and Regional Research* 42 (5): 807–27.

Du Bois, W. E. B. 1899. *The Philadelphia Negro: A Social Study*. Philadelphia, PA: Published for the University.

Du Bois, W. E. B. 1903. *The Souls of Black Folk*. Chicago: A. C. McClurg.

Du Bois, W. E. B. 1920. *Darkwater: Voices from Within the Veil*. New York: Harcourt, Brace and Howe.

Duneier, Mitchell. 2016. *Ghetto: The Invention of a Place, the History of an Idea*. New York: Macmillan.

Dunning, Claire. 2022. *Nonprofit Neighborhoods: An Urban History of Inequality and the American State*. Chicago: University of Chicago Press.

DuPuis, Nicole, Trevor Langan, Christiana McFarland, Angelina Panettieri, and Brooks Rainwater. 2018. "City Rights in an Era of Preemption: A State-by-State Analysis." *National League of Cities: Center for City Solutions*. https://www.nlc.org.

Dynamo Metrics, LLC. 2015. *Estimating Home Equity Impacts from Rapid, Targeted Residential Demolition in Detroit, MI: Application of a Spatially-Dynamic System for Decision Support*. Dynamo Metrics, LLC. http://www.demolitionimpact.org.

The Economist. 2013a. "Can Motown be Mended? Detroit's Bankruptcy." July 27.

The Economist. 2013b. "Skid Row; Detroit." February 23.

Editors. 2012. "The State of Detroit." *Bloomberg*, May 15. https://www.bloomberg.com.

Eisenberg, Alexa, Roshanak Mehdipanah, and Margaret Dewar. 2020. "'It's Like They Make It Difficult for You on Purpose': Barriers to Property Tax Relief and Foreclosure Prevention in Detroit, Michigan." *Housing Studies* 35 (8): 1415–41.

Elden, Stuart. 2006. *Speaking Against Number: Heidegger, Language and the Politics of Calculation*. Edinburgh: Edinburgh University Press.

Ellman, Jeffrey B., and Daniel J. Merrett. 2011. "Pensions and Chapter 9: Can Municipalities Use Bankruptcy to Solve Their Pension Woes." *Emory Bankruptcy Development Journal* 27 (2): 365–414.

Embrick, David G. 2011. "The Diversity Ideology in the Business World: A New Oppression for a New Age." *Critical Sociology* 37 (5): 541–56.

Embrick, David G., and Wendy Leo Moore. 2020. "White Space(s) and the Reproduction of White Supremacy." *American Behavioral Scientist* 64 (14): 1935–45.

Engel, Kathleen C., and Patricia A. McCoy. 2008. "From Credit Denial to Predatory Lending: The Challenge of Sustaining Minority Homeownership." In *Segregation: The Rising Costs for America*, edited by James H. Carr and Nandinee K. Kutty, 81–123. New York: Routledge.

Evans, Shani Adia. 2025. *We Belong Here: Gentrification, White Spacemaking, and a Black Sense of Place*. Chicago: University of Chicago Press.

Executive Office of the President. 2016. *Building and Restoring Civic Capacity: The Obama Administration's Federal-Local Partnership with Detroit (2011–2016)*. Washington, DC: Executive Office of the President. https://obamawhitehouse.archives.gov.

Faber, Jacob W. 2013. "Racial Dynamics of Subprime Mortgage Lending at the Peak." *Housing Policy Debate* 23 (2): 328–49.

Faber, Jacob W., and Ingrid Gould Ellen. 2016. "Race and the Housing Cycle: Differences in Home Equity Trends Among Long-term Homeowners." *Housing Policy Debate* 26 (3): 456–73.

Farley, Reynolds. 2015. "The Bankruptcy of Detroit: What Role Did Race Play?" *City & Community* 14 (2): 118–37.

Farley, Reynolds, Sheldon Danziger, and Harry J. Holzer. 2000. *Detroit Divided*. New York: Russell Sage Foundation.

Fasenfest, David, and Theodore Pride. 2016. "Emergency Management in Michigan: Race, Class and the Limits of Liberal Democracy." *Critical Sociology* 42 (3): 331–34.

Feagin, Joe R. 2020. *The White Racial Frame: Centuries of Racial Framing and Counter-Framing*. New York: Routledge.

Feagin, Joe R., Hernan Vera, and Pinar Batur. 2020. *White Racism: The Basics*. New York: Routledge.

Feagin, Joe R., and José A. Cobas. 2008. "Latinos/as and White Racial Frame: The Procrustean Bed of Assimilation." *Sociological Inquiry* 78 (1): 39–53.

Federal Insurance Office, US Department of Treasury. 2017. *Study on the Affordability of Personal Automobile Insurance*. N.p.: Federal Insurance Office, US Department of the Treasury. https://home.treasury.gov.

Federal Reserve. 2022. "Community Reinvestment Act Proposal Fact Sheet." May. https://www.federalreserve.gov.

Feltner, Tom, and Douglas Heller. 2015. *Price of Mandatory Auto Insurance in Predominantly African American Communities*. N.p.: Consumer Federation of America. http://consumerfed.org.

Ferretti, Christine. 2016. "Council Questions Consultant Payments." *Detroit News*, September 30.

Fields, Desiree. 2023. "Speculative Urbanism." *Environment and Planning A: Economy and Space*, 55 (2): 511–16.

Fields, Desiree, and Elora Lee Raymond. 2021. "Racialized Geographies of Housing Financialization." *Progress in Human Geography* 45 (6): 1625–45.

Finley, Allysia. 2013. "Kevyn Orr: How Detroit Can Rise Again." *Wall Street Journal*, August 2. https://www.wsj.com.

Finley, Nolan. 2014. "Banks Paid for Detroit's Bankruptcy." *Detroit News*, November 9. https://www.detroitnews.com.

Flores-González, Nilda. 2017. *Citizens but Not Americans*. New York: New York University Press.

Florida, Richard. 2012a. "Detroit Rising Episode Two: Creative Potential." YouTube video, November 1. https://www.youtube.com/watch?v=tl1RLfh0NyE.

Florida, Richard. 2012b. "Detroit Rising Episode One: The State of Detroit." YouTube video, November 1. https://youtu.be/tw2mfhCM11Y.

Florida, Richard. 2017. *The New Urban Crisis: How Our Cities Are Increasing Inequality, Deepening Segregation, and Failing the Middle Class—and What We Can Do About It*. New York: Basic Books.

Foley, Eileen. 1970. "Pool Pals Shoot to Save Center." *Detroit Free Press*, January 30.

Forbes, Lauren. 2024. "Rooted Resistance: The Struggle for Black Liberation through Food Cultivation." *Journal of Race, Ethnicity and the City* 5 (2): 164–90.

Forester, John F. 2021. "Introduction: Place Making, Not Plan Making-Learning from What Takes Place." In *How Spaces Become Places: Place Makers tell their Stories*, edited by John F. Forester, 1–14. New York: New Village Press.

Foster, Alec, and Joshua P. Newell. 2019. "Detroit's Lines of Desire: Footpaths and Vacant Land in the Motor City." *Landscape and Urban Planning* 189 (September): 260–73.

Freund, David. 2010. *Colored Property*. Chicago: University of Chicago Press.

Frey, William H. 2021. "2020 Census: Big Cities Grew and Became More Diverse, Especially Among Their Youth." Brookings Institution, October 28. https://www.brookings.edu.

Gallagher, John. 1991. "Who Needs Detroit?" *Detroit Free Press*, October 13.

Gallagher, John. 2011. "Detroit Works Re-launched." *Detroit Free Press*, December 4.

Gallagher, John. 2013a. "Are They Ignoring the Way Out?" *Detroit Free Press*, October 27.

Gallagher, John. 2013b. "Tale of Two Futures." *Detroit Free Press*, January 13.

Gallagher, John. 2017. "'Two Detroits': Even Far from Downtown, Contrasts Abound in City Neighborhoods." *Detroit Free Press*, July 22. https://www.freep.com.

Gallagher, John. 2019. "A Farewell." *Detroit Free Press*, December 22.

Galster, George C. 2019. *Making Our Neighborhoods, Making Our Selves*. Chicago: University of Chicago Press.

Galster, George, and Patrick Sharkey. 2017. "Spatial Foundations of Inequality: A Conceptual Model and Empirical Overview." *RSF: The Russell Sage Foundation Journal of the Social Sciences* 3 (2): 1–33.

Gans, Herbert J. 2002. "The Sociology of Space: A Use-Centered View." *City & Community* 1 (4): 329–39.

Ghertner, D. Asher, and Robert W. Lake. 2021. *Land Fictions: The Commodification of Land in City and Country.* Ithaca: Cornell University Press.

Gibson, Chris, Crystal Legacy, and Dallas Rogers. 2023. "Deal-Making, Elite Networks and Public-Private Hybridisation: More-than-Neoliberal Urban Governance." *Urban Studies* 60 (1): 183–99.

Gieryn, Thomas F. 2000. "A Space for Place in Sociology." *Annual Review of Sociology* 26 (1): 463–96.

Gilmore, Ruth Wilson. 2002. "Fatal Couplings of Power and Difference: Notes on Racism and Geography." *Professional Geographer* 54 (1): 15–24.

Gilmore, Ruth Wilson. 2007. *Golden Gulag: Prisons, Surplus, Crisis, and Opposition in Globalizing California.* Berkeley: University of California Press.

Gilmore, Ruth Wilson. 2019. "Making Abolition Geography in California's Central Valley." *The Funambulist* 21 (Jan–Feb.): 14–19.

Gladwell, Malcolm. 2024. "The Tipping Point I Got Wrong." TED, October. https://www.ted.com.

Glock, Judge. 2016. "The Rise and Fall of the First Government-Sponsored Enterprise: The Federal Land Banks, 1916–1932." *Business History Review* 90 (4): 623–45.

Go, Julian. 2023. "Unveiling Power, or Why Social Science's Task is Explanation." *British Journal of Sociology*, 1–5. https://doi.org/10.1111/1468-4446.13056.

Goings, Kenneth W. 1994. *Mammy and Uncle Mose: Black Collectibles and American Stereotyping.* Bloomington: Indiana University Press.

Gold, Michael, and Alan Rappeport. 2024. "Trump Speech Meanders to Its Point: New Tax Cut." *New York Times*, October 12.

Goldman, Michael. 2023. "Speculative Urbanism and the Urban-Financial Conjuncture: Interrogating the Afterlives of the Financial Crisis." *Environment and Planning A: Economy and Space* 55 (2): 367–87.

Gonzales, Phillip B., Renato Rosaldo, and Mary Louise Pratt. 2021. Introduction to *Trumpism, Mexican America, and the Struggle for Latinx Citizenship*, edited by Phillip B. Gonzales, Renato Rosaldo and Mary Louise Pratt, ix–xxix. Albuquerque: University of New Mexico Press.

Gonzales, Teresa Irene. 2017. "Two Sides of the Same Coin: The New Communities' Program, Grassroots Organizations, and Leadership Development in Two Chicago Neighborhoods." *Journal of Urban Affairs* 39 (8): 1138–54.

Gonzales, Teresa Irene. 2021. *Building a Better Chicago: Race and Community Resistance to Urban Redevelopment.* New York: New York University Press.

Gonzales, Teresa Irene. 2022. "Ratchet-Rasquache Activism: Aesthetic and Discursive Frames within Chicago-based Women-of-Color activism." *Social Problems* 69 (2): 380–97.

Gonzales, Teresa Irene, Elizabeth M. Thissell, and Soumitra Thorat. 2022. "'The Stories We Tell: Colorblind Racism, Classblindness, and Narrative Framing in the Rural Midwest." *Rural Sociology* 87 (4): 1274–301.

Gonzalez, Erualdo R. 2017. *Latino City: Urban Planning, Politics, and the Grassroots*. London: Routledge.

Gordillo, Luz María. 2010. *Mexican Women and the Other Side of Immigration: Engendering Transnational Ties*. Austin: University of Texas Press.

Gordon, Lewis R. 1997. "Race, Biraciality, and Mixed Race-In Theory." In *Her Majesty's Other Children: Sketches of Racism from a Neocolonial Age*, edited by Lewis R. Gordon, 51–71. Lanham, MD: Rowman & Littlefield.

Gordon, Colin. 2004. "Blighting the Way: Urban Renewal, Economic Development, and the Elusive Definition of Blight." *Fordham Urban Law Journal* 31 (2): 305–37.

Gordon, Daanika. 2022. *Policing the Racial Divide: Urban Growth Politics and the Remaking of Segregation*. New York: New York University Press.

Grabar, Henry. 2016. "Can America's Worst Transit System Be Saved?" *Slate*, June 7. https://slate.com.

Graeber, David. 2014. *Debt: The First 5,000 Years*. Brooklyn: Melville House.

Greene, Jay. 2014. "A Growing Issue." *Crain's Detroit Business*, January 20.

Greenwood, Tom. 2014a. "Bank Boss: Detroit Can Have a Real Renaissance." *Detroit News*, May 22.

Greenwood, Tom. 2014b. "Dimon's Plan Extols City's Future." *Detroit News*, May 22.

Gregory, Siobhan. 2012. "Detroit is a Blank Slate: Metaphors in the Journalistic Discourse of Art and Entrepreneurship in the City of Detroit." *Ethnographic Praxis in Industry Conference Proceedings* 2012 (1): 217–33.

Grodzins, Morton. 1957. "Metropolitan Segregation." *Scientific American*, 33–41.

Gross, Allie. 2019. "Developers the Real Winners in this Game: Wayne County Effort to Help People Keep Homes Actually Doesn't." *Detroit Free Press*, March 17.

Guilhot, Nicolas. 2007. "Reforming the World: George Soros, Global Capitalism and the Philanthropic Management of the Social Sciences1." *Critical Sociology* 33 (3): 447–77.

Hackman, Rose. 2015. "'Detroiters Stay Out': Racial Blockades Divide a City and its Suburbs." *The Guardian*, February 3. https://www.theguardian.com.

Hackney, Suzette. 2010. "Bing Starts Land Discussion." *Detroit Free Press*, September 9.

Hackney, Suzette, and Naomi R. Patton. 2010. "Bing: City Needs Detroiters' Help." *Detroit Free Press*, August 18.

Hackworth, Jason. 2002. "Local Autonomy, Bond-Rating Agencies and Neoliberal Urbanism in the United States." *International Journal of Urban and Regional Research* 26 (4): 707–25.

Hackworth, Jason. 2015. "Rightsizing as Spatial Austerity in the American Rust Belt." *Environment and Planning A: Economy and Space* 47 (4): 766–82.

Hackworth, Jason. 2019. *Manufacturing Decline: How Racism and the Conservative Movement Crush the American Rust Belt*. New York: Columbia University Press.

Hackworth, Jason, and Prentiss Dantzler. 2024. "Racial Capitalism in Urban Studies: From Spaces of Victimisation to Spaces of Benefit." *Urban Studies* 62 (4): 772–85. https://doi.org/10.1177/00420980241262197.

Hall, Matthew, Kyle Crowder, and Amy Spring. 2015. "Variations in Housing Foreclosures by Race and Place, 2005–2012." *ANNALS of the American Academy of Political and Social Science* 660 (1): 217–37.

Hall, Matthew, Kyle Crowder, Amy Spring, and Ryan Gabriel. 2018. "Foreclosure Migration and Neighborhood Outcomes: Moving Toward Segregation and Disadvantage." *Social Science Research* 70 (February): 107–14.

Halvorson, Britt E., and Joshua O. Reno. 2022. *Imagining the Heartland: White Supremacy and the American Midwest*. Oakland: University of California Press.

Haney-López, Ian. 2014. *Dog Whistle Politics: How Coded Racial Appeals Have Reinvented Racism and Wrecked the Middle Class*. New York: Oxford University Press.

Harcourt, Bernard E. 2009. *Illusion of Order: The False Promise of Broken Windows Policing*. Cambridge, MA: Harvard University Press.

Harris, Cheryl. 1993. "Whiteness as Property." *Harvard Law Review* 106 (8): 1707–91.

Hartigan, John, Jr. 1999. *Racial Situations: Class Predicaments of Whiteness in Detroit*. Princeton, NJ: Princeton University Press.

Hartman, Saidiya. 2019. "The Plot of Her Undoing." https://feministartcoalition.org.

Hartman, Saidiya. 2022. *Scenes of Subjection: Terror, Slavery, and Self-Making in Nineteenth-century America*. New York: W. W. Norton.

Harvey, David. 2003a. "Accumulation by Dispossession." In *New Imperialism*, edited by David Harvey, 137–82. New York: Oxford University Press.

Harvey, David. 2003b. "The Right to the City." *International Journal of Urban and Regional Research* 27 (4): 939–41.

Harvey, David. 2014a. "Spacetime and the World." In *The People, Place, and Space Reader*, edited by Jen Jack Gieseking, William Mangold, Cindi Katz, Setha Low, and Susan Saegert, 12–16. New York: Routledge.

Harvey, David. 2014b. *Seventeen Contradictions and the End of Capitalism*. Oxford: Oxford University Press.

Hawthorne, Camilla. 2019. "Black Matters are Spatial Matters: Black Geographies for the Twenty-First Century." *Geography Compass* 13 (11): e12468. https://doi.org/10.1111/gec3.12468.

Haydon, Steph, Tobias Jung, and Shona Russell. 2021. "'You've Been Framed': A Critical Review of Academic Discourse on Philanthrocapitalism." *International Journal of Management Reviews* 23 (3): 353–75.

Hebbert, Michael. 2003. "New Urbanism—The Movement in Context." *Built Environment* 29 (3): 193–209.

Hedman, Carl, and Rolf Pendall. 2018. "Rebuilding and Sustaining Homeownership for African Americans." Urban Institute, June. https://www.urban.org/.

Heimer, Matt. 2017. "Making a Motown Miracle." *Fortune*, September 15.

Helmore, Edward. 2017. "Detroit Redefined: City Hires America's First Official 'Chief Storyteller.'" *The Guardian*, September 5. https://www.theguardian.com.

Helps, David, and Christine Hwang. 2024. "'See Detroit Like We Do': White Savior Capitalism and the Myth of Black Obsolescence." *American Quarterly* 76 (1): 103–26.

Henderson, Stephen. 2008. "People & Politics: For Mayor and City, Lies Undermine So Much Potential." *Detroit Free Press*, January 24.

Henderson, Stephen. 2013a. "Detroit Future City." PBS, November 3. https://video.pbswisconsin.org.

Henderson, Stephen. 2013b. "Detroit Works Project." PBS, January 13. https://www.pbs.org.

Herbert, Claire W. 2021. *A Detroit Story: Urban Decline and the Rise of Property Informality*. Oakland: University of California Press.

Herbert, Claire, and Jay Orne. 2021. "No Lawless Place: Foregrounding Property in Sociology." *Socius* 7. https://doi.org/10.1177/23780231211045448.

Herman, Edward S. 2021. "Still Manufacturing Consent: The Propaganda Model at Thirty." In *Power and Inequality*, edited by Levon Chorbajian, 207–13. New York: Routledge.

Hernández, Tanya Katerí. 2022. *Racial Innocence: Unmasking Latino Anti-Black Bias and the Struggle for Equality*. Boston, MA: Beacon Press.

Herstad, Kaeleigh. 2017. "'Reclaiming' Detroit: Demolition and Deconstruction in the Motor City." *Public Historian* 39 (4): 85–113.

Heyman, Josiah. 2017. "Contributions of US-Mexico Border Studies to Social Science Theory." In *The US-Mexico Transborder Region. Cultural Dynamics and Historical Interactions*, edited by Carlos Vélez-Ibánez and Josiah Heyman, 44–64. Tucson: University of Arizona Press.

Hoffman, Alexander von. 2012. "The Past, Present, and Future of Community Development in the United States." In *Investing in What Works for America's Communities: Essays on People, Place & Purpose*, edited by Federal Reserve Bank, 10–54. San Francisco, CA: Federal Reserve Bank of San Francisco.

HoSang, Daniel, and Natalia Molina. 2019. "Introduction: Toward a Relational Consciousness of Race." In *Relational Formations of Race: Theory, Method, and Practice*, edited by Natalia Molina, Daniel Martinez HoSang and Ramón A. Gutiérrez, 1–18. Oakland, CA: University of California Press.

Howell, Junia, and Elizabeth Korver-Glenn. 2018. "Neighborhoods, Race, and the Twenty-First-Century Housing Appraisal Industry." *Sociology of Race and Ethnicity* 4 (4): 473–90.

Howell, Ocean. 2019. *Making the Mission: Planning and Ethnicity in San Francisco*. Chicago: University of Chicago Press.

Howes, Daniel. 2004. "Dissing Detroit is a Convenient but Ill-Informed National Pastime." *Detroit News*, October 15.

Hulett, Sarah. 2010. "Inchvesting in Detroit: A Virtual Reality." NPR, March 4. https://www.npr.org.

Humphrey, Norman D. 1943. "The Migration and Settlement of Detroit Mexicans." *Economic Geography* 19 (4): 358–61.

Hunter, George. 2019. "Once Homeless, Vets Swelter in Apartments with Bed Bugs." *Detroit News*, July 24, A1, A3.

Hunter, Marcus Anthony. 2013. "A Bridge Over Troubled Water: W. E. B. Du Bois's *The Philadelphia Negro* and the Ecological Conundrum." *Du Bois Review: Social Science Research on Race* 10 (1): 7–27.

Hunter, Marcus Anthony, and Zandria F. Robinson. 2018. *Chocolate Cities*. Oakland, CA: University of California Press.

Hyde, Zachary. 2022. "Giving Back to Get Ahead: Altruism as a Developer Strategy of Accumulation through Affordable Housing Policy in Toronto and Vancouver." *Geoforum* 134 (August): 187–96.

Hyman, Mikell. 2020. "When Policy Feedback Fails: 'Collective Cooling' in Detroit's Municipal Bankruptcy." *Theory and Society* 49 (4): 633–68.

Ikonomova, Violet. 2018. "Get to Know the City of Detroit's Propaganda Arm." *Detroit Metro Times*, January 31. https://www.metrotimes.com.

Immergluck, Dan. 2008. "From the Subprime to the Exotic: Excessive Mortgage Market Risk and Foreclosures." *Journal of the American Planning Association* 74 (1): 59–76.

Itzigsohn, José, and Karida L. Brown. 2020. *The Sociology of W. E. B. Du Bois: Racialized Modernity and the Global Color Line*. New York: New York University Press.

Jackson, Janet Thompson. 2010. "What Is Property? Property Is Theft: The Lack of Social Justice in US Eminent Domain Law." *St. John's Law Review* 84 (1): 63–116.

Jackson, Zakiyyah Iman. 2020. *Becoming Human: Matter and Meaning in an Antiblack World*. New York: New York University Press.

Jacobs, Jane. 1961. *The Death and Life of Great American Cities*. New York: Random House.

Jamal, Frank Imani. 2002. "Town Meeting Debates Home Rule Issue." *Michigan Citizen*, November 2.

Jay, Mark, and Philip Conklin. 2020. *A People's History of Detroit*. Durham, NC: Duke University Press.

Jay, Martin. 2023. *Immanent Critiques: The Frankfurt School Under Pressure*. Brooklyn: Verso Books.

Jenkins, Destin. 2021. *The Bonds of Inequality: Debt and the Making of the American City*. Chicago: University of Chicago Press.

Jiménez Román, Miriam, and Juan Flores, eds. 2010. *The Afro-Latin@ Reader: History and Culture in the United States*. Durham, NC: Duke University Press.

JPMorgan Chase & Co. n.d.a. "Investing in Detroit." Video presented by JPMorgan Chase & Co. and produced by Atlantic Re:Think. www.theatlantic.com.

JPMorgan Chase & Co. n.d.b. "PolicyCenter." JPMorgan Chase & Co. https://www.jpmorganchase.com.

JPMorgan Chase & Co. 2014. *Annual Report 2014*. New York: JPMorgan Chase & Co. https://www.jpmorganchase.com.

JPMorgan Chase & Co. 2016. "JPMorgan Chase Commits $5 Million to Detroit's New $30 Million Strategic Neighborhood Fund." October 19. https://www.jpmorganchase.com.

JPMorgan Chase & Co. 2017a. "JPMorgan Chase & Co. Announces $10 Million Investment to Drive Inclusive Growth in Underserved Washington, D.C. Neighborhoods." September 25. https://www.jpmorganchase.com.

JPMorgan Chase & Co. 2017b. "JPMorgan Chase Commits More Than $1.2 Million to Help Revitalize Detroit's Neighborhoods." February 23. https://www.jpmorganchase.com.

JPMorgan Chase & Co. 2017c. *Annual Report 2017*. New York: JPMorgan Chase & Co. https://www.jpmorganchase.com.

JPMorgan Chase & Co. 2019. "JPMorgan Chase Exceeds Five-Year, $150 Million Investment in Detroit, Announces New Commitment to Reach $200 Million Total by 2022." June 26. https://www.jpmorganchase.com.

JPMorgan Chase & Co. 2021. "JPMorgan Chase Commits $350 Million to Grow Black, Latinx and Women-Owned Small Businesses." February 25. https://www.jpmorganchase.com.

JPMorgan Chase & Co. 2023. "JPMorgan Chase & Co. Marks 90 Years of Service in Detroit and 10-Year Anniversary of $200 Million Commitment to City's Economic Recovery." September 19. https://www.jpmorganchase.com.

Kahrl, Andrew W. 2024. *The Black Tax: 150 Years of Theft, Exploitation, and Dispossession in America*. Chicago: University of Chicago Press.

Kang, Leanne. 2020. *Dismantled: The Breakup of an Urban School System: Detroit, 1980–2016*. New York: Teachers College Press.

Katz, Bruce, and Jennifer Bradley. 2009. "The Detroit Project." *New Republic*, December 2.

Kelley, Robin D. G. 2015. "Beyond Black Lives Matter." *Kalfou* 2 (2): 330–37.

Kelley, Robin D. G. 2020. "Foreword: Why Black Marxism? Why Now?" In *Black Marxism*, edited by Cedric J. Robinson, xi–xxxiii. Chapel Hill: University of North Carolina Press.

Kellogg, Alex P. 2010a. "Detroit Shrinks Itself, Historic Homes and All." *Wall Street Journal*, May 14.

Kellogg, Alex P. 2010b. "Detroit's Smaller Reality: Mayor Plans to Use Census Tally Showing Decline as Benchmark in Overhaul." *Wall Street Journal*, February 27.

Kendi, Ibram X. 2023. *How to Be an Antiracist*. New York: One World.

Kickert, Conrad. 2019. *Dream City: Creation, Destruction, and Reinvention in Downtown Detroit*. Cambridge, MA: MIT Press.

Kinder, Kimberley. 2016. *DIY Detroit: Making Do in a City Without Services*. Minneapolis: University of Minnesota Press.

King, Martin Luther, Jr. 2018. *Letter from Birmingham Jail*. London: Penguin Classics.

Kinkead, Dan. 2016. "Detroit Case Study." In *Remaking Post-Industrial Cities*, edited by Donald K. Carter, 46–65. New York: Routledge.

Kinney, Rebecca J. 2016. *Beautiful Wasteland: The Rise of Detroit as America's Postindustrial Frontier*. Minneapolis: University of Minnesota Press.

Kinzer, Stephen. 2004. "Debating a Plan for a Blacks-Only Fund to Finance an 'Africa Town' in Detroit." *New York Times*, October 13.

Klein, Naomi. 2007. *The Shock Doctrine: The Rise of Disaster Capitalism*. New York: Metropolitan Books.

Kling, Karen, Amanda Nothaft, and Sam Stragand. 2024. "Where Research Meets the Real World: How Detroit Communities Inform the Poverty Solutions Research Agenda." Panel, July 12, University of Michigan, University of Michigan Detroit Center, https://events.umich.edu/event/123243.

Knight Foundation. 2003. *2003 Annual Report*. Miami: John S. and James L. Knight Foundation. https://knightfoundation.org.

Knight Foundation. 2005. "Detroit Education, Arts and Community Service Receive $2.7M Investment." September 29. https://knightfoundation.org.

Knight Foundation. 2008. "New Investments of $24.3 Million from Knight Foundation Improve Detroit Neighborhoods, Expand Regional Arts Access." December 18. https://knightfoundation.org.

Kohler, Scott. 2007a. "Living Cities." In *Casebook for The Foundation: A Great American Secret*, edited by Joel L. Fleishman, J. Scott Kohler, and Steven Schindler, 217–18. New York: Public Affairs.

Kohler, Scott. 2007b. "Local Initiative Support Corporation (LISC)." In *Casebook for The Foundation: A Great American Secret*, edited by Joel L. Fleishman, J. Scott Kohler, and Steven Schindler, 151–55. New York: Public Affairs.

Kornberg, Dana. 2016. "The Structural Origins of Territorial Stigma: Water and Racial Politics in Metropolitan Detroit, 1950s–2010s." *International Journal of Urban and Regional Research* 40 (2): 263–83.

Korver-Glenn, Elizabeth. 2021. *Race Brokers: Housing Markets and Segregation in 21st Century Urban America*. New York: Oxford University Press.

Korver-Glenn, Elizabeth, and Sarah Mayorga. 2024. *A Good Reputation: How Residents Fight for an American Barrio*. Chicago: University of Chicago Press.

Koscielniak, Michael. 2020. "Ground Forces: Dirt, Demolition, and the Geography of Decline in Detroit, Michigan." PhD diss., University of Michigan.

Krinks, Andrew. 2024. *White Property, Black Trespass: Racial Capitalism and the Religious Function of Mass Criminalization*. New York: New York University Press.

Krippner, Greta R. 2005. "The Financialization of the American Economy." *Socio-Economic Review* 3 (2): 173–208.

Krippner, Greta R. 2011. *Capitalizing on Crisis: The Political Origins of the Rise of Finance*. Cambridge, MA: Harvard University Press.

Kurashige, Scott. 2017. *The Fifty-Year Rebellion*. Oakland: University of California Press.

Laskey, Allison B., and Walter Nicholls. 2019. "Jumping off the Ladder: Participation and Insurgency in Detroit's Urban Planning." *Journal of the American Planning Association* 85 (3): 348–62.

Lee, Shawna J., Amy Krings, Sara Rose, Krista Dover, Jessica Ayoub, and Fatima Salman. 2016. "Racial Inequality and the Implementation of Emergency Management Laws in Economically Distressed Urban Areas." *Children and Youth Services Review* 70 (November): 1–7.

Lefebvre, Henri. 1984. *The Production of Space*. Translated by Donald Nicholson-Smith. Maiden, MA: Blackwell.

Lepore, Jill. 2018. *These Truths: A History of the United States*. New York: W. W. Norton.

Lewis, Martin W., and Kären Wigen. 1997. *The Myth of Continents*. Berkeley: University of California Press.

Lewis, Oscar. 1966. "The Culture of Poverty." *Scientific American* 215 (4): 19–25.

Lewis-Colman, David M. 2008. *Race Against Liberalism: Black Workers and the UAW in Detroit*. Urbana: University of Illinois Press.

Lighthill, Stephen. 1980. *Taking Back Detroit*. Icarus Films.

Lincoln Institute of Land Policy. 2020. *50-State Property Tax Comparison Study for Taxes Paid in 2019*. N.p.: Lincoln Institute of Land Policy and Minnesota Center for Fiscal Excellence. https://www.lincolninst.edu.

Lipsitz, George. 2011. *How Racism Takes Place*. Philadelphia, PA: Temple University Press.

Lipsitz, George. 2018. *The Possessive Investment in Whiteness: How White People Profit from Identity Politics*. Philadelphia, PA: Temple University Press.

Livengood, Chad. 2019. "Detroit's 40-Square-Mile Question—And Opportunity." *Crain's Detroit Business*, September 23.

Livengood, Chad, and Annalise Frank. 2020. "Serve and Protect. Then Go Home. 2020's Tensions Revive an Old Debate: Should Police Live in Communities Where they Work?" *Crain's Detroit Business*, July 27.

Locker, Katy. 2013. "Community Persistence Pays off in Detroit." Knight Foundation, December 18. https://knightfoundation.org.

Lockridge, Mark W. 2020. "Memo to The Honorable City of Detroit City Council Re: Detroit Land Bank Limited Scope Forensic Audit." Memo dated July 27, 2020, from Mark W. Lockridge, Auditor General, to the Detroit City Council. https://detroitmi/gov.

Logan, John R. 2012. "Making a Place for Space: Spatial Thinking in Social Science." *Annual Review of Sociology* 38 (1): 507–24.

Logan, John R., and Harvey Molotch. 2007. *Urban Fortunes: The Political Economy of Place*. Berkeley: University of California Press.

Londoño, Johana. 2020. *Abstract Barrios: The Crises of Latinx Visibility in Cities*. Durham, NC: Duke University Press.

Long-Bey, Jesse. 2003. "WRO Fights Seizure of Kids After Utility Shutoffs." *Michigan Citizen*, January 18.

López, Nancy, and Howard Hogan. 2021. "What's Your Street Race? The Urgency of Critical Race Theory and Intersectionality as Lenses for Revising the U.S. Office of Management and Budget Guidelines, Census and Administrative Data in Latinx communities and Beyond." *Genealogy* 5 (3): 75. https://doi.org/10.3390/genealogy5030075.

Loughran, Kevin. 2015. "*The Philadelphia Negro* and the Canon of Classical Urban Theory." *Du Bois Review: Social Science Research on Race* 12 (2): 249–67.

Löw, Martina. 2016. *The Sociology of Space: Materiality, Social Structures, and Action*. New York: Palgrave Macmillan.
Low, Setha M. 2023. *Why Public Space Matters*. New York: Oxford University Press.
Lowe, Lisa. 2015. *The Intimacies of Four Continents*. Durham, NC: Duke University Press.
Lupher, Eric. 2024. "Allowing the Detroit DDA's Captured Tax Revenues to Again Fund Government Services." Citizens Research Council of Michigan, September. https://crcmich.org.
MacDonald, Christine. 2010. "Detroit Talk to Focus on Land Use." *Detroit News*, May 12.
MacDonald, Christine, and Darren A. Nichols. 2010. "Bing Moves to Jump-Start Plans to Reshape Detroit." *Detroit News*, August 18.
MacDuffie, John Paul, Kent Smetters, and Morris Cohen. 2018. "The Auto Bailout 10 Years Later: Was It the Right Call?" *Knowledge at Wharton*, September 12. https://knowledge.wharton.upenn.edu.
Maclean, Mairi, Charles Harvey, Ruomei Yang, and Frank Mueller. 2021. "Elite Philanthropy in the United States and United Kingdom in the New Age of Inequalities." *International Journal of Management Reviews* 23 (3): 330–52.
Maggio, Christopher. 2021. "State-Level Immigration Legislation and Social Life: The Impact of the 'Show Me Your Papers' Laws." *Social Science Quarterly* 102 (4): 1654–85.
Mahu, Robert J., and Lyke Thompson. 2014. "Detroit: The Financial Crisis and the Emergency Manager." In *Local Politics and Mayoral Elections in 21st Century America*, edited by Marcia L. Godwin and Sean D. Foreman, 115–31. New York: Routledge.
Marchiel, Rebecca K. 2020. *After Redlining: The Urban Reinvestment Movement in the Era of Financial Deregulation*. Chicago: University of Chicago Press.
Markus, Gregory B., and Amy Krings. 2020. "Planning, Participation, and Power in a Shrinking City: The Detroit Works Project." *Journal of Urban Affairs* 42 (8): 1141–63.
Martin, Elizabeth Anne. 1993. *Detroit and the Great Migration, 1916-1929*. Ann Arbor: Bentley Historical Library, University of Michigan.
Martin, Ron. 2011. "The Local Geographies of the Financial Crisis: From the Housing Bubble to Economic Recession and Beyond." *Journal of Economic Geography* 11 (4): 587–618.
Marx, Karl. 1973. *Grundrisse: Foundations of the Critique of Political Economy*. Translated and with a foreword by Martin Nicolaus. New York: Random House.
Marx, Karl. 1978a. "The German Ideology: Part I." In *The Marx-Engels Reader*, edited by Robert C. Tucker, 146–202. New York: W. W. Norton.
Marx, Karl. 1978b. "Capital, Volume One." In *The Marx-Engels Reader*, edited by Robert C. Tucker, 294–438. New York: W. W. Norton.
Massey, Douglas S., and Nancy A. Denton. 1993. *American Apartheid: Segregation and the Making of the Underclass*. Cambridge, MA: Harvard University Press.

Mayorga-Gallo, Sarah. 2014. *Behind the White Picket Fence: Power and Privilege in a Multiethnic Neighborhood*. Chapel Hill: University of North Carolina Press.

Mayorga-Gallo, Sarah. 2019. "The White-Centering Logic of Diversity Ideology." *American Behavioral Scientist* 63 (13): 1789–809.

Mayorga, Sarah. 2023. *Urban Specters: The Everyday Harms of Racial Capitalism*. Chapel Hill: University of North Carolina Press.

McGoey, Linsey. 2012. "Philanthrocapitalism and Its Critics." *Poetics* 40 (2): 185–99.

McGoey, Linsey. 2016. "The Philanthropic State: Market-State Hybrids in the Philanthrocapitalist Turn." *Third World Quarterly* 35 (1): 109–25.

McGoey, Linsey. 2021. "Philanthrocapitalism and the Separation of Powers." *Annual Review of Law and Social Science* 17 (October): 391–409.

McGraw, Bill. 2018. "Coleman Young at 100: The 10 Greatest Myths." *Detroit Free Press*, May 27.

McKinney, Dave. 2015. "Knocking down Detroit to Revive It Comes at a Price." Reuters, December 15. https://www.reuters.com.

McKittrick, Katherine. 2006. *Demonic Grounds: Black Women and the Cartographies of Struggle*. Minneapolis: University of Minnesota Press.

McKittrick, Katherine. 2011. "On Plantations, Prisons, and a Black Sense of Place." *Social & Cultural Geography* 12 (8): 947–63.

McKittrick, Katherine. 2013. "Plantation Futures." *Small Axe* 17 (3): 1–15.

McKittrick, Katherine. 2021. *Dear Science and Other Stories*. Durham, NC: Duke University Press.

McMillan, Tracie. 2024. *The White Bonus: Five Families and the Cash Value of Racism in America*. New York: Henry Holt.

Mele, Christopher. 2017. *Race and the Politics of Deception: The Making of an American City*. New York: New York University Press.

Menjívar, Cecilia. 2013. "When Immigration Policies Affect Immigrants' Lives: Commentary." *Demography* 50 (3): 1097–99.

Metro Times Editorial Staff. 2020. "30 People Who Are Only Famous in Detroit." *Detroit Metro Times*, March 20. https://www.metrotimes.com.

Merrifield, Andy. 2002. *Dialectical Urbanism: Social Struggle in the Capitalist City*. New York: Monthly Review Press.

Mezzadra, Sandro, and Brett Neilson. 2013. *Border as Method, or the Multiplication of Labor*. Durham, NC: Duke University Press.

Michigan Department of Insurance and Financial Services. 2024. "Michigan Sees Largest Decrease in Uninsured Motorists in the Nation." January 4. https://www.michigan.gov.

Mignolo, Walter. 2011. *The Darker Side of Western Modernity: Global Futures, Decolonial Options*. Durham, NC: Duke University Press.

Mills, Charles W. 2019. *The Racial Contract*. Ithaca: Cornell University Press.

Milov, Sarah. 2019. *The Cigarette: A Political History*. Cambridge, MA: Harvard University Press.

Molotch, Harvey. 2012. "Objects and the City." In *The New Blackwell Companion to the City*, edited by Sophie Watson and Gary Bridge, 66–78. Malden, MA: John Wiley & Sons.

Montgomery, Alesia. 2016. "Reappearance of the Public: Placemaking, Minoritization and Resistance in Detroit." *International Journal of Urban and Regional Research* 40 (4): 776–99.

Montgomery, Alesia. 2020. *Greening the Black Urban Regime: The Culture and Commerce of Sustainability in Detroit*. Detroit: Wayne State University Press.

Motor City Mapping. 2014. "Motor City Mapping, Winter 2013–2014 Certified Results." December 30. https://portal.datadrivendetroit.org.

Moore, Jason W. 2016. "Nature/Society & the Violence of Real Abstraction." October 4. https://jasonwmoore.wordpress.com.

Moore, Natalie Y. 2004. "Hispanics Protest Black Economic Plan." *Detroit News*, September 29.

Moore, Wendy Leo. 2008. *Reproducing Racism: White Space, Elite Law Schools, and Racial Inequality*. Lanham, MD: Rowman & Littlefield.

Moore, Wendy Leo. 2020. "The Mechanisms of White Space(s)." *American Behavioral Scientist* 64 (14): 1946–60.

Moraga, Cherríe. 2021. "Enough Is Enough: Preface to the Fortieth Anniversary Edition." In *This Bridge Called My Back: Writings by Radical Women of Color*, edited by Cherríe Moraga and Gloria Anzaldúa, xv–xxii. Albany: State University of New York Press.

Morris, Aldon. 2015. *The Scholar Denied*. Oakland: University of California Press.

Moskowitz, Peter. 2015. "The Two Detroits: A City Both Collapsing and Gentrifying at the Same Time." *The Guardian*, February 5. https://www.theguardian.com.

Moskowitz, Peter E. 2018. *How to Kill a City: Gentrification, Inequality, and the Fight for the Neighborhood*. New York: Nation Books.

Moynihan, Daniel P. 1967. "Crisis in the City." *Massachusetts Review* 8 (3): 492–98.

Mozena, John C. 2020. "Real Cost of Economic Development." *Detroit News*, January 15.

Muller, Joann. 2010. "Detroit Must Shrink to Grow." *Forbes*, November 8.

Murray, Martin J. 2021. "Ruination and Rejuvenation: Rethinking Growth and Decline Through an Inverted Telescope." *International Journal of Urban and Regional Research* 45 (2): 348–62.

Myers, Ella. 2022. *The Gratifications of Whiteness: W. E. B. Du Bois and the Enduring Rewards of Anti-Blackness*. New York, NY: Oxford University Press.

National Academies of Sciences, Engineering, and Medicine. 2018. *Proactive Policing: Effects on Crime and Communities*. Washington, DC: National Academies Press. https://doi.org/10.172226/24928.

Neidert, Lisa, Reynolds Farley, and Jeffrey Morenoff. 2025. "How Census Undercount Became a Civil Rights Issue and Why It Is Increasingly Important." *RSF: The Russell Sage Foundation Journal of the Social Sciences* 11 (1): 26–43.

Neavling, Steve. 2020a. "Detroit City Council Renews Contract for Racially Biased Facial Recognition Surveillance Software." *Detroit Metro Times*, September 29. https://www.metrotimes.com.

Neavling, Steve. 2020b. "Struggling to Breathe in 48217, Michigan's Most Toxic ZIP Code." *Detroit Metro Times*, January 8. https://www.metrotimes.com.

New York Advisory Committee to the US Commission on Civil Rights. 2018. *The Civil Rights Implications of "Broken Windows" Policing in NYC and General NYPD Accountability to the Public*. N.p.: New York Advisory Committee to the US Commission on Civil Rights. https://www.usccr.gov.

Nicolaides, Becky M. 2024. *The New Suburbia: How Diversity Remade Suburban Life in Los Angeles After 1945*. New York: Oxford University Press.

Norris, Davon. 2023. "Embedding Racism: City Government Credit Ratings and the Institutionalization of Race in Markets." *Social Problems* 70 (4): 914–34.

Novak, Paolo. 2017. "Back to Borders." *Critical Sociology* 43 (6): 847–64.

Office of the Auditor General, City of Detroit. 2019. *Audit of Demolition Activities Interim Report on Contract Administration for City-funded Residential Demolitions*. November. https://detroitmi.gov.

Oeur, Freeden Blume, and Zawadi Rucks-Ahidiana. 2024. "*The Philadelphia Negro* at 125 Years: A Critical Commemoration." *City & Community* 23 (4): 269–79.

Okechukwu, Amaka. 2021. "Watching and Seeing: Recovering Abolitionist Possibilities in Black Community Practices of Safety and Security." *Du Bois Review: Social Science Research on Race* 18 (1): 153–80.

Okechukwu, Amaka. 2024. "From the Block to the World: Black Placemaking in New York City over Three Generations." *Journal of Race, Ethnicity and the City*, December, 1–25. https://doi.org/10.1080/26884674.2024.2425078.

Omi, Michael, and Howard Winant. 2015. *Racial Formation in the United States*. New York: Routledge.

Pacewicz, Josh. 2016. "The City as a Fiscal Derivative: Financialization, Urban Development, and the Politics of Earmarking." *City & Community* 15 (3): 264–88.

Pacewicz, Josh, and John N. Robinson III. 2021. "Pocketbook Policing: How Race Shapes Municipal Reliance on Punitive Fines and Fees in the Chicago Suburbs." *Socio-Economic Review* 19 (3): 975–1003.

Paffendorf, Jerry. 2010a. "LOVELAND Season 2 Pre-Game: The Legend of The Ghost Inches." May 11. https://www.kickstarter.com.

Paffendorf, Jerry. 2010b. "LOVELAND Season 2 Pre-Game Continued: Ghost Inches Unleash Ravishing Forces." May 11. https://www.kickstarter.com.

Pardo, Steve, and Francis X. Donnelly. 2013. "Napoleon Targets Detroit Crime—Mayoral Candidate Unveils Plan for Safer Neighborhoods." *Detroit News*, September 11.

Park, Robert. 1950. *Race and Culture*. Glencoe, IL: Free Press.

Park, Robert, and Ernest W. Burgess. 1925. *The City*. Chicago: University of Chicago.

Pattillo, Mary. 2021. "Black Advantage Vision: Flipping the Script on Racial Inequality Research." *Issues in Race & Society* 10 (1): 5–39.

Pattillo, Mary, Rosa Emilia Bermúdez Rico, and Ana María Mosquera Guevara. 2021. "Estamos Distanciados: The Black Middle Class and Politics in Cali, Colombia." *Du Bois Review: Social Science Research on Race* 18 (1): 49–72.

Peck, Jamie. 2010. "Zombie Neoliberalism and the Ambidextrous State." *Theoretical Criminology* 14 (1): 104–10.

Peck, Jamie, and Heather Whiteside. 2016. "Financializing Detroit." *Economic Geography* 92 (3): 235–68.

Perkins, Tom, and Lee DeVito. 2019. "New Management Takes over El Club After Founder Accused of Wage Theft and Racial Discrimination." *Detroit Metro Times*, February 25. https://www.metrotimes.com.

Perry, Andre M. 2020. *Know Your Price: Valuing Black Lives and Property in America's Black Cities*. Washington, DC: Brookings Institution Press.

Phillips-Fein, Kim. 2017. *Fear City: New York's Fiscal Crisis and the Rise of Austerity Politics*. New York: Metropolitan Books.

Phinney, Sawyer. 2018. "Detroit's Municipal Bankruptcy: Racialised Geographies of Austerity." *New Political Economy* 23 (5): 609–26.

Pickett, Justin T., Amanda Graham, and Francis T. Cullen. 2022. "The American Racial Divide in Fear of the Police." *Criminology* 60 (2): 291–320.

Piper, Karen Lynnea. 2002. *Cartographic Fictions: Maps, Race, and Identity*. New Brunswick, NJ: Rutgers University Press.

Polanyi, Karl. 2001. *The Great Transformation: The Political and Economic Origins of Our Time*. Boston: Beacon Press.

Ponder, C. S., and Mikael Omstedt. 2019. "The Violence of Municipal Debt: From Interest Rate Swaps to Racialized Harm in the Detroit Water Crisis." *Geoforum* 132 (June): 271–80.

Ponder, C. S. 2023. "'Cuando Colón Baje el Dedo': The Role of Repair in Urban Reproduction." *Urban Geography* 44 (9): 1853–73.

Porter, Michael, and Mark Kramer. 2011. "Creating Shared Value." *Harvard Business Review* 89 (1/2): 62–77.

Porter, Michael E. 2002. "The Competitive Advantage of Corporate Philanthropy." *Harvard Business Review* 80 (December): 56–69.

Purifoy, Danielle M., and Louise Seamster. 2021. "Creative Extraction: Black Towns in White Space." *Environment and Planning D: Society and Space* 39 (1): 47–66.

Rector, Josiah. 2022. *Toxic Debt: An Environmental Justice History of Detroit*. Chapel Hill: University of North Carolina Press.

Quijano, Aníbal. 2007. "Coloniality and Modernity/Rationality." *Cultural Studies* 21 (2–3): 168–78.

Quinn, Sarah L. 2019. *American Bonds: How Credit Markets Shaped a Nation*. Princeton, NJ: Princeton University Press.

Quizar, Jessi. 2019. "Land of Opportunity: Anti-Black and Settler Logics in the Gentrification of Detroit." *American Indian Culture and Research Journal* 43 (2): 113–33.

Quizar, Jessi. 2020. "A Bucket in the River: Race and Public Discourse on Water Shutoffs in Detroit." *Social Identities* 26 (4): 429–45.

Ramsey, Clare Pfeiffer. 2006. "Kwame Kilpatrick: Growing the 'Next Detroit.'" Model D, April 25. https://www.modeldmedia.com.

Reid, Carolina K., Debbie Bocian, Wei Li, and Roberto G. Quercia. 2017. "Revisiting the Subprime Crisis: The Dual Mortgage Market and Mortgage Defaults by Race and Ethnicity." *Journal of Urban Affairs* 39 (4): 469–87.

Reindl, J. C. 2020. "New Paradise Valley Luxury Apartments Planned: City District Will Pay Homage to Black-Owned Businesses." *Detroit Free Press*, November 7.

Rendon, Maria G. 2019. *Stagnant Dreamers: How the Inner City Shapes the Integration of the Second Generation*. New York: Russell Sage Foundation.

Renn, Aaron M. 2009. "Detroit: Urban Laboratory and the New American Frontier." *NewGeography*, November 4. https://www.newgeography.com.

Reed, Adolph, Jr. 1999. *Stirrings in the Jug: Black Politics in the Post-segregation Era*. Minneapolis: University of Minnesota Press.

Ritchie, Andrea J. 2017. *Invisible No More: Police Violence against Black Women and Women of Color*. Boston: Beacon Press.

Roane, J. T. 2023. *Dark Agoras: Insurgent Black Social Life and the Politics of Place*. New York: New York University Press.

Robinson, Cedric J. 2020. *Black Marxism*. 3rd ed. Chapel Hill: University of North Carolina Press.

Robinson, John N., III. 2020. "Capitalizing on Community: Affordable Housing Markets in the Age of Participation." *Politics & Society* 48 (2): 171–98.

Robinson, John N., III. 2021. "Surviving Capitalism: Affordability as a Racial 'Wage' in Contemporary Housing Markets." *Social Problems* 68 (2): 321–39.

Rodriguez, Marc Simon. 2011. *The Tejano Diaspora: Mexican Americanism and Ethnic Politics in Texas and Wisconsin*. Chapel Hill: University of North Carolina Press.

Rodriguez, Maria Elena. 2011. *Detroit's Mexicantown*. Charleston, SC: Arcadia Publishing.

Rosa, Vanessa A. 2023. *Precarious Constructions: Race, Class, and Urban Revitalization in Toronto*. Chapel Hill: University of North Carolina Press.

Rothstein, Richard. 2017. *The Color of Law: A Forgotten History of How Our Government Segregated America*. New York: Liveright.

Rucks-Ahidiana, Zawadi. 2022. "Theorizing Gentrification as a Process of Racial Capitalism." *City & Community* 21 (3): 173–92.

Rucks-Ahidiana, Zawadi. 2023. "Housing as Capital: US Policy, Homeownership, and the Racial Wealth Gap." In *The Sociology of Housing: How Homes Shape Our Social Lives*, edited by Brian J. McCabe and Eva Rosen, 15–28. Chicago: University of Chicago Press.

Rucks-Ahidiana, Zawadi. 2024. "Controlling Images of Neighborhoods in Gentrification Coverage." *Social Problems* 72 (3): 1260–79. https://doi.org/10.1093/socpro/spae014.

Rugh, Jacob S. 2015. "Double Jeopardy: Why Latinos Were Hit Hardest by the US Foreclosure Crisis." *Social Forces* 93 (3): 1139–84.

Rugh, Jacob S., and Matthew Hall. 2016. "Deporting the American Dream: Immigration Enforcement and Latino Foreclosures." *Sociological Science* 3:1053–76.

Rugh, Jacob S., and Douglas S. Massey. 2010. "Racial Segregation and the American Foreclosure Crisis." *American Sociological Review* 75 (5): 629–51.

Ryssdal, Kai, and Paulina Velasco. 2017. "Detroit's Chief Storyteller Says It's Time to Talk About Neighborhoods That Persevered." Marketplace, July 24. https://www.marketplace.org.

Ryzewski, Krysta. 2021. *Detroit Remains: Archaeology and Community Histories of Six Legendary Places*. Tuscaloosa: University of Alabama Press.

Safransky, Sara. 2014. "Greening the Urban Frontier: Race, Property, and Resettlement in Detroit." *Geoforum* 56 (September): 237–48.

Safransky, Sara. 2017. "Rethinking Land Struggle in the Postindustrial City." *Antipode* 49 (4): 1079–100.

Safransky, Sara. 2018. "Land Justice as a Historical Diagnostic: Thinking with Detroit." *Annals of the American Association of Geographers* 108 (2): 499–512.

Safransky, Sara. 2020. "Geographies of Algorithmic Violence: Redlining the Smart City." *International Journal of Urban and Regional Research* 44 (2): 200–218.

Safransky, Sara. 2022. "Grammars of Reckoning: Redressing Racial Regimes of Property." *Environment and Planning D: Society and Space* 40 (2): 292–305.

Safransky, Sara. 2023. *The City after Property: Abandonment and Repair in Postindustrial Detroit*. Durham, NC: Duke University Press.

Sampson, Robert J. 2008. "Collective Efficacy Theory: Lessons Learned and Directions for Future Inquiry." In *Taking Stock*, edited by Francis T. Cullen, John Paul Wright and Kristie R. Blevins, 149–67. New Brunswick, NJ: Routledge.

Sampson, Robert J. 2012. *Great American City: Chicago and the Enduring Neighborhood Effect*. Chicago, IL: University of Chicago Press.

Sampson, Robert J., Jeffrey D. Morenoff, and Thomas Gannon-Rowley. 2002. "Assessing 'Neighborhood Effects': Social Processes and New Directions in Research." *Annual Review of Sociology* 28 (1): 443–78.

Sampson, Robert J., and Stephen W. Raudenbush. 2004. "Seeing Disorder: Neighborhood Stigma and the Social Construction of 'Broken Windows.'" *Social Psychology Quarterly* 67 (4): 319–42.

Sampson, Robert J., and Stephen W. Raudenbush. 2005. "Neighborhood Stigma and the Perception of Disorder." *Focus* 24 (1): 7–11.

Sandoval-Strausz, A. K. 2019. *Barrio America: How Latino Immigrants Saved the American City*. New York: Basic Books.

Sassen, Saskia. 2008. *Territory, Authority, Rights*. Princeton: Princeton University Press.

Saulny, Susan. 2010. "Razing the City to Save the City: Detroit Tries the Once Unthinkable." *New York Times*, June 21, A16–17.

Schelling, Thomas C. 1971. "Dynamic Models of Segregation." *Journal of Mathematical Sociology* 1 (2): 143–86.

Scher, Peter L. 2019. "How Detroit Became a Model for Urban Renewal." *Fortune*, June 2. https://fortune.com.

Schindler, Seth. 2014. "Detroit after Bankruptcy: A Case of Degrowth Machine Politics." *Urban Studies* 53 (4): 818–36.

Schultz, Marisa. 2013. "Mich. Set to Receive $100M in Fed Funds for Demolitions." *Detroit News*, June 6.

Scott, James C. 2008. *Seeing Like a State*. New Haven: Yale University Press.

Seamster, Louise. 2018. "When Democracy Disappears: Emergency Management in Benton Harbor." *Du Bois Review: Social Science Research on Race* 15 (2): 295–322.

Seamster, Louise, and Danielle Purifoy. 2020. "What is Environmental Racism For? Place-Based Harm and Relational Development." *Environmental Sociology* 7 (2): 1–12.

Seamster, Louise. Forthcoming. *The Flint Water Coup: Debt at the End of Democracy*. New York: Columbia University Press.

Seelye, Katharine Q. 2011. "Detroit Census Figures Confirm a Grim Desertion Like No Other." *New York Times*, March 23.

Seigel, Ron. 2002. "Takeovers Raise Land, Civil Rights Issues." *Michigan Citizen*, July 27.

Seuss, Dr. 1958. *Yertle the Turtle and Other Stories*. New York: Random House.

Seymour, Eric, and Joshua Akers. 2019. "Portfolio Solutions, Bulk Sales of Bank-owned properties, and the Reemergence of Racially Exploitative Land Contracts." *Cities* 89 (June): 46–56.

Seymour, Eric, and Joshua Akers. 2021. "Building the Eviction Economy: Speculation, Precarity, and Eviction in Detroit." *Urban Affairs Review* 57 (1): 35–69.

Seymour, Eric, and Joshua Akers. 2024. "Judged by Their Deeds: Outcomes for Properties Acquired by Contract Sellers Following the Foreclosure Crisis in Detroit." *Housing Policy Debate* 34 (6): 870–90.

Shabazz, Rashad. 2015. *Spatializing Blackness: Architectures of Confinement and Black Masculinity in Chicago*. Urbana: University of Illinois Press.

Shachar, Ayelet, and Ran Hirschl. 2007. "Citizenship as Inherited Property." *Political Theory* 35 (3): 253–87.

Shaw, Todd C., and Lester K. Spence. 2004. "Race and Representation in Detroit's Community Development Coalitions." *Annals of the American Academy of Political and Social Science* 594 (1): 189–92.

Sheller, Mimi. 2017. "From Spatial Turn to Mobilities Turn." *Current Sociology* 65 (4): 623–39.

Sheller, Mimi, and John Urry. 2006. "The New Mobilities Paradigm." *Environment and Planning A* 38 (2): 207–26.

Shields, Yvette. 2020. "Investors Return to Detroit." *Bond Buyer* 392 (35396): 1–2.

Shields, Yvette. 2021. "Investors Swarm over Junk-Rated Detroit GO bonds." *Bond Buyer*, February 5. https://www.bondbuyer.com.

Silver, Hilary. 2015. "The Urban Sociology of Detroit." *City & Community* 14 (2): 97–101.

Silverman, Robert Mark. 2005. "Caught in the Middle: Community Development Corporations (CDCs) and the Conflict between Grassroots and Instrumental Forms of Citizen Participation." *Community Development* 36 (2): 35–51.

Silverman, Robert Mark, Henry Louis Taylor Jr, Li Yin, Camden Miller, and Pascal Buggs. 2019. "Place Making as a form of Place Taking: Residential Displacement and Grassroots Resistance to Institutional Encroachment in Buffalo, New York." *Journal of Place Management and Development* 12 (4): 566–80.

Simms, Angela M. Forthcoming. *Fighting for a Foothold: How Government and Markets Undermine Black Middle-Class Suburbia*. New York: Russell Sage Foundation.

Simon, Bob. 2013. "Detroit on the Edge." *60 Minutes*, October 13. https://www.cbsnews.com.

Small, Mario L., and Laura Adler. 2019. "The Role of Space in the Formation of Social Ties." *Annual Review of Sociology* 45 (1): 111–32.

Smith, Neil. 2001. "Global Social Cleansing: Postliberal Revanchism and the Export of Zero Tolerance." *Social Justice* 28 (3): 68–74.

Smith, Neil. 2005. *The New Urban Frontier: Gentrification and the Revanchist City*. London: Routledge.

Smith, Naomi, and Peter Walters. 2018. "Desire Lines and Defensive Architecture in Modern Urban Environments." *Urban Studies* 55 (13): 2980–95.

Snell, Robert. 2014. "Talks on $140M in Ch. 9 Fees to Start." *Detroit News*, December 3.

Sohn-Rethel, Alfred. 2020. *Intellectual and Manual Labour: A Critique of Epistemology*. Atlantic Highlands, NJ: Humanities Press.

Soja, Edward W. 1980. "The Socio-Spatial Dialectic." *Annals of the Association of American Geographers* 70 (2): 207–25.

Sorentino, Sara-Maria. 2019. "The Abstract Slave: Anti-Blackness and Marx's Method." *International Labor and Working-Class History* 96 (Fall): 17–37.

Spivak, Gayatri Chakravorty. 2023. "Can the Subaltern Speak?" In *Imperialism*, edited by Peter H. Cain and Mark Harrison, 171–219. New York: Routledge.

Sroka, Robert. 2024. "Subsidizing a Sports Arena in a Bankrupt City: Detroit's Little Caesars Arena." *Social Science Quarterly* 105 (5): 1691–705.

Stafford, Kat, and Kristi Tanner. 2020. "Demolitions Put Kids at Risk." *Detroit News*, October 18.

Stahl, Lesley. 2019. "Jamie Dimon's Data-Focused Investment in Detroit." *60 Minutes*, November 10. https://www.cbsnews.com.

Stech, Katy. 2014. "Detroit's Orr Describes City's 'Rebirth' in Chapter 9; Detroit's Bankruptcy Filing in July made it the Largest U.S. City Ever to File for Bankruptcy." *Wall Street Journal*, April 25. https://www.wsj.com/.

Steil, Justin P., Len Albright, Jacob S. Rugh, and Douglas S. Massey. 2018. "The Social Structure of Mortgage Discrimination." *Housing Studies* 33 (5): 759–76.

Stern, Gary H., and Ron J. Feldman. 2004. *Too Big to Fail: The Hazards of Bank Bailouts*. Washington, DC: Brookings Institution Press.

Stovall, Maya, and Alex B. Hill. 2016. "Blackness in Post-Bankruptcy Detroit: Racial Politics and Public Discourse." *North American Dialogue* 19 (2): 117–27.

Sugrue, Thomas J. 2008. *Sweet Land of Liberty: The Forgotten Struggle for Civil Rights in the North*. New York: Random House.

Sugrue, Thomas J. 2014. *The Origins of the Urban Crisis*. Princeton, NJ: Princeton University Press.

Summers, Brandi Thompson. 2019. *Black in Place: The Spatial Aesthetics of Race in a Post-Chocolate City*. Chapel Hill: University of North Carolina Press.

Svoboda, Sandra. 2014. "Term Limits and Bankruptcy." *Michigan Citizen*, March 9.
Tabb, William K. 2015. "If Detroit is Dead, Some Things Need to be said at the Funeral." *Journal of Urban Affairs* 37 (1): 1–12.
Talen, Emily. 2018. *Neighborhood*. New York: Oxford University Press.
Taylor, Keeanga-Yamahtta. 2019. *Race for Profit: How Banks and the Real Estate Industry Undermined Black Homeownership*. Chapel Hill: University of North Carolina Press.
Taylor, Ralph. 2018. *Breaking Away from Broken Windows: Baltimore Neighborhoods and the Nationwide Fight against Crime, Grime, Fear, and Decline*. New York: Routledge.
The Neighborhoods. N.d. "About." http://www.theneighborhoods.org.
Thomas, June Manning. 2013. *Redevelopment and Race: Planning a Finer City in Postwar Detroit*. Detroit, MI: Wayne State University Press.
Thomas, June Manning. 2022. "Racism and US Urban Planning." In *Infrastructure, Wellbeing and the Measurement of Happiness*, edited by Hoda Mahmoudi, Jenny Roe, and Kate Seaman, 63–85. New York: Routledge.
Thompson, Bankole. 2004a. "African Town Killed." *Michigan Citizen*, October 24–30.
Thompson, Bankole. 2004b. "African Town Supporters Outgun Opponents." *Michigan Citizen*, October 17–23.
Thompson, Heather Ann. 2017. *Whose Detroit? Politics, Labor, and Race in a Modern American City*. Ithaca: Cornell University Press.
Thomson, Dale E. 2012. "Targeting Neighborhoods, Stimulating Markets: The Role of Political, Institutional, and Technical Factors in Three Cities." In *The City after Abandonment*, edited by June Manning Thomas and Margaret Dewar, 104–32. Philadelphia: University of Pennsylvania Press.
Thomson, Dale E. 2019. "Donor-Driven Democracy? Governance Implications of Foundation-Dependent Revitalization." *Journal of Urban Affairs* 41 (4): 551–69.
Torres-Saillant, Silvio. 1998. "The Tribulations of Blackness: Stages in Dominican Racial Identity." *Latin American Perspectives* 25 (3): 126–46.
Treitler, Vilna Bashi. 2013. *The Ethnic Project: Transforming Racial Fiction into Ethnic Factions*. Stanford, CA: Stanford University Press.
Trujillo-Pagán, Nicole. 2019. "Marking Walls and Borders: Latina/o/x Youth, Graffiti and Competing Visions of Community Development." *International Journal of Sociology and Social Policy* 39 (11/12): 975–94.
Turbeville, Wallace C. 2013. "The Detroit Bankruptcy." *Dēmos*, November 20. https://www.demos.org.
Turbeville, Wallace C. 2014. "Lessons from The Detroit Bankruptcy." *Dēmos*, July 16. https://www.demos.org.
Underkuffler, Laura S. 1990. "On Property: An Essay." *Yale Law Journal* 100 (1): 127–48.
Urban Institute. 2017. "The Tipping Point." September 12. https://www.urban.org.
USA Today. 2023. "Most Recent Readers' Choice Awards Results, #1: Best Riverwalk." https://10best.usatoday.com.
USA Today. 2025a. "Most Recent Readers' Choice Awards Results, #1: Best Public Square." https://10best.usatoday.com.

USA Today. 2025b. "Most Recent Readers' Choice Awards Results, #2: Best Art Museum." https://10best.usatoday.com.

US Attorney's Office, Eastern District of Michigan. 2023. "The Detroit Land Bank Authority Pays $1.5 Million To Resolve False Claims Act Allegations Relating to Blight Elimination Costs." Press release, February 10. https://www.justice.gov.

US Census Bureau. 2000. "Profile of General Demographic Characteristics: 2000." *Decennial Census, DEC Summary File 4*, Table DP1. https://data.census.gov.

US Census Bureau. 2010a. "Demographic Characteristics for Occupied Housing Units." *American Community Survey, 2010: ACS 5-Year Estimates Subject Tables*, Table S2502. https://data.census.gov.

US Census Bureau. 2010b. "Hispanic or Latino, and Not Hispanic or Latino by Race." *Decennial Census, DEC Summary File 1*, Table P9. https://data.census.gov.

US Census Bureau. 2010c. "Median Income in the Past 12 Months (in 2010 Inflation-Adjusted Dollars)." *American Community Survey, 2010: ACS 5-Year Estimates Subject Tables*, Table S1903. https://data.census.gov.

US Census Bureau. 2010d. "Median Value (Dollars)." *American Community Survey, 2010: ACS 5-Year Estimates Detailed Tables*, Table B25077. https://data.census.gov.

US Census Bureau. 2010e. "Poverty Status in the Past 12 Months." *American Community Survey, 2010: ACS 5-Year Estimates Subject Tables*, Table S1701. https://data.census.gov.

US Census Bureau. 2012. "Poverty Status in the Past 12 Months." *American Community Survey, 2012: ACS 5-Year Estimates Detailed Tables*, Table S1701. https://data.census.gov.

US Census Bureau. 2014. "Presence and Types of Internet Subscriptions in Household." *American Community Survey, 2014: ACS 1-Year Estimates Detailed Tables*, Table B28002. https://data.census.gov.

US Census Bureau. 2017. "Presence and Types of Internet Subscriptions in Household." *American Community Survey, 2017: American Community Survey 5-Year Estimates Detailed Tables*, Table B28002. https://data.census.gov.

US Census Bureau. 2018. "Census Tracts for the 2020 Census-Final Criteria." *Federal Register* 83 (219): 56277.

US Census Bureau. 2019. "Poverty Status in the Past 12 Months." *American Community Survey, 2019: ACS 5-Year Estimates Subject Tables*, Table S1701. https://data.census.gov.

US Census Bureau. 2020. "Hispanic or Latino, and Not Hispanic or Latino by Race." *Decennial Census, 2020: DEC Demographic and Housing Characteristics*, Table P9. https://data.census.gov.

US Census Bureau. 2022a. "Demographic Characteristics for Occupied Housing." *American Community Survey, 2022: ACS 5-Year Estimates Subject Tables*, Table S2502. https://data.census.gov.

US Census Bureau. 2022b. "Mean Income in the Past 12 Months (in 2022 Inflation-Adjusted Dollars)." *American Community Survey, 2022: ACS 5-Year Estimates Subject Tables*, Table S1902. https://data.census.gov.

US Census Bureau. 2022c. "Median Income in the Past 12 Months (in 2022 Inflation-Adjusted Dollars)." *American Community Survey, 2022: ACS 5-Year Estimates Subject Tables*, Table S1903. https://data.census.gov.

US Census Bureau. 2022d. "Median Value (Dollars)." *American Community Survey, 2022: ACS 5-Year Estimates Detailed Tables*, Table B25077. https://data.census.gov.

US Census Bureau. 2022e. "Poverty Status in the Past 12 Months." *American Community Survey, 2022: ACS 5-Year Estimates*, Table S1701. https://data.census.gov.

US Federal Housing Administration. 1938. *Underwriting Manual*. Washington, DC: US Government Printing Office.

US Government Accountability Office. 2020. "Troubled Asset Relief Program: Treasury Continues Winding Down Housing Programs." December 8. https://www.gao.gov.

US Department of Justice. 2013. "Justice Department, Federal and State Partners Secure Record $13 Billion Global Settlement with JPMorgan for Misleading Investors About Securities Containing Toxic Mortgages." Press release, November 19. https://www.justice.gov.

US House Committee on Un-American Activities. 1952. *Communism in the Detroit Area—Part I*. Washington, DC: US Government Printing Office.

US National Advisory Commission on Civil Disorders. 1968. *Report of the National Advisory Commission on Civil Disorders*. Washington, DC: US Government Printing Office.

US Special Inspector General for the Troubled Asset Relief Program. 2016. *Quarterly Report to Congress: - Q3 2016*. N.p.: Office of the Special Inspector General for the Troubled Asset Relief Program. https://www.oversight.gov.

US Special Inspector General for the Troubled Asset Relief Program. 2017. *Quarterly Report to Congress - Q3 2017*. N.p.: Office of the Special Inspector General for the Troubled Asset Relief Program. https://www.oversight.gov.

Vargas, Edward D., Melina Juarez, Lisa Cacari Stone, and Nancy Lopez. 2021. "Critical 'Street Race' Praxis: Advancing the Measurement of Racial Discrimination Among Diverse Latinx Communities in the U.S." *Critical Public Health* 31 (4): 381–91.

Vargas, Zaragosa. 1993. *Proletarians of the North: A History of Mexican Industrial Workers in Detroit and the Midwest, 1917–1933*. Berkeley: University of California Press.

Vergara, Camilo José. 1995a. "Downtown Detroit: 'American Acropolis' or Vacant Land-What to Do with the World's Third Largest Concentration of Pre-Depression Skyscrapers?" *Metropolis*, April, 32–38.

Vergara, Camilo José. 1995b. *The New American Ghetto*. New Brunswick, NJ: Rutgers University Press.

Vergara, Camilo José. 1999. *American Ruins*. New York: Monacelli Press.

Vergara, Camilo José. 2016. *Detroit is No Dry Bones: The Eternal City of the Industrial Age*. Ann Arbor: University of Michigan Press.

Villarreal, Ana. 2021. "Reconceptualizing Urban Violence from the Global South." *City & Community* 20 (1): 48–58.

Vogel, Steven. 1996. *Against Nature. The Concept of Nature in Critical Theory*. Albany: SUNY Press.

Wacquant, Loïc. 2001. "Deadly Symbiosis: When Ghetto and Prison Meet and Mesh." *Punishment & Society* 3 (1): 95–133.
Wacquant, Loïc. 2010. "Urban Desolation and Symbolic Denigration in the Hyperghetto." *Social Psychology Quarterly* 73 (3): 215–19.
Wacquant, Loïc. 2022. *The Invention of the 'Underclass': A Study in the Politics of Knowledge*. Cambridge: Polity.
Wacquant, Loïc. 2023. *Bourdieu in the City: Challenging Urban Theory*. Cambridge: Polity.
Walsh, Tom. 2006. "Neighborhoods Next to Rise." *Detroit Free Press*, December 19.
Walsh, Tom, and John Gallagher. 2014. "New Econ Chief Lewand Hustles to Deliver on Duggan's To-Do List." *Detroit Free Press*, February 13.
Watson, JoAnn. 2004. "The 'African Town' Proposal." *Michigan Citizen*, October 3–9.
We the People of Detroit Community Research Collective. 2016. *Mapping the Water Crisis*. Detroit: We the People of Detroit Community Research Collective.
Weber, Max. 1978. *Economy and Society: An Outline of Interpretive Sociology*. Vol. 1. Berkeley: University of California Press.
Weheliye, Alexander G. 2014. *Habeas Viscus: Racializing Assemblages, Biopolitics, and Black Feminist Theories of the Human*. Durham, NC: Duke University Press.
Weil, Julie Zauzmer. 2021. "Wards 7 and 8 Have Long Represented Poor, Black D.C. Neighborhoods. What Does It Mean to Redistrict Them?" *Washington Post*, November 3. https://www.washingtonpost.com.
Welch, Sherri. 2017. "A Career in Social Justice; Southwest Solutions CEO to Cap 45-year Tenure Next Year." *Crain's Detroit Business*, June 12.
Welch, Sherri. 2019. "Southwest Solutions Slims Down in Bid to Stabilize." *Crain's Detroit Business*, February 25.
Westbrook, Dene. 2013. "League President Jacqueline Noonan Issues Media Statement on Detroit Bankruptcy Court Ruling." Michigan Municipal League, December 4. https://mml.org.
Whitaker, David. 2016. "Memo to The Honorable City of Detroit City Council Re: Possible Use of Hardest Hit Funds (HHF) for Tax Foreclosure Prevention." Memo dated April 28, 2016, from David Whitaker, Director of Legislative Policy Division, to the Detroit City Council. https://detroitmi/gov.
White, Hylton. 2020. "How is Capitalism Racial? Fanon, Critical Theory and the Fetish of Antiblackness." *Social Dynamics* 46 (1): 22–35.
White, Monica M. 2011. "D-Town Farm: African American Resistance to Food Insecurity and the Transformation of Detroit." *Environmental Practice* 13 (4): 406–17.
Williams, Paige. 2014. "Drop Dead, Detroit!" *New Yorker*, January 27.
Wilson, James Q., and George L. Kelling. 1982. "Broken Windows." *Atlantic Monthly* 249 (3): 29–38.
Wilson, William Julius. 1980. *The Declining Significance of Race: Blacks and Changing American Institutions*. Chicago: University of Chicago Press.
Wilson, William Julius. 2012. *The Truly Disadvantaged: The Inner City, the Underclass, and Public Policy*. Chicago: University of Chicago Press.

Winling, LaDale C., and Todd M. Michney. 2021. "The Roots of Redlining: Academic, Governmental, and Professional Networks in the Making of the New Deal Lending Regime." *Journal of American History* 108 (1): 42–69.

Woods, Clyde. 2017a. *Development Arrested: The Blues and Plantation Power in the Mississippi Delta*. London: Verso Books.

Woods, Clyde. 2017b. *Development Drowned and Reborn: The Blues and Bourbon Restorations in Post-Katrina New Orleans*. Athens: University of Georgia Press.

WXYZ-TV. 2025. "Frustration Mounts Over Pothole-Riddled Detroit Road." YouTube video, July 10. https://www.youtube.com/watch?v=EIKxJRrNDs4.

Wylie, Jeanie. 1989. *Poletown: Community Betrayed*. Urbana: University of Illinois Press.

Wylie-Kellermann, Bill. 2010. "Looking for Real Justice." *Detroit Metro Times*, December 8. https://www.metrotimes.com.

Wynter, Sylvia. 2003. "Unsettling the Coloniality of Being/Power/Truth/Freedom: Towards the Human, After Man, its Overrepresentation—An Argument." *CR: The New Centennial Review* 3 (3): 257–337.

Young, Alfohlrd A. 2004. *The Minds of Marginalized Black Men: Making Sense of Mobility, Opportunity, and Future Life Chances*. Princeton, NJ: Princeton University Press.

Young, Carlito H. 1997. "Constant Struggle: Coleman Young's Perspective on American Society and Detroit Politics." *Black Scholar* 27 (2): 31–41.

Young, Coleman A., and Lonnie Wheeler. 1994. *Hard Stuff: The Autobiography of Coleman Young*. New York: Viking.

Zuberi, Tukufu, and Eduardo Bonilla-Silva. 2008. *White Logic, White Methods: Racism and Methodology*. Lanham, MD: Rowman & Littlefield.

Zukin, Sharon. 2010. *Naked City: The Death and Life of Authentic Urban Places*. New York: Oxford University Press.

Zunz, Olivier. 1982. *The Changing Face of Inequality: Urbanization, Industrial Development, and Immigrants in Detroit, 1880–1920*. Chicago: University of Chicago Press.

INDEX

Page numbers in *italics* indicate Figures, Tables, and Pictures

abstractions, 30–31, 199; African Town proposal struggles, 144–48; blight, 6, 13, 38, 74; as bordering and crossing practices, 21–24; of Detroit, 7–10, 13–16; doubleness of, 13–14, 191, 193, 221n65; ignoring conditions, 24–25; Lefebvre on production of space, 12, 14, 17, 222n70; media, 7, 8, 142; in *Plessy v. Ferguson* on separate but equal, 19; powerful groups dependence on, 16–17, 37; property claims as, 91–122; property relations and, 18–21, 96, 194; public-private partnerships promotion by, 21; of race and space relations, 6, 10, 11–17; reality through lived experiences, 13–15; as reflection of reality, 7, 10, 220n28; of space, 36; of threat and exclusion, 147; tipping point, 6, 13, 38; white supremacy and, 223n91

ACLU. *See* American Civil Liberties Union

AdvancingCities initiative, of JPMC, 188

affirmative action, 150; Michigan constitutional amendment outlawing, 126; Williams on, 234n2

African Americans. *See* Blacks

African Town proposal (2002): abstraction struggles, 144–48; affirmative action issue, 150; as African-centered retail and entertainment community, 143; Anderson proposal in Empowerment Zone, 143; Asian, Hispanic, Arab business owner opposition to, 146, 147; Black entrepreneurship promotion, 39; Black-led development model, 142–43, 146; civil rights activists support of, 147; collaboration and protests against, 149–50; *The Detroit News* on, 39, 141–42; Harvey and Willis plans for, 143; JPMC Entrepreneurs of Color Fund, 149; political support for, 143; on public funds for specific race, 148–49; Reyes criticism of, 147; Vivian tie to civil rights for, 144; Watson and Boggs on Black entrepreneurs, 145

Ambassador Bridge, 84; displacement of Mexicantown, 114; as international border crossing dividing SWD, 6, 22, 41–42, 92, 105; SWD street access from, 41–42, *42*

American Civil Liberties Union (ACLU), actions against racial profiling and surveillance, 84

American Dream, 5, 35; Detroit embodiment of, 91, 165; of immigrants, 3–4; property as, 121; SWD struggle for, 38, 101, 114; whiteness association, 4

Anderson, Claud, 39; African Town proposal in Empowerment Zone, 143; on underserved Blacks, 144–45

anti-Blackness, 33, 39, 118, 142, 193, 194, 198

273

Baldwin, James, 150
bankruptcy (2013), 55–56; attempt to produce new Detroit after, 63; Black governance limitations and, 38; blamed on decades of mismanagement, 9; bordering practice of government and, 123–24; Bunge maps on money transfers in and out of city, 137, *138*, 144–45; credit swaps impact on, 130–31; demolition program compared to, 138; emergency management blamed for, 126–27; Jones Day attorneys financial benefits from, 129, 197; media on explanations for, 1–2; Obama and federal response to, 151–52; Orr on opportunity for rebirth from, 131; pensioners pitted against city assets, 128–30, 197; neighborhood count pre- and post-, 60; quality of life improvement after, 25; racial difference and dispossession, 123; regime change after, 142–43; shift in metropolitan area, 123, 127; Snyder filing for, 32; state and city government shaped by, 123

Bing, David "Dave," 132, 152, 193, 196; Detroit Works Project and, 160, 183

Black Bottom: Black population displacement from, 5; Blacks development of, 4; Detroit 1960s razing of, 96

Black communities, DFC plan for displacement of, 77

Black entrepreneurship, 145, 149; African Town proposal promotion of, 38

Blacks, 92; Anderson on underserved, 144–45; Black Bottom and Paradise Valley developments, 4; blight blamed on, 78; bordering practices prevention of political influence, 140; Detroit largest Black city in overall population, 1–2; displacement of governance, 20; Feikens on era of development of, 220n44; intervention with emergency management, 127; largest middle class in US, 4; NAACP largest branch in Detroit, 4; rebellion of 1967 for civil rights of, 116–17; representation struggle in Detroit, 20; struggle for space, 11; Taylor on public-private partnerships at expense of, 223n86. *See also* dispossession; inclusive growth

blight: as abstraction, 6, 13, 38, 74; Blacks blamed for, 78; defined, 78, 229n63; property values perspective for removal of, 134; questions about benefit from, 165. *See also* Detroit Blight Removal Task Force

Boggs, Grace Lee, 145, 147–48
Bomey, Nathan, 132
Bonilla-Silva, Eduardo, 13
bordering practices, 38, 139, *205*, 226n10; abstractions as, 21–24; bankruptcy and government, 123–24; Blacks political influence prevention, 140; gerrymandering as, 124–25; international crossings between US and Canada, 22; Latina/o/x youth in SWD defensive, 93; neighborhoods and, 59–60, 90; policing and redlining example, 22; policing as SWD urban, 44–47; through race and ethnicity, 48, 56; socio-spatial mobility, 37; of Southwest Solutions, 88–89; SWD mapping as spatial and sociocultural, 55; tied to SWD, 23–24

The Bridge Called My Back, 41
broken windows theory, of Wilson and Kelling, 63–66, 199
Bunge, William, 137, *138*, 144–45

CDCs. *See* community development corporations
CDFIs. *See* Community Development Financial Institutions Funds
Census Bureau, US, 237n69; on census tracts, 60, 101–5, *102*, *103*, 109, 227n3; Latina/o/x population undercount by,

124; on poverty, 219n12; references to race, 149
census tracts, for SWD: businesses in, 109; city and resident defined boundaries for, 104–5; city disregard for areas, 105; population decline by, 101–3, *103*; SNF funding, 101, *102*
certificates of participation (COP), Kilpatrick and pension obligation, 130
Chang, Joyce, 155
civil rights: activists support of African Town proposal, 147; African Town proposal tied to, 144; rebellion of 1967 and Black, 116–17; Young as first Black mayor, 5, 117
class: Foley reference to, 83; Hartigan on whiteness relation to, 226n150
Coates, Ta-Nehisi, 3
Cockerel, Kenneth Sr., 118–19
community, neighborhood compared to, 59
community development corporations (CDCs), 66, 67
Community Development Financial Institutions Funds (CDFIs), 175–76, 178–79, 238n96
Community Reinvestment Act (1977), 66
conditions, abstractions ignoring of, 24–25
container theory of space, 7, 193–94
COP. *See* certificates of participation
county and city land banks controversy, 152, 219n11
creative development approach, of foundations, 159
credit swaps, bankruptcy impacted from, 130–31
crime versus lived experience of safety, in SWD: block and neighborhood distinction, 48–49, 54; having skill and degree distinction, 49–50; Project Green Light camera surveillance, 51–52, 64, 84, 94; social ties to promote public order and control crime, 51
crossing practices, 38, 139, 140; abstractions as, 21–24; of Latina/o/x youth, 23, 28; production of race and space struggles, 23; of Southwest Solutions, 88–89; in SWD, 23–24, 58
Cunningham, Eugene "Gene," 190, 191

DARE. *See* Detroit Alliance for a Rational Economy
Data Driven Detroit (2008): challenges of, 74; Kresge and Skillman Foundations support, 73; Kresge funding of, 162; Metzger and, 73, 162–66; Paffendorf land repackaging, 163; work with National Neighborhood Indicators Partnership, 165
data-driven interventions, 61, 90, 161–62
"Defining Blight" report, of Detroit Blight Removal Task Force, 79, 79–80
DEGC. *See* Detroit Economic Growth Corporation
delinquency, dispossession and, 30–31
demolition program, 38, 123, 132–33, 136–39; bankruptcy compared to, 138; concerns of Detroit Land Bank Authority, 135; contractors and workforce requirements, 137; Detroit Blight Removal Task Force tipping point for, 80–81, *81*; FBI and US Attorney found rigged bidding for contracts, 135; HHF fraud, bid rigging, 135; HHF funding directed to, 36, 133, 233n48; Lockridge negative findings on, 136; problem of static space production, 134–35; residents concerns about, 135; socio-spatial transformation, 123; targeted areas for, 134
Department of Justice: JPMC collaboration with city government, 36; JPMC settlement with, 171–72, 183, 196

Department of Neighborhoods (DON), 81–84, 134, 194–95; Duggan development of, 60, 81–82; planners shaping of area in SWD, 55–56
Detroit: embodiment of American Dream, 91, 165; Financial Review Commission oversight until 2027, 21; Finley on mismanagement, corruption of, 138–39; as global city, 4, 219n17; highest national average car insurance premium, 43; manufacturing-centered economy, 91; Peck and Whiteside on financialized urbanism in, 18–19; positive reviews on, 1; urban decline and transformation study, 239n1; Vergara on people of future in, 24
Detroit Alliance for a Rational Economy (DARE), 119
Detroit Blight Busters NPO, 135
Detroit Blight Removal Task Force, 34, 78, 82, 132, 133, 153, 195; on blight and elimination generation of revenue, 229n66; broad definition of blight, 229n63; "Defining Blight" report, 79, 79–80; Gilbert appointed to, 150, 154; lack of data validity and reliability, 80; MCM survey published by, 163–64, 197; Obama and, 150; tipping point and, 80–81, *81*, 228n28; U Snap Bac leadership on, 77–78
Detroit Economic Growth Corporation (DEGC), 118, 180–81, 196
Detroit Free Press, lack of consensus on neighborhood names, 67–69
Detroit Future City (DFC) report, 74, 169–70; fifty-year plan of, 166; lack of resident feedback and, 167–68; media favorable review of, 168; vacancy focus of, 75, 166–67
Detroit Future City (DFC) strategic framework, 168–69, 193–95; abstraction of blight and, 74; Black communities displacement concerns, 77; concern over anticipated vacancy areas, 75; creative use of empty lots, 74, 75; criticism of, 74–75, 196; Detroit Blight Removal Task Force report and, 153; framework zones, 75, *76*; Kresge investment in, 76; lack of coordination in, 75–76; promotion of wealth for white outside investors, 152–53; racial inequity disregard in urban planning, 74; on vacancy as abstraction, 154–55
Detroit Land Bank Authority, 196; demolition program concerns of, 135
Detroit Medical Center (DMC), sale to Vanguard Health Systems, 173
The Detroit News, on African Town proposal, 39, 141–42
"Detroit on the Edge" *60 Minutes* program, 133
Detroit Resurrected (Bomey), 132
Detroit Water and Sewer Department (DWSD): EPA lawsuit against, 115; inflated charges of, 115; metropolitan area growth support, 115; predatory interest rate swap agreements, 131; protests and litigation against, 30
Detroit Works Project, 196; Bing and, 160, 183; DFC report on fifty-year plan, 166; Rapson and, 183; residents concern for, 160–61; two components of, 183
DFC. *See* Detroit Future City
Dimon, Jamie, 154–55; Bomey on, 132; on Duggan leadership, 182, 196; as JPMC CEO, 131; on JPMC gift to Detroit, 157; on public policy, 185–87, 196; reference to Obama, 187–88; *60 Minutes* episode on JPMC exceptionalism, 175, 177–78
discrimination: in policing, 45, 227n11; with segregation of Blacks and whites in metropolitan area, 45
disjuncture: between belonging and property, 38; between lived experiences and abstraction, 37

disjuncture, events as, 25–34; of development and mobility, 29; of Latina/o/x youth and unemployment or urban decline, 27; national foreclosure crisis in 2008, 26; SWD 2008 good quality product, 27; SWD Latina/o/x population and, 25–26; of SWD nonprofits, 27–28; undermining ability to redress extractive relations, 30; uneven city development, 33

displacement: abstraction and action explanation of, 24; from Black Bottom, 5

dispossession, 20, 38, 98–99, 194, 195; abstraction and action explanation of, 24; bankruptcy and racial difference in, 123; delinquency and, 30–31; under Financial Review Commission, 21; foreclosure and, 97; foreclosure crisis and, 110–13; Latina/o/x property, 92; state promotion of accumulation by, 18; tax foreclosures and, 93, 110–11

diversity programs, of Duggan, 60–61, 228n7

DMC. *See* Detroit Medical Center

DON. *See* Department of Neighborhoods

doubleness, of abstractions, 13–14, 191, 193, 221n65

Du Bois, W. E. B., 25; on doubleness of abstractions, 191; race and space relational analysis, 61–62; on Seventh Ward of Philadelphia, 11–12, 61, 221n51, 226n155; on slums, 11–12, 62, 221n52; on urban space overlook of racism, 63; on whiteness ownership of earth, 221n65

Duggan, Michael "Mike," 126; confusion about philanthropy and profit, 176–77; Dimon and JPMC on leadership of, 182, 196; diversity programs of, 60–61, 228n7; DON development, 60, 82; Foley as chief storyteller for, 82; neglect of predominantly Black neighborhoods, 83; people trust in, 185; sale of DMC to Vanguard Health Systems, 173; twenty-minute neighborhood idea, 156, 197, 227n6

DWSD. *See* Detroit Water and Sewer Department

economic inequality, from targeting and branding neighborhoods, 37, 90

emergency management: bankruptcy blame by, 126–27; Black residents intervention with, 127; gerrymandering facilitation of, 38; Orr and, 126, 127–28; Public 4 and 436 laws on, 125–26

eminent domain, for development projects, 95

Enterprise Foundation, to promote affordable housing, 67

Entrepreneurs of Color (EOC), JPMC fund of, 149, 179, 182

Environmental Protection Agency (EPA), suit against DWSD wastewater, 115

EOC. *See* Entrepreneurs of Color

EPA. *See* Environmental Protection Agency

"Every Neighborhood Has a Future . . . and It Doesn't Include Blight" report (2014), 78

Fair Housing Act (1968), 119

Federal Bureau of Investigations (FBI), evidence of rigged demolition contract bidding, 135

Federal Housing Administration (FHA), 66–67

Feikens, John, 115–16, 120

FHA. *See* Federal Housing Administration

Financial Review Commission, 21

Finley, Nolan, 138–39

Florida, Richard, 32, 159, 199

Foley, Aaron, 82–84

278 | INDEX

foreclosure: Detroit involuntary ownership transfers through, 20; dispossession and, 97; JPMC lending leading to, 131, 172–73; Latina/o/x disproportionate impact of, 111–12; predatory mortgage lending and, 7–8, 111; racial segregation capitalized from, 131; tax, 10, 93, 110–11, 136, 195
foreclosure crisis: dispossession and, 110–13; Florida on Detroit quick recovery from, 32; JPMCs contribution to, 177–78; Latina/o/x move to suburbs after, 35, 36; vacancy and jobs lost from, 8
foundations: absent local groups relationships, 158; creative development approach, 159; efforts to attract entrepreneurs, 159; funding directed to NPOs, 158; mapping projects funding, 166; place- and impact-based investing by, 73, 74, 158–59; spending outpaced federal expenditures, 158. *See also* nonprofit organizations
foundations, Detroit neighborhoods production, 68–78; Knight Foundation, 68, 69, 85, 158; Kresge and Skillman Foundations support of Data Driven Detroit, 72–73; NDNI, *71*, 71–73, 229n49; public-private partnerships targeted neighborhood investments, 69, *70–71*; Skillman Foundation and LISC, 72
fraud and racketeering conviction, of Kilpatrick, 128, 129, 152
Free the Water graffiti, 30, *31*

gentrification: Foley reference to psychological, 83–84; in SWD, 33
gerrymandering of districts: as bordering practice, 124–25; emergency management facilitated from, 38; REDMAP project, 123
Gilbert, Dan, 20, 34; appointment to Detroit Blight Removal Task Force, 150, 154; as Quicken Loans founder, 77–78, 163–64, 195
Global Cities Initiative, of JPMC, 188
global city, Detroit as, 4, 219n17
GLWA. *See* Great Lakes Water Authority
Google map labels, for SWD, 56–58, *57*
Gordie Howe Bridge international crossing, 96, 105, 114, 169, 170
Government Accounting Office analysis, 36
grassroots organizations, NPOs relation to, 194, 225n134
Great Lakes Water Authority (GLWA), 31, 132
Great Migration (1916–1930), of Blacks from South to North, 4
Great Recession (2008), 2, 4, 26, 131
Griffin, Toni, 153, 161

Hardest Hit Fund (HHF) federal funds, 78, 195; demolition program fraud and bid rigging, 135; for homeowners help, 133–34; to promote city demolition program, 36, 133, 233n48; resident concerns about, 136
Harvey, Dorian, 143
Henderson, Stephen, 193
HERA. *See* Housing and Economic Recovery Act
HHF. *See* Hardest Hit Fund
Hispanic Development Corporation, 147
Hitler, Adolf, 141, 142
Home Mortgage Disclosure Act (1975), 66
homeownership: HHF funds for, 133–34; TARP for, 133; Taylor on citizenship conception tied to, 224n104
Home Owners' Loan Corporation, mapping by, 167, 197
home rule, 116–19
Housing and Economic Recovery Act (HERA) (2008), 72
"How Detroit Became a Model for Urban Renewal" (Scher), 175–76

Hudson-Webber foundation, population-centered approach, 159
human capital investment, of JPMC, 157, 184–85

immigrants: American Dream of, 3–4; Flor move to suburbs experience, 96–97; Latina/o/x for industrial labor, 114; policing undocumented, 47–48; recent Latin Americans to SWD, 5. *See also* Latina/o/x
inclusive capitalism, of JPMC investment, 181
inclusive growth, Black borrowers and, 179–80, 184–88; Detroit Works Project and, 183; EOE and, 182; JPMC and Dimon abstract concepts of, 182; JPMC references to underserved neighborhoods, 181
international crossing: Ambassador Bridge, 5–6, 22, 41–42, 92, 105; Gordie Howe Bridge, 96, 105, 114, 169, 170
investments: foundations place- and impact-based, 73, 74, 158–59; inclusive capitalism of JPMC, 181; JPMC human capital, 157, 184–85; of JPMC in CDFIs, 175–76, 178–79; public-private partnerships target of neighborhood, 69, *70–71*; shared value of JPMC, 175, 185, 187; trust relationship with, 225n133; vacancy as opportunity for, 123; Young on racism undermining, 238n110

"Jamie Dimon's Data-Focused Investment in Detroit" *60 Minutes* episode, 131–32, 175, 177–78
John S. and James L. Knight Foundation (Knight Foundation), 85; place-based investment by, 158; six neighborhood revitalization, 68, 69
Johnson, Lyndon B., 117
Johnson v. McIntosh (1823), 92, 95

Jones Day attorneys, 196; financial benefits from bankruptcy, 129, 197
JPMorgan Chase (JPMC): AdvancingCities initiative, 188; Chang head of research, 155; city government collaboration with, 36; contribution to foreclosure crisis, 177–78; Department of Justice settlement with, 171–72, 183, 196; Dimon as CEO of, 131; Dimon on unfair penalties for toxic assets, 237n79; discriminatory and predatory lending practices, 178, 182; on Duggan leadership, 182, 196; EOC funded by, 149, 179, 182; *Fortune* magazine on, 172; Global Cities Initiative of, 188; grant for SWD, 85; human capital investment, 157, 184–85; inclusive capitalism of, 181; investment in CDFIs, 175–76, 178–79; lending leading to foreclosures, 131, 172–73; local investments of, 182; philanthrocapitalism of, 156, 171–75, *174*; press releases on loans to Black households, 236n18; Scher oversight of Detroit, 174; urban renewal effort, 65

Kelley, Robin D. G., 18
Kelling, George L., 63–65
Kerner Report, on urban racism, 117
Kilpatrick, Kwame: fraud and racketeering conviction, 128, 129, 152; NDNI of, 71, 71–72, 229n49; pension financing through COP, 130
Knight Foundation. *See* John S. and James L. Knight Foundation
Korver-Glenn, Elizabeth, 17
Kresge Foundation, 196; critical to EOC initiative, 182; Data Driven Detroit support, 73, 162; DFC investment by, 76; New Economy Initiative of 2007, 158; place-based investment by, 158–59; Rapson as CEO of, 153

land contracts, for SWD property, 113
Latina/o/x: blight blamed on, 78; Census Bureau undercount of, 124; defined, 220n24; DeGenaro on self perspective by, 226n149; dispossession of property, 92; disproportionate impact of foreclosures on, 111–12; homeowners negative equity, 112; immigrants for industrial labor, 114; laws compromising social mobility of, 96–97; representation struggle in Detroit, 20; SWD homeownership, 106–8, *107*; value on holding property in SWD, 92–93
Latina/o/x youth, in SWD, 198; bordered by police, 42; crime versus lived experience of safety, 48–52; crossing practices of, 23, 28; defensive bordering of, 93; lack of freedom to go to suburbs, 45; on metropolitan area white and Black residents, 23, 33; neighborhood boundaries and official maps differences, 42; perceived as unsafe, 42, 43; policing as urban bordering practice, 44–47; on property and belonging, 121; sense of community, 99; struggle to hold onto property and produce space, 37, 38; SWD described, 52–58
law, whiteness as object of, 95
Lefebvre, Henri: on abstractions production of space, 12, 14, 16, 222n70; on Marx conception of concrete abstractions, 16, 222n82; on mystification, 222n77
Lewis, Oscar, 62
LISC. *See* Local Initiatives Support Corporation
local community control: erosion of, 128–32; Young on, 117
Local Initiatives Support Corporation (LISC): focus on SWD market opportunities, 85; high-risk loans for affordable housing development by, 67; Skillman Foundation and, 72
Locke, John, 91–92
Lockridge, Mark, 136
Logan, John R., 16
Londoño, Johana, 17
Loveland Technologies: MCM survey, 163–64, 197; Paffendorf founding of, 162
Lower Woodward Corridor Initiative, of Kresge Foundation, 159

Majority Black Detroit Matters protests, 60, *61*
mapping projects: efforts to monetize Detroit through, 15–16; foundations funding of, 166; of Home Owners' Loan Corporation, 167, 197; MCM survey and, 163–64, 197; Safransky on high-vacancy areas, 16; SWD as spatial and sociocultural bordering practice, 55; of SWD by residents, 55–57
Marathon Refinery, 105
Marx, Karl, 28; on movement from abstract to concrete, 15, 16–17, 222n82; on space, 17, 222n82
McKittrick, Katherine, 17, 23
MCM. *See* Motor City Mapping
MDEQ. *See* Michigan Department of Environmental Quality
media: abstractions, 7, 8, 142; bankruptcy explanations, 1–2; DFC report favorable review, 168
Mein Kampf (Hitler), 39, 141, 142
Mele, Christopher, 13
metropolitan area, of Detroit, 5, 45, 64; bankruptcy shift in, 123, 127; DWSD support of growth in, 115; Latina/o/x on white and Black residents in, 23, 33; policing in, 44; public-private partnerships for growth in, 115
Metropolitan Statistical Area (MSA), 111
Metzger, Kurt, 72, 73, 162–66

Mexicantown, 54, 56–58, 103–4, 114, 149
Mexicantown Community Development Corporation, 85
Michigan Constitution: amendment outlawing affirmative action, 126; home rule state established in 1908, 116–17; on property taxes limitation in 1963, 93, 110
Michigan Department of Environmental Quality (MDEQ), 136
Mills, Karen: on Dimon letter in JPMC annual report, 185–86; at Harvard Business School, 175; Scher conversation with, 175–76, 179, 183
Molotch, Harvey, 16
Motor City, 4, 43; Latina/o/x youth crossing borders of, 28
Motor City Mapping (MCM) survey, 163–64, 197
Moynihan, Patrick, 22
MSA. *See* Metropolitan Statistical Area
mystifications, abstractions of, 10, 16; Lefebvre on, 222n77

National Association for the Advancement of Colored People (NAACP), 4
National Community Development Initiative (NCDI), 67
national identity, in relation to whiteness, 100
National Neighborhood Indicators Partnership, work with Data Driven Detroit, 165
naturalization, of whiteness, 192
NCDI. *See* National Community Development Initiative
NDNI. *See* Next Detroit Neighborhoods Initiative
Neighborhood Housing Services (NHS), of Pittsburg model, 66
neighborhood improvement program, of Young, 66

Neighborhood Integrity Act (2021), New York, 60
Neighborhood Reinvestment Corporation Act (1978), 66
neighborhoods: as abstractions without scientific definition, 89, 194; background on, 59–60; bordering practices and, 59–60, 90; community compared to, 59; Detroit Blight Removal Task Force and, 78–82; Detroit lack of consensus on names for, 68; DON and, 55–56, 60, 82–84, 134, 194–95; foundations production of, 68–78; investment targets of public-private partnerships, 61, 69, *70–71*; NPOs, 84–88; powerful groups production as abstraction, 37; production of, 59–90; public-private partnerships production of, 65–67, *70–71*; racial and economic inequality from targeting, 37, 90; racialized association of, 59; scholars production of, 62–65, 89–90; US Census Bureau on census tracts, 60, 226n3
Neighborhood Stabilization Program (NSP), 72; map of, *73*; SWD federal funds from, 84–85
neoliberal governance: public-private partnerships and, 18, 195, 224n94; urban policy and, 124
New Economy Initiative (2007), of Kresge Foundation, 158
Next Detroit Neighborhoods Initiative (NDNI), *71*, 69–72, 229n49
NHS. *See* Neighborhood Housing Services
nonprofit organizations (NPOs): CDCs mergers, 86; Detroit Blight Busters, 135; foundations funding directed to, 158; grassroots relationship with, 194, 225n134; residents concerns about, 87; Southwest Solutions and Van Camp, 84–89, 194; Urban Neighbor

nonprofit organizations (*cont*)
   hood Initiatives, 86–87; U Snap Bac, 77–78
NSP. *See* Neighborhood Stabilization Program

Obama, Barack, 38; Dimon reference to, 187–88; federal funds through Detroit Blight Removal Task Force, 150; response to bankruptcy, 151–52; Strong Cities, Strong Communities program, 127
Orr, Kevyn, 126, 139, 192–93; on Black people stereotype, 128; law firm and partners financial benefit from bankruptcy, 129; on municipal pension errors, 128–29, 197; on outsiders necessary for turnaround, 196

Paffendorf, Jerry, 162–64, 197
Paradise Vally, 4, 5, 96
Patterson, Brooks, 115–16
Peck, Jamie, 18–19
philanthrocapitalism, 190; of JPMC, 156, 171–75, *174*
philanthropic foundations, in public-private partnerships, 152, 154; philanthrocapitalism, 156, 171–75, *174*, 190; power from economic to social and politics, 171
Piquette Square for Veterans (PSV), 88
place- and impact-based investing, 37; by foundations, 72–74, 158–59
Plessy v. Ferguson (1896), 19
police: foot patrols for crime reduction, 63, 65; patrols in SWD, 52–54; Secure Communities program on arrests, 112; slave patrols origins of, 221n50, 228n20; STRESS task force rebellion reponse, 118; Wilson and Kelling on community controls reinforced by, 63–64
policing: as bordering practice example, 22; racial profiling, 44; racial relation between Black city and white state, 48; SWD lack of freedom to go to suburbs, 45, 227n11; as SWD urban bordering practice, 44–47; undocumented immigrants, 47–48
Pollock, Marcus, 228n28
population: change in Detroit city and Wayne County, 36; Detroit and abstraction of loss of, 14–15; loss, 1–2; shift, 3
population-centered approach, of Hudson-Webber Foundation, 159
poverty, 2, 4, 63; average status of, *112*; Census Bureau on, 219n12; SWD rates of, 5–6, 105–6, *106*, 108
powerful groups, neighborhood produced as abstraction by, 37
PowerNomics (Anderson), 39, 143
"A Powernomics Economic Development Plan for Detroit's Under-Served Majority Population" (Anderson), 144
predatory mortgage lending, 127; CDFI and, 238n96; foreclosed homes and, 7–8, 111; of JPMC and Dimon, 178, 182
Project Green Light camera surveillance, 51–52, 64, 83–84, 94
property: abstraction and relation to, 18–21, 96, 194; as American Dream, 121; claims as abstractions, 91–122; defined through right to exclude, 92; disjuncture between belonging and, 39; Kelley on neoliberal variant of racial capitalism, 18; laws originated in slavery for whiteness, 19; as mutually dependent relation between opposed interest, 18; privatizing and transferring public assets to private companies, 18; Robinson on mass violence and pursuit of, 223n93; tax increments and property tax revenues from values of, 13, 221n64
property, as bundle of rights, 94; Black Bottom and Paradise Valley razed, 96; eminent domain for development projects, 95; Flor immigrant move

to suburbs experience, 96–97; Gabi housing instability experience, 97–100; Young on, 117–18

property, in SWD, 109; census tracts of SNF, 101, *102*; high-earning households, 108; Hispanic homeownership, 106–8, *107*; home rule, local control, 116–19; informal options for homeownership, 113; land contracts and, 113; Latina/o/x youth struggle to hold onto, 38; loss of property value, 119–21; Marathon Refinery and, 105; population decline by census tract, 101–3, *103*; poverty rates and, 5–6, 105–6, *106*, 108; property claims, 114–16; vacancies, 108

property taxes: high rates of, 92–93, 230n5; Michigan 1963 Constitution on limitations to, 93, 110; white flight and loss of revenue from, 48

property value: loss of, 119–21; perspective focus on blight removal, 134

PSV. *See* Piquette Square for Veterans

psychological gentrification, Foley reference to, 83–84

public-private partnerships: abstractions promotion of, 21; Black borrower and inclusive growth, 179–88; city and county land banks, 152, 219n11; Detroit Works Project to DFC, 160–62; DFC report, 166–70; experimentation, 175–79; federal support for, 39; foundation funding outsizing public spending, 157–60; JPMC Dimon and, 154–55; land transfers, 152; naturalist theories racialization of urban spaces, 66; neoliberal governance and, 18, 195, 224n94; philanthropic foundation spending, 152, 154; private sector dominance over public policy, 39; of Project Green Light, 51–52, 64, 84, 94; from property vacancy to density, 162–66; of redlining, 167, 178; shared value, inclusive growth, virtuous circles abstractions, 170–75; targeted neighborhood investments, 61, 69, *70–71*; tax increment incentive packages, 152; Taylor on residential segregation with, 17; for urban reform, 188

quality of life laws, broken windows theory and, 65–66

Quicken Loans, Gilbert as founder of, 77–78, 163–64, 195

race and ethnicity: bordering practices distinguished through, 48, 56; urban renewal and inequities in, 62

race and space: case study and methods, 34–37; crossing practices struggles to produce, 23; Du Bois relational analysis of, 62; McKittrick on naturalizing of, 17; scholars on abstractions of, 11–17; state promotion of relations between, 19; trust and, 196

Race: The Power of Illusion documentary, 12

racial capitalism, 223nn92–93; Kelley on neoliberal variant of, 18

racial inequality, 3; Bonilla-Silva on, 13; DFC report disregard in urban planning, 74; life experiences through space and, 11; from targeting and branding neighborhoods, 37

racial profiling, 198; ACLU actions against, 84; policing traffic laws and selective enforcement, 44

racial segregation: from foreclosure, 131; *Plessy v. Ferguson* on separate but equal for, 19

racism: policies and practices producing slum, 62; Scher colorblind, 180; in urban planning, 196; Young charge of reverse, 120–21

Rapson, Rip, 153, 155–56; data-driven plans promotion, 161–62; on outsiders necessary for turnaround, 196

Reagan, Ronald, 67

real-estate-owned property (REO), MSA density for, 111
reality: abstractions as reflection of, 7, 10, 220n28; through lived experience abstractions, 14–15
rebellion (1967): Black civil rights and, 116–17; Black Detroiters loss of property value, 119–21; due to white flight and postindustrial decline, 4, 117; residents forced from city after, 20; STRESS police task force response to, 118; white supremacy and anti-Blackness, 118; Young on white people reaction to, 118
REDistricting Minority Project (REDMAP), 123, 124–26, 140
redlining, 66, 91, 180, 197; as bordering practice, 22; public-private partnership and, 167, 178
REO. *See* real-estate-owned property
representation: abstractions of, 20–21; Blacks and Latina/o/x struggle for, 20
Residential Mortgage-Backed Securities (RMBS) Settlement, Chase, 184
residential segregation, 11; Korver-Glenn and Londoño on, 17; Rosa on, 12–13; social isolation produced by, 225n136
residents: census tracts for SWD defined boundaries for, 104–5; demolition program concerns, 135; Detroit Works Project concerns, 160–61; emergency management intervention by Black, 127; feelings of frequent study but lack of understanding, 192; forced from city after rebellion of 1967, 20; HHF federal funds concerns, 136; lack of feedback on DFC report, 167–68; mapping projects of SWD, 55–57; NPOs concerns, 87; perceptions at university event, 190
Reyes, Angela, 147
Ritchie, Andrea, 199
RMBS. *See* Residential Mortgage-Backed Securities Settlement
Robinson, Cedric, 223n93

Roosevelt, Franklin D., 167; on Detroit as arsenal of democracy, 4
Rosa, Vanessa, 12–13
Rutkowski, Ed, 228n28

Safransky, Sara, 16
Sampson, Robert, 62–63
"Say Nice Things About Detroit" campaign of 1970s, 2
Scher, Peter, 65, 174, 175–76, 179–80
scholars: on neighborhoods, 62–64, 89–90; on race and space abstractions, 11–17
Secure Communities program, on police sharing arrest information, 112
Seventh Ward in Philadelphia, Du Bois analysis of, 11–12, 62, 221n51, 226n155
shared value, 188; JPMC investment and, 175, 185, 187
Skillman Foundation, 72, 73
slave codes, whiteness defined by, 91–92
slums: Du Bois on, 11–12, 62, 221n52; racism policies and practices producing, 62
SNF. *See* Strategic Neighborhood Fund
Snyder, Rick, 32, 196; Orr emergency manager appointment by, 126, 127–28
social isolation, residential segregation producing, 225n136
social relations, space produced through, 21–22
Southwest Detroit "Southwest" (SWD): Ambassador Bridge and street access in, 41–42, 42; Ambassador Bridge international border crossing, 5–6, 22, 41–42, 92, 105; American Dream struggle in, 38, 101, 114; bordering and crossing practices tied to, 23–24; code violations in, 231n46; crossing practices in, 23–24, 58; cultural hubs of racial and ethnic groups, 56; described, 52–58; expressway building prioritization, 43; Google map

labels for, 56–58, *57*; inadequate public transportation system, 43; Latina/o/x population in, 5; LISC on market opportunities in, 85; lost population between 2000 and 2020, 61; mapping as spatial and sociocultural bordering practice, 55; Mexican ancestry residents in, 5; Mexicantown and, 56–58; negative daily experiences of, 93–94; NPOs in, 27–28; NSP federal funds for, 84–85; police patrols and community safety, 52–54; poverty rate in, 5–6, 105–6, *106*, 108; property and, 101–9; recent Latin America immigrants in, 5; renamed as sixth district, 83; residents mapping of, 55–57; scale of space and safety feeling, 55; slow gentrification in, 33; Southwest Pride place identity, 6; target for development, 61; transportation problems, 43–44. *See also* Latina/o/x youth

Southwest Housing Corporation, Southwest Solutions operating as, 87–88

Southwest Solutions, 84–89, 194

space, 3, 224n112; abstractions of, 36; Black and white, 22; Black people struggle for, 11; as cause or consequence of social, 7, 220n27; container theory of, 7, 193–94; embodiment and abstraction struggles in, 37; Hartigan on whiteness relation to, 226n150; Lefebvre on abstractions production of, 12, 14, 17, 222n70; Logan and Molotch on growth machine for, 17; Marx and Lefebvre on, 17, 222n82; racial inequality and, 34; in relation to individuals and groups, 99; residential segregation, 11; social relations production of, 21–22; white supremacy control over, 11

state: described, 224n99; monopoly over legitimate use of violence to enforce order, 19–20; promotion of accumulation by dispossession, 18; promotion of race and space relation, 19; role in social groups relations, 18

"The State of Detroit" series, by Florida, 199

Stop the Robberies, Enjoy Safe Streets (STRESS) police task force, 118

Strategic Neighborhood Fund (SNF), 230n94; SWD census tracts for, 101, *102*

STRESS. *See* Stop the Robberies, Enjoy Safe Streets

Strong Cities, Strong Communities program, of Obama, 127

suburb areas: city migration to, 119–20; Flor moving experience to, 96–97; Latina/o/x move to after foreclosure crisis, 35, *36*; Latina/o/x youth lack of freedom to go to, 45; policing and lack of freedom to go to, 45, 227n11; values in relation to racial and ethnic background, 44–45

SWD. *See* Southwest Detroit "Southwest"

TARP. *See* Troubled Asset Relief Program

tax foreclosures, 10, 136, 195; dispossession and, 93, 110–11

Taylor, Keeanga-Yamahtta, 17, 223n86, 224n104

threat and exclusion, abstractions on, 147

tipping point: as abstraction, 6, 13, 38; broken windows theory on, 64–65; Detroit Blight Removal Task Force and, 80–81, *81*, 228n28

transportation problems, in SWD: car insurance socioeconomic factors to set premium, 43–44; lack of car ownership, 43; personal injury insurance claims, 44; potholes and vehicle destruction, 44; public transportation system inadequacy, 43; state favored outside interests decisions, 44; uninsured drivers and insurance fraud, 44, 226n1

Troubled Asset Relief Program (TARP), 133

trust: investment relationship with, 225n133; of people in Duggan, 185; race and space, 196
twenty-minute neighborhood idea, of Duggan, 156, 197, 227n6

university event, resident perceptions and: Cunningham on city as agent of inequalities, 190; on public perception of crime, 190
urban development, Mele on, 13
Urban Institute report, 65
Urban Neighborhood Initiatives, 86
urban planning, racism in, 196
urban policy, neoliberal governance and, 124
urban reform, public-private partnerships for, 188
urban renewal: Baldwin on negro removal in, 150; Black communities displacement with, 77; demolition and slum clearance in, 66; JPMC effort for, 65; place- and impact-based investing practices, 37; racial and ethnic inequities from, 62, 96; Reagan on government intervention, 67
urban revitalization, Kresge Foundation on, 155
urban spaces, 63, 224n112
urban sprawl, 115, 121
US Attorney, evidence of rigged demolition contract bidding, 135
U Snap Bac NPO, 77–78
US Special Inspector General for the Troubled Asset Relief Program, 233n49

vacancy: blight removal over affordable housing, 133; DFC report focus on, 75, 166–67; foreclosure crisis and jobs lost, 8; as investment opportunity, 123; Paffendorf creation of index for, 164; Paffendorf efforts monetize areas of, 162–63; in SWD, 108
Van Camp, John, 85–86
Vergara, Camilo José, 24, 190, 198
Vivian, C. T., 144

Wacquant, Loïc, 193
Warren, Gwendolyn, 137, *138*
Watson, JoAnn, 143, 145
white flight, 4, 48, 117, 153
whiteness: association with American Dream, 4; courts protection of property interest of, 19; defined through right to exclude, 92; Du Bois on ownership of earth and, 221n65; Hartigan on relation to space and class, 226n150; *Johnson v. McIntosh* meaning of, 92; national identity in relation to, 100; naturalization of, 192; as object of law, 95; slave codes defining, 91–92
white power groups, white supremacy promoted by, 61
Whiteside, Heather, 18–19
white supremacy, 18, 39, 142, 194, 198, 223n91, 239n11; controlling over space, 11; Foley references to diversity and, 82; rebellion of 1967 and, 118; white power groups promotion of, 61
Williams, Kidada, 234n2
Willis, Terence, 143
Wilson, James Q., 63–65

Young, Coleman, 9, 180–81, 196; charge of reverse racism, 120–21; Cockerel on, 118–19; critics of, 118–19; DEGC creation, 118; as first Black mayor, 5, 117; home rule and local control for Black Detroiters, 117; neighborhood improvement program of, 66; on property bundle of rights, 117–18; on racism undermining investment, 238n110

ABOUT THE AUTHOR

NICOLE E. TRUJILLO-PAGAN is Associate Professor of Sociology at Wayne State University. She is a native New Yorker transplanted to the alternate postindustrial production of Detroit. She is a proud Puerto Rican focused on issues of race and colonization and the author of *Modern Colonization by Medical Intervention: U.S. Medicine in Puerto Rico*.